RAVEL
Life & Works

THE AUTOGRAPH OF RAVEL'S "HABANERA"
AS IT FIRST APPEARED IN 1895

RAVEL AT HOME

RAVEL

Life & Works

BY

ROLLO H. MYERS

GREENWOOD PRESS, PUBLISHERS
WESTPORT, CONNECTICUT

The Library of Congress has catalogued this publication as follows:

Library of Congress Cataloging in Publication Data

Myers, Rollo H
  Ravel: life and works.

  Reprint of the 1960 ed., New York.
  1. Ravel, Maurice, 1875-1937.
[ML410.R23M9 1973]   789'.92'4 [B]   73-2340
ISBN 0-8371-6841-4

© *Rollo H. Myers 1960*

Originally published in 1960 by Thomas Yoseloff, New York

Reprinted with the permission of A. S. Barnes & Co.

Reprinted by Greenwood Press,
a division of Williamhouse-Regency, Inc.

First Greenwood Reprinting 1973
Second Greenwood Reprinting 1975

Library of Congress Catalog Card Number 73-2340

ISBN 0-8371-6841-4

Printed in the United States of America

CONTENTS

LIST OF ILLUSTRATIONS

FOREWORD

THIS book does not claim to present its subject in any sense in a " new light "; nor have I made any special effort to discover, or give prominence to, incidents or events in the private life of the composer that do not directly contribute to our knowledge of the man considered in relation to his art. In the case of an introvert like Ravel whose life, as regards externals at least, could be described as uneventful by comparison, for example, with the lives of Liszt or Berlioz or Wagner, the main task of the biographer is clearly to stress as far as possible the connexion between the " inner " life of the artist, with all its secret tensions, aspirations and deceptions, and its outward projection as revealed in his works. But with Ravel, as we shall see, this connexion is far less evident than in the case of the majority of composers; for it is difficult to think of any other great musician whose attitude towards his art has been so rigorously objective and detached. Stravinsky, it is true, once startled the world by asserting that it is not the function of music to " express " anything at all outside itself; but was it not also Stravinsky who declared: " For myself, I cannot begin to take an interest in the phenomenon of music except in so far as it emanates from the integral man "? Perhaps the truth lies somewhere between these two apparently conflicting statements; and whether or not the composer of *Gaspard de la Nuit* would have endorsed the first, it is my own agreement with the thought expressed in the second that has led me to undertake this study and try to discover to what extent the music of Maurice Ravel can be said to represent the " integral man ".

My thanks are due especially to Mr. Felix Aprahamian and United Music Publishers Ltd. and to Mr. R. D. Gibson of J. & W. Chester Ltd. for their courtesy in allowing me to borrow freely from their libraries; to MM. Durand & Cie. of Paris for permission to reproduce extracts from the following: *Trois Poèmes de Mallarmé*, the *Piano Trio*, the *String Quartet*, the *Sonatas* for *Violin and Piano* and *Violin and 'Cello*; the *Valses Nobles et Sentimentales, Gaspard de la Nuit, Minuet on the name of Haydn*, the two *Piano Concertos, Daphnis et Chloë* and *Boléro* and *Histoires Naturelles*; to Messrs. Schott & Co. Ltd. and Editions Max Eschig of Paris for permission to print the extract from *Jeux d'Eau*; and last, but not least, to Madame Hélène Jourdan-Morhange who has very kindly allowed me to reproduce photographs and documents from her private collection.   I am also grateful to Monsieur Manuel Rosenthal of Paris for very kindly allowing me to reproduce the first page of the manuscript of *Habanera,* which he owns, and to the publishers of *La Revue Musicale* for permission to quote from and translate articles and documents from back numbers of the *Revue.*   The words of all the songs quoted are reproduced by permission of their respective publishers: Durand & Cie. for *Trois Chansons* (Ravel); Editions Salabert for *Noël des Jouets* (Ravel); Hamelle & Cie. for *Manteau de Fleurs* (Gravelot); Librairie Ernest Flammarion for *Histoires Naturelles* (J. Renard); Librairie Gallimard for *Rêves* (L. P. Fargue); Mercure de France for three poems from *Shéhérazade* (Tristan Klingsor) and *Les Grands Vents venus d'Outre-mer* (Henri de Régnier).

R. H. M.

London. *April* 1960.

PART I

THE LIFE

CHAPTER ONE

1875—1895

MAURICE-JOSEPH RAVEL was born on March 7, 1875, at Ciboure, a small fishing port in the Basses-Pyrénées between St. Jean-de-Luz and the Spanish frontier. He was of mixed Swiss-Basque descent; Swiss on his father's side, Basque on his mother's. His father, Pierre-Joseph Ravel, was born at Versoix, near Geneva, in 1832, but the Ravel family originally came from a village on the French side of the border, in Haute-Savoie, called Collonges-sous-Salève. The name was variously spelt at different times; thus Ravel's grandfather Aimé spelt his name Ravex when his son (the composer's father) was baptized, and became Ravet four years later.* Ravez is yet another alternative spelling. It is unlikely that there is any connexion between the composer's family and a certain comic actor named Pierre-Alfred Ravel who became famous in the Bordeaux region at the end of the nineteenth century, although this may be taken as an indication that the name was perhaps not uncommon in the south-west provinces of France. It was in this region, too, that the composer's mother, who came from the Basses-Pyrénées, was born; she was, in fact, of Basque descent, as her name Delouart denotes—this being clearly a

---

* The following is an extract from the Act of Baptism of Maurice Ravel's grandfather from the Register of the Parish Church of Collonges-sous-Salève, Diocese of Annecy:
"L'an mil huit cent et le quinze janvier environ neuf heures du soir est né et le vingt-six a été baptisé sous condition dans l'église, malgré la persécution, par je soussigné Missionaire, Aimé, fils de François Ravex et de Jeanne Cottet mariés. Le parrain a été Aimé Cottet de Meigny-en-Chablais, et la marraine Claudine Dupraz de Corsy. Ainsi est.

"Signé au Registre:
"HUMBERT, prêtre et Missionaire."

It is interesting to note that the word " persécution " has been written in in place of the word "Revolution", effaced but clearly legible. (Reproduced from *Ravel*, by Roland-Manuel, by kind permission of Librairie Gallimard, Paris.)

French variant of the Spanish-Basque Deluarte (or Eluarte).
And, as it happened, it was in Spain that Marie Delouart, in
1873, first met the young Swiss engineer whom she was to
marry the following year. The encounter took place at Aranjuez where Pierre-Joseph Ravel was helping to build a railway
for the Spanish Government.

Aranjuez, famous for its asparagus and for its miniature
Palace and lovely gardens which used to be the summer resort
of the Spanish sovereigns, is a romantically beautiful spot,
and it therefore seems appropriate that it should have been the
trysting place of the parents of the composer of the *Rapsodie
Espagnole*.

The marriage took place a year later, and the young couple
went to live at Ciboure, at 12 Quai de la Nivelle. Maurice
was their first child; three months after his birth the Ravels
moved to Paris and settled at 40 Rue des Martyrs, on the
slopes of Montmartre. Here, three years later, a second son
was born, the composer's younger brother Edouard. Pierre-
Joseph Ravel seems to have been a man of singular charm and
of wide culture with many interests,* while his brother
Edouard was a painter of repute whose pictures can be seen
in galleries and museums at Geneva, Lausanne and Neuchâtel,
as well as in Lille and Marseilles. Thus the family background
was an artistic and cultivated one, and the young Maurice
received every encouragement from his father when it became
evident that music was going to be his vocation. He took his
first piano lessons at the age of six. His master, Henri Ghys,
noted in his diary that Maurice " appeared to be an intelligent
boy ", but added that it was evidently his fate to have to teach
children. Six years later Maurice began to study harmony
with Charles René, who had been a pupil of Delibes, and in

---

* He invented, it would seem, the first internal combustion engine and was thus a
pioneer of the automobile industry. On September 2, 1868, he took out a patent, No.
82263 J. R., for a " générateur à vapeur chauffé par les huiles minérales appliqué à la
locomotion ", and in the same year constructed a vehicle propelled in this way which he
drove " from the Route de la Révolte to St. Denis and back in two hours ", escorted by
two policemen on foot. The vehicle was expected to attain the record speed of six
kilometres per hour. In 1904 Joseph Ravel presented at the Casino de Paris a sensational
number known as " Le Tourbillon de la Mort " in which a motor-car was thrown up
into the air and after turning a complete somersault landed on its four wheels.

1889 he entered the Paris Conservatoire and was placed in Anthiôme's preparatory piano class, from which he emerged two years later with a *premier prix* and medal. Promoted to Charles de Bériot's class, the young Ravel first met there the pianist Ricardo Viñes, who was to become a lifelong friend as well as the most faithful and sympathetic interpreter of his works.

1889 was the year of the Great Exhibition and, although then only a boy of fourteen, Ravel must have been enthralled, as was Debussy then aged twenty-seven, by the oriental and other exotic music that could be heard in the foreign countries' pavilions on the Esplanade des Invalides. It is difficult for us to realize the strength of the impact made by this unfamiliar music on Parisian artists at the time, but there is no doubt that the famous Javanese *gamelang* orchestras, the Annamite dancers and the Hungarian Tziganes attracted all the musicians in Paris to the Exhibition. Apart from Claude Debussy, who was wholly subjugated by these fascinating revelations of Eastern art, these included Chabrier, Satie and Rimsky-Korsakov, who was then visiting Paris to conduct the Colonne orchestra in two symphony concerts of Russian music, much of which must have been new to Ravel at the time, thus providing him with yet another kind of musical experience.

Yet the direct influence of this exotic music, apart from the " gapped " scale

Ex.1

of which the composer of *Ma Mère l'Oye* was especially fond, is on the whole less discernible in Ravel's music than in that of Debussy. For instance, Ravel seldom if ever employs the pentatonic or whole-tone scale on which Debussy's harmony was so largely based. His music, in fact, is far more modal than Debussy's, and takes its colour less from the East than from early European sources. Moreover, the oriental gapped scale can also be considered as a variant of the Dorian mode—the mode which lends its peculiar flavour to so many of Ravel's melodies and is one of the composer's most characteristic " finger-prints ". Incidentally, this mode is also typical of much of the music of the Basque country, in contradistinction to that of the rest of Spain, especially Andalucia, where the prevailing mode is the Phrygian, of which Ravel also makes use when he is being particularly " Spanish ", as in the *Habanera* or the *Rapsodie Espagnole*.

Nevertheless, it cannot be doubted that the Exhibition of 1889 left its mark on the young Ravel, who was then at an impressionable age, as it did on all his generation. It came at a time when Paris was leading the world in literature and the plastic arts. In painting the Impressionists, Symbolists and the Neo-Realists were in their heyday; Seurat, van Gogh, Lautrec and the Douanier Rousseau were exhibiting at the Fifth Salon des Indépendants; Antoine in his *Théâtre Libre* was staging plays by the Goncourts, E. A. Poe and Zola; Mallarmé was holding his Tuesday receptions in his flat in the Rue de Rome, which were attended by painters and musicians —for example, Whistler and Debussy—as well as by all the most famous men of letters in the capital; Verlaine, then aged forty-five, had just published *Parallèlement* and had been set by both Fauré and Debussy; Marcel Proust, as a youth of eighteen, was serving his apprenticeship in high society in the Faubourg Saint-Germain, while Anatole France was being lionized in the fashionable literary salon of Mme de Caillavet. Meanwhile Debussy had already composed *La Damoiselle Elue* and the *Cinq Poèmes de Baudelaire*; Massenet's *Esclarmonde* had just been produced at the Opéra-Comique, and Fauré's *Requiem* at the Madeleine in the previous year. Up in Montmartre Toulouse-Lautrec was painting *Au Bal du Moulin de la Galette* and Erik Satie playing the piano in Rudolf de Salis' cabaret *Au Chat Noir*, having already published his *Sarabandes* and *Gymnopédies* and now writing the *Gnossiennes* under the influence, no doubt, of the oriental music he had heard in the sideshows of the Great Exhibition.

In politics, this was the year of General Boulenger's abortive

MAURICE RAVEL'S FATHER WITH HIS SONS

MUSIC IN THE HOME—RAVEL ON THE RIGHT

RAVEL AS A STUDENT IN 1905

coup d'état; but when the Exhibition opened on May 1 the General had already fled the country. And, as if to symbolize all this ferment of artistic and intellectual activity, this escape from outworn conventions and the birth of a new and questing spirit in the arts and in human enterprise, there on the Champs de Mars, for all to see, stood the brand-new Tower, the highest building in Europe, built at a cost of 15 million gold francs by the genius of Gustave Eiffel, a striking symbol of France's second material and spiritual renaissance and, as a feat of engineering, still without a parallel. As an expression of national aspirations it certainly fully justified the boast made by its creator that the French flag was now the only flag in the world to fly from a mast 300 metres high! No wonder, then, that painters like the Douanier Rousseau never tired of painting this new symbol of France's expanding aspirations, which had given to Paris, overnight as it were, a new and distinctive look that seemed to presage the shape of things to come.

Such, then, was the background of Ravel's boyhood and early youth. He was growing up at a time when new ideas were in the air and music, no less than painting, was waking to a new life and preparing to break down the barriers imposed upon it by stuffy nineteenth-century conventions. Naturally, then, it was the *avant-garde* that attracted him most strongly, and so his earliest models were independent pioneers, outside official musical circles, such as Emmanuel Chabrier, Erik Satie and, to a lesser degree, Claude Debussy. Chabrier was fifty in 1891 when the young Ravel, together with his new friend, the pianist Ricardo Viñes, had the honour of playing to the composer of *Le Roi Malgré Lui* his *Trois Valses Romantiques* for two pianos. Ravel had discovered and been fascinated by the bold originality of the *Trois Valses* while still a student at the Conservatoire, and his admiration for Chabrier never waned in after life. And so, referring to his first (unpublished) composition written when he was eighteen, he did not hesitate later to acknowledge the source of his youthful inspiration. " The influence of Chabrier " (in this piece), he wrote,* " is apparent, as is that of Satie in the *Ballade de la Reine Morte d'Aimer* " (also unpublished and dating from the same year).

Soon after his encounter with Chabrier, Ravel met Satie for the first time. It was his father, whose circle of acquaintances was wide and catholic, who first introduced him to that strange and enigmatic figure who, for the next thirty years, was to become the *éminence grise* behind the modernistic movement in French music. The meeting took place in the famous Montmartre café, *La Nouvelle Athènes*, much frequented at that time by artists and musicians. That meeting with the composer of the *Sarabandes* and the *Gymnopédies*, which had so impressed the young Ravel when they first came out in 1887–1888, was, as he was never tired of repeating, an event which had a decisive effect on his future development. Throughout his life, indeed, Ravel was one of Satie's staunchest supporters, and he showed his admiration not only by dedicating to the " Bon Maître " (in 1913) the last of the *Trois Poèmes de Stéphane Mallarmé,* but by openly imitating his style in such things as the early song *Sainte* (Mallarmé, 1896) and the *Belle et la Bête* episode in *Mother Goose*, which Roland-Manuel even goes so far as to call " that delightful ' Fourth ' *Gymnopédie* ". Moreover, as we shall see later,† Ravel was one of the first to play Satie's music in public at a time when he himself was at the height of his reputation—a gesture of disinterested generosity that was characteristic of the man.

With Debussy, on the other hand, Ravel's relations were of a rather different kind. He was his junior by some thirteen years, but the two composers were for a time on friendly, if not intimate, terms and admired each other's works. Debussy thought highly of Ravel's string quartet, and when Ravel had doubts about it in the face of some hostile criticism (notably from Fauré, who thought the last movement a failure) Debussy

---

* In a biographical sketch written by himself and communicated to Roland-Manuel in 1928 and subsequently published in *La Revue Musicale* of December 1938. Further quotations from this document in the pages that follow will be indicated by the initials " B.S.". For a full account of how this document came to be compiled, see Appendix I.
† Chapter III.

adjured him: " In the name of the gods of music and in mine, do not touch a note of what you have written." Ravel, on his side, thought there was nothing in music more beautiful than the *Prélude à l'Après-midi d'un Faune*, which he said he would like to have played to him on his deathbed. In later years, however, they became estranged, without desiring it, in circumstances which will be described in another chapter. The estrangement did not affect in any way Ravel's admiration and respect for Debussy, although it would be misleading to suggest that he was ever directly influenced by him as he admittedly was by Chabrier and Satie. There were points of resemblance, but nothing more. I shall return to this question when considering the general characteristics of Ravel's style.

It is time now to resume the chronological thread of events and close this digression, the object of which has been to set the scene of Ravel's first contacts with the musical milieu in which he found himself, and to show what formative influences were at work in shaping his future development.

CHAPTER TWO

1895—1905

At the Conservatoire Ravel was in some ways a model pupil and set himself deliberately to learn everything there was to learn about the technique of composition, studying harmony and counterpoint, and analysing classical scores so as to make himself thoroughly familiar with the musician's craft. At the same time he had, of course, no illusions as to the intrinsic value of the conventions and rules of academic instruction, and although he was quite ready to accept the discipline they imposed in order to perfect his technique, he did so in a spirit of critical detachment and complete independence. He knew already instinctively that the kind of music he intended to write would bear little resemblance to the models approved of in academic circles. Technique was what interested him, then as always, and he was particularly delighted with a remark made by Massenet at one of his lectures on composition to the effect that " in order to know your own technique you must learn the technique of other people ". Ravel never forgot this saying, and quoted it frequently.

He was a pupil at the Conservatoire, as were so many of France's leading composers of his generation, of André Gédalge, of whom he thought highly; he also attended Fauré's composition class, which had a great vogue at that time and was more like a kind of musical salon than a professor's class. Here are his impressions of these two masters: " In 1897, while studying counterpoint with André Gédalge, I entered the composition class of Gabriel Fauré. I am pleased to say I owe all the most valuable elements of my technique to André Gédalge. As to Fauré, I profited no less from his advice *as an artist.*" (B.S.) In other words, he took what he wanted from every source without sacrificing anything of his own individuality.

Alfred Cortot, who was a fellow student of Ravel's at the Conservatoire, says of him that he was at that time " a deliberately sarcastic, argumentative and aloof young man, who used to read Mallarmé and associate with Erik Satie ".

As to his tastes in literature, we learn from his principal biographer, M. Roland-Manuel, that Mallarmé was his favourite poet, and Baudelaire and Poe the prophets of his aesthetic creed. He also greatly admired Villiers de l'Isle Adam, especially *Eve Future*, and Huysmans' *A Rebours*; these authors satisfied his taste for fantasy and sophistication. We shall examine later in their context a number of other literary sources which provided a foundation for so many of his best-known works, ranging from Ronsard to Jules Renard, and from Charles Perrault to Colette. But enough has been said already to show that his early orientation in both literature and music left little doubt as to the lines on which he was going to develop. In this respect he resembled Debussy, whose tastes in his student days were very similar. With less genius, however, but perhaps more talent Ravel was the quicker starter of the two and seems to have found his characteristic style and acquired all the essential elements of his technique in his very earliest works.

In this he was exceptional among composers, for his first published compositions were astonishingly mature. For him there was no fumbling " first period " to be followed by a riper middle and still more highly evolved " third " period, as with Beethoven and Wagner and, to mention only two or three of his contemporaries, with Fauré, d'Indy and Debussy, all of whom were much slower in reaching maturity. Thus, at the age of twenty Ravel had already composed the famous *Habanera** which not only contains the essence of his whole musical personality, but is a striking example of his

---

* Incorporated later in the orchestral *Rapsodie Espagnole* (1907).

extraordinary technical accomplishment at an age when most students are only feeling their way. Writing of this work in later life, the composer himself said: " I consider that this work contains in embryo several of the elements that were to be most characteristic of my later compositions." (B.S.) From the same year dates the *Menuet Antique*, a mixture of pastiche and experimental harmony, which Ravel later referred to as " this somewhat retrograde work ".

Habanera, together with another piece (unpublished) entitled *Entre Cloches*, was originally written for two pianos, and, under the collective (and provocative) title of *Sites Auriculaires* (Ravel was obviously taking a leaf out of Satie's book), these two pieces were first performed on March 5, 1898, at a concert of the Société Nationale.* Needless to say, they were not favourably received: the Parisian public, and especially the older generation of musicians, were not then ready to accept as serious music anything that savoured of the *avant-garde*, which did not in those days have the following which it almost automatically has today among, at any rate, the so-called intelligentsia.

The following year Ravel came before the public again, this time with an Overture to an opera he was then working on to be entitled *Shéhérazade*; for this he had himself sketched out a libretto based on the Sindbad episode in the *Arabian Nights*, using Galland's translation. The opera, of which Ravel said later that it " showed strong Russian influences ", was never completed, and no part of it was ever published; and when the Overture was performed under his direction at a Société Nationale concert on May 27, 1899, the audience and the critics reacted even more strongly than they had to the *Sites Auriculaires*. Pierre Lalo, writing in *Le Temps*, spoke of " incoherence in the general plan and in the tonal relationships carried to excess ", and compared " the structural approach " to that of Grieg or Rimsky-Korsakov. With this verdict Ravel himself concurred in after years, adding that the Over-

* Founded on February 25, 1871, by Camille Saint-Saëns and a group of his contemporaries to uphold the traditions and interests of French music.

ture was so full of whole-tone scales that he had had " enough of them for a lifetime ". Nevertheless, in a letter to Florent Schmitt (who was then preparing his cantata for the Grand Prix de Rome which he won next year) written just after the concert, Ravel expressed himself as " satisfied " with the orchestration and, while admitting that a section of the audience had " sifflé ferme ", went on to say that " the truth obliges me to admit that those who applauded outnumbered the hostile members of the audience, since I was recalled twice to the platform ". He adds that d'Indy, who was present, " was delighted that it was still possible to get excited over something ", although his attitude towards the composer " was perfectly correct ".

Although the Overture was never published, Ravel did in fact use some of the material in his later song-cycle of the same name (1903), which in all other respects, however, is a work of an entirely different character.

If, then, his first symphonic work, the Overture to *Shéhérazade*, could hardly be considered a success, his next composition, written the same year, had a very different reception and almost made the young composer's reputation overnight. This was the *Pavane pour une Infante Défunte*, which very soon found its way into countless drawing-rooms and became extremely popular with the general public and with amateur pianists everywhere. Once again Ravel was outspoken in his criticism of this early work when he came to write about it later (in the Bulletin of the S.I.M.—*Société Internationale de Musique*—of February 1912). He said then that he no longer perceived its virtues from that distance, but could see its faults only too well, and he attributed the success of what he called " this inconclusive and conventional work " to the " remarkable interpretations " which it had received. The allusion here, of course, is to the title which inspired so many fanciful interpretations, literary, pictorial, choreographical, of the story it is supposed to tell, whereas in reality, as Ravel was never tired of explaining, the only thing that interested him when he made it up was " the pleasure of alliteration ".

The work is curiously untypical of Ravel, and he never wrote anything like it again.

The year 1900 seems to have been a quiet year of study and is marked by no new creation, but in 1901 Ravel made history with a remarkable virtuoso piece for the piano which, with one eye no doubt on Liszt and the fountains in the Villa d'Este, he entitled *Jeux d'Eau*. Even Debussy at that date had written nothing comparable for the piano, and *Jeux d'Eau* is generally considered to have inaugurated a new era in the evolution of the technical resources of the instrument.

All this time, it must be remembered, Ravel was still a student at the Conservatoire, and so in 1901 it was only natural that he should become a candidate for the Grand Prix de Rome for composition, which ensured for the winner of the coveted prize three carefree years of study at the Villa Medicis which the French Institut (Academy of Fine Arts) maintained in Rome as a cultural centre and nursery for prize-winning sculptors, painters, engravers and musicians. The subject of the Cantata (the traditional form of the test-piece) for that year was *Myrrha*, a poem by one Fernand Beissier which seems to have been more than ordinarily loaded with clichés and absurdities. Nevertheless Ravel set about this task with his usual application, but doubtless with a certain sly inclination to parody the outmoded, effusive style of the poem —only to be rewarded with a second prize, in spite of Massenet's backing. The winner that year was André Caplet, afterwards to become a close friend of Debussy, one of his most trusted interpreters, and himself a composer of great distinction.

The following year Ravel tried again. This time the Cantata to be set was entitled *Alcyone* and contained the remarkable alexandrine:

Alcyone! Alcyone! Aimée! Aimée! Hélas!

Again he was unsuccessful, the winner that year being a notably obscure composer, Aymé Kunc, whose name is not even mentioned in the musical dictionaries and whose only claim to fame appears to be his victory over Ravel in this academic contest.

But Ravel was not wasting his time, for it was in this same year that he began to compose his String Quartet (completed the following year), one of his most perfect compositions and one that put him in the front rank of contemporary composers. " My String Quartet in F ", wrote Ravel in after years, " reflects a definite preoccupation with musical structure, imperfectly realized, no doubt, but much more apparent than in my previous compositions." (B.S.)

In 1903, having already won fame with his Quartet, Ravel was once more a candidate for the prize and composed a Cantata entitled *Alyssa*, but again he was not placed. The prize-winner that year was Raoul Laparra, a good musician, who later became a successful composer of operas—his *Habanera* is still in the repertory of the Opéra-Comique—until he was killed in tragic circumstances during a bombardment in 1943.

The next year Ravel decided not to compete. Instead he wrote his song-cycle *Shéhérazade* on poems by Tristan Klingsor which had its first performance at the Société Nationale on May 17, 1904, with Mme Hatto as soloist and Alfred Cortot conducting. Ravel said later of this work that it showed the influence, in spirit at all events, of Debussy, adding that in writing it he had yielded to the profound fascination the Orient had always held for him ever since his childhood. This work, together with others mentioned in this chapter, is discussed in greater detail elsewhere in this book.

In 1905 Ravel, now a fully fledged composer and the author of at least two masterpieces, decided to make one more attempt at the Prix de Rome and entered his name as candidate. This time he was not even admitted to sit for the preliminary examination.

He was by now, *because* of the *Quartet, Shéhérazade* and *Jeux d'Eau*, looked upon as suspect and a dangerous revolutionary by the more bigoted members of the Institute, one of whom* went so far as to declare: "M. Ravel may look upon us as old fogeys if he pleases, but he will not with impunity make fools of us." This time the Institute had gone too far. There were violent protests in the national Press, led by Alfred Edwards of *Le Matin*, and musicians of all shades of opinion were shocked by what had now become " l'affaire Ravel ". The thing had become a public scandal, and to the chorus of protestations and indignation at official obscurantism the distinguished writer Romain Rolland now added his voice.

His protest took the form of a letter to the Director of Fine Arts, Paul Léon, and was couched in the following uncompromising terms: " I am absolutely disinterested in this affair. I am not a friend of Ravel's; I can even say that I am not personally in sympathy with his subtle and refined art. But what in justice I am compelled to say is that Ravel is not merely a promising pupil; he is already one of the most distinguished of our younger school of composers, which cannot claim many like him. . . The competition was honoured by the presence of a musician of his standing, and even if by some unfortunate chance, which I would find it difficult to account for, his compositions were, or appeared to be, inferior to those of his fellow competitors, he ought all the same to have been admitted. . . I admire the composers who dared to judge him. Who will judge them in return? Forgive me for interfering in a question which does not concern me, but it is the duty of each one of us to protest against a judgment which, even if strictly legal, nevertheless is an offence against real justice and against art."

Romain Rolland's intervention turned the scales heavily against the " die-hards ", and was probably largely instrumental in bringing about the resignation before the end of the year of Théodore Dubois, one of the last pillars of conservatism, who had been directing, or misdirecting, the Paris Conservatoire since 1896. He was succeeded by Gabriel Fauré, under whose enlightened direction the old Conservatoire took

* Emile Paladilhe, 1844-1926.

on a new lease of life, and the standard of musical instruction in France was thereby immeasurably improved.

Meanwhile, whatever Ravel's feelings may have been, he said nothing, took no action and remained aloof from the controversy that raged round him. He must nevertheless have been glad to accept the invitation of Alfred and Misia Edwards to accompany them on a cruise in their yacht to Holland.

Edwards, who was the son of a very wealthy man, physician-in-chief to the Sultan Abdul Hamid, was at that time a prominent figure in Parisian society, a millionaire and proprietor of the great Parisian daily *Le Matin*. His wife, Misia, the half-sister of Cyprien (" Cipa ") Godebski, one of Ravel's most intimate friends, whose name will occur frequently in these pages, was a great patron of the arts and a fervent admirer of Ravel. She had previously been married to Thadée Natanson, founder of the famous literary journal *La Revue Blanche* (of which Debussy was for a short time the music critic), and was later to become the wife of the Catalan painter J. M. Sert. A woman of striking personality, elegance and charm, she was in every sense a leader of fashion, not only in material things such as dress and interior decoration, but also in the sphere of art and literature; and her *salon* was one of the most brilliant in Paris.

The Edwards possessed a luxurious yacht called the *Aimée*, and for the next six weeks or so Ravel was their guest on board this floating palace as it made its way through the canals of France and Flanders to Holland, ending with a trip up the Rhine as far as Frankfurt. The return journey was made through Holland once more to Ostend, and thence by sea to Le Havre, where Ravel took leave of his friends. The painter Bonnard was his fellow guest on this cruise, but unfortunately a picture he painted while on the yacht disappeared during the second world war.

Eleven letters written by Ravel to various friends from the " Yacht Aimée " have been preserved. Apart from his evident delight in the pictures he saw in Holland and Germany

("... des Franz Hals qui sont une révélation! ... un admirable Rembrandt, des Cranach et surtout un Velasquez! "), what impressed him most were the great factories and smoking chimneys in the industrial areas of Belgium and Germany. At Liége he notes " strange, magnificent factories, one, especially, like a sort of Romanesque cathedral of cast iron emitting a reddish smoke and slender flames ". On the Rhine, near Düsseldorf, he encounters the same vision again; he calls it " ce spectacle prodigieux ". He is writing to his great friend Maurice Delage: " How can I convey to you the impression of these castles of iron, these incandescent cathedrals, the marvellous symphony of conveyor belts, whistles and mighty hammer-blows by which one is surrounded. Everywhere the sky is red, dark and threatening... How full of music all this is (" ce que tout cela est musical ") and I have every intention of making use of it." In another letter he comments on the windmills: "... on all sides you see nothing but their sails going round and round. Looking at this mechanical landscape one begins to feel one is an automaton oneself. With all this, needless to say, I am doing absolutely nothing. But I'm storing it all up, and I think quite a lot will come out of this voyage."

These letters are already an indication of Ravel's aesthetic outlook, and for that reason alone are worth quoting. The poetry and drama of machinery impress him more than the beauties of nature; the reference to the " mechanical landscape " and to being an " automaton " reveal the natural bent of his mind towards mechanical toys, automata of all kinds, puppets and everything artificial, and seem to foreshadow the ticking clocks in *L'Heure Espagnole*, the pagoda bells in *Ma Mère l'Oye*, the *Noël des Jouets*, the cricket winding up his watch in the *Histoires Naturelles* and all the phantasmagoria of furniture coming to life, striking grandfather clocks, talking teapots and waltzing chairs which captured his imagination in *L'Enfant et les Sortilèges*. The furnishings and contents of his house at Montfort L'Amaury bear witness, too, to his love for *chinoiserie*, mechanical toys, bric-à-brac and pastiche of every kind—an essential trait in his character which provides a clue to a better understanding of the man and his music.

By the end of July 1905 the cruise was over and Ravel, back in Paris after some visits to friends in the country, settled down once more to work and make plans for the future.

CHAPTER THREE

1905–1913

THE storm aroused by the Institute's exclusion of Ravel from the Prix de Rome contest in 1905 had at least served to focus the limelight on the thirty-year-old composer, who now found himself a celebrity. But when the hubbub had died down, he settled to work, and the next ten years of his life were a period of intense creative activity. Many of his best works were, in fact, composed during these years. I would list the following as the most important: for the piano, *Miroirs* and the *Sonatine* (1905), *Ma Mère l'Oye* (1908) and the *Valses Nobles et Sentimentales* (1911); for voice and piano, *Histoires Naturelles* (1906); for orchestra, *Rapsodie Espagnole* (1907); for the theatre, *L'Heure Espagnole* (1907) and *Daphnis et Chloë* (1909–1912), and, finally, the *Piano Trio* (1914). Had he written nothing more, these works alone would have sufficed to establish him as one of France's, indeed of Europe's, foremost composers. It only remained for his fame, thus assured, to be enhanced and consolidated by the works of his last period, notably *Le Tombeau de Couperin* (1917), *L'Enfant et les Sortilèges* (1925), *Chansons Madécasses* (1926) and the two Piano Concertos (1930–1931).

The ten years that followed his leaving the Conservatoire up to the outbreak of war in 1914 were also the years in which Ravel found his freedom and his place in the artistic world of Paris. He began to lead a bohemian existence in the company of congenial friends, but his "bohemianism" was never of the sordid, if picturesque, *vie de bohème*, life-in-a-garret type; it was a far more sophisticated and dandified brand of bohemianism that he affected, and he moved in the most select and distinguished literary, musical and artistic circles.

At the centre of the little band of Ravel's closest friends were the Godebski family, Ida and Cyprien (" Cipa ") Godebski and their children Mimi and Jean (for whom Ravel wrote *Ma Mère l'Oye*). Cyprien Godebski's father was a Pole who had settled in France and married a French wife; they were people of great culture and refinement and had transmitted these qualities to their son. In this way, Cyprien and his wife, who was also of Polish origin, although by no means wealthy, were able to take an active part in the artistic and intellectual life of the French capital, where their flat in the Rue d'Athènes was the rendezvous of the *élite* of the Parisian world of writers, artists and musicians. Among those who were regular visitors to the Godebski's Sunday evenings were Jean Cocteau and André Gide, Léon-Paul Fargue, Paul Valéry and Valéry-Larbaud, Jean Aubry and Arnold Bennett, Ambroise Vollard, the painters La Fresnaye and d'Espagnat, Valentine Gross (now Valentine Hugo), the musicians Albert Roussel, Florent Schmitt, Déodat de Sévérac, Darius Milhaud, Georges Auric, Maurice Delage, Roland-Manuel, Ricardo Viñes, Alfredo Casella, Manuel de Falla, Igor Stravinsky, Erik Satie, and sometimes Diaghilev and Nijinsky.

There was also another circle of friends with whom Ravel was even more intimately associated; these used to meet at the house of the painter Paul Sordes and, later, in Maurice Delage's studio in Auteuil. The " Club des Apaches ",* as they called themselves, numbered among its members (in addition to several of those mentioned above, such as Léon-Paul Fargue, Florent Schmitt, Maurice Delage and Ricardo Viñes) the poets Tristan Klingsor and Charles Guérin, the composers André Caplet, Paul Ladmirault and D. E. Inghelbrecht, the critics Emile Vuillermoz and M. D. Calvocoressi, Lucien Garban, of the Maison Durand and Ravel's lifelong friend, the Abbé Léonce Petit, a well-known figure in the

* The story goes that on one occasion the little band were coming away from a concert when they were jostled by a newspaper-seller who cried out: " Attention, aux apaches ! " This pleased them enormously, and from then on the nickname remained with them.

Paris musical world, the brothers Paul and Charles Sordes and another painter, Edouard Benedictus, artist, dandy and inventor—one of his inventions being safety glass.

The Apaches had a private code of communication and used to greet one another by whistling softly the theme of the first movement of Borodin's Second Symphony. They could often be heard referring to another, but imaginary, member of the group, a certain " Gomez de Riquet ", who had been invented by Ravel so that he and his friends could always pretend a rendezvous with this non-existent personage to escape from tedious company or avoid an unwanted invitation.

Ravel at this time wore side-whiskers and a beard, and was always elegantly dressed. The Baudelairian cult of the dandy was exactly suited to his temperament—a mixture of fastidiousness, extreme reserve and a certain preciosity which is everywhere apparent in his music. He was known to his intimate friends as " Rara". Léon-Paul Fargue has sketched the following portrait of Ravel as he was at this epoch:*

> Already his career was beginning to take shape. He joined us in our *cafés* and in our wanderings through Paris, and shared our enthusiasms and our crazes of the moment. Like us, he was determined to go to every performance of *Pelléas* to the last. He liked Mallarmé, Marcel Schwob, the tenth arrondissement, the old gates of the Central market, exhibitions of precious objects, the coarse black tobacco that used to be weighed in scales made of horn, the horses on the merry-go-round, the Eiffel Tower, the little theatres of Belleville, and the great ladies in society without understanding of any kind. We were happy, cultivated and aggressive, especially at concerts where we never hesitated to demonstrate, red in the face and chin in the air like a drawbridge, the burning and spontaneous justice of our point of view.
>
> It was in this passionate atmosphere of conflicting ideas and sensations, during these crowded hours where everything was worth its weight in richness and dignity, that the works of Ravel took shape, silently, in his patient and heroic soul. Here there was no question of failure or mediocrity, of favour-seeking or jobbery or of music for drawing-rooms, bars or of the type which panders to fashionable sentimentality. Only of works, in the purest sense of the term. After the miraculous freshness of the piano works he

* *Ravel par quelques-uns de ses familiers.* Editions du Tambourinaire, Paris, 1939.

had now entered on his dramatic period, and everyone was talking of his great successes—the *Rapsodie Espagnole*, *L'Heure Espagnole*, *L'Enfant et les Sortilèges*, *Daphnis et Chloë*—the fruit of some thirty years of devotion to art and the inner life. And always, everywhere, in the simplest bar as in the strongest climaxes, that same fragile, smiling grace, that spirit at once tender and severe, that same clarity, that rich flower garden full of memories of Bach and Rameau, Mozart and Chabrier, mingled with allusions to America...

Ravel had a pawky sense of humour of his own. I can see him now, like a sort of debonair wizard, sitting in his corner at the *Grand Ecart* or the *Bœuf sur le Toit*, telling endless stories which had the same sort of elegance, richness and clarity as his compositions. He could tell a story as well as he could write a waltz or an adagio. One of the most remarkable traits of this curious Pyrenean was his passion for perfection. This man, who was profoundly intelligent, versatile, precise and as learned as it was possible to be and who did everything with a facility which was proverbial, had the character and qualities of an artisan—and there was nothing he liked better than to be compared to one. He liked doing things, and doing things well; everything that issued from his brain, whatever reservations the critics may make about his inspiration, bears the stamp of perfection, a certain perfection. He knew that a thing, a poem, a novel, a picture, a garden, a love-affair or a ceremony— all such events or dramas can have what is called "finish", to employ a term used in the workshop. And it was his passion to offer the public works which were " finished " and polished to the last degree. Such a high degree of professional conscientiousness is becoming more and more rare in our time.

This picture of Ravel is as good a likeness of him at the age of thirty—the year we have now arrived at—as at any other period of his life. The truth is that both his character and his tastes were formed early and underwent little change as he grew older. The essential Ravel, indeed, is to be found no less in the words of the period we are now considering than in those composed at the end of his life. Thus, the " miraculous freshness " of the early piano pieces referred to by Léon-Paul Fargue in the passage just quoted is a term that could equally well be applied to *L'Enfant et les Sortilèges* or even *Boléro*. However, Fargue was thinking no doubt of such things as *Jeux d'Eau*, *Miroirs* and the *Sonatine*, of which the last two date from 1905. Writing later about *Miroirs* Ravel said: ". . . they represent such a considerable change in my harmonic development that even musicians who were accustomed to my manner up to then were somewhat disconcerted." (B.S.)

The *Sonatine* could be described as a typically Ravelian piece of pastiche, exquisitely wrought and impregnated with the nostalgic fragrance of some old forgotten potpourri, but with an added piquancy due to the skilful infusion of new harmonic blood into the old veins of classical form. Yet with all its charm, this music is as brittle and impersonal as some rare piece of porcelain.

Very different were the *Histoires Naturelles*, which followed close upon the *Sonatine*. Here Ravel was definitely breaking new ground. To many people it seemed madness to attempt to set to music the dry, precise prose of that master of irony and acute observation, Jules Renard (the author, *inter alia*, of *Poil de Carotte*); but, to quote Ravel's own words: " For a long time I had been attracted by the clear, direct language and deep hidden poetry of these sketches by Jules Renard. The text itself demanded a particular kind of declamation, closely bound to the inflexions of the French language. The first performance of the *Histoires Naturelles* at the Société Nationale provoked a veritable scandal, which gave rise to lively polemics in the musical Press at the time." (B.S.)

The date of this performance was January 12, 1907, and the singer was Madame Jane Bathori, the champion of new music in France, who was always ready to serve with her great talent and musicianship the cause of the *avant-garde* by interpreting to an often uncomprehending public whatever she judged worthy to be heard. Later she was to be the faithful interpreter of Satie and the " Six ", and it was to her that Ravel almost invariably entrusted his *premières auditions*. On this occasion she was accompanied by Ravel at the piano, but a section of the audience jeered and hissed, and the critics were uncomplimentary. Pierre Lalo of *Le Temps* talked of " café-concert music, with chords of the ninth ". The hostility shown by the public of 1907 to Ravel's witty and allusive settings of Jules Renard's delightful and imaginative thumb-nail sketches of the *Peacock*, the *Cricket*, the *Swan*, the *King-fisher* and the *Guinea-fowl* is difficult for us to understand today, but it must be remembered that, for one thing, Ravel in these pieces had thrown overboard melody in the accepted sense of the term, leaving in its place hardly more than a spoken de-clamation following closely the inflexions of the speaking voice and ignoring the conventional laws of prosody according to which, in a musical setting, the mute final *e* should never be elided. This alone was enough to shock the purists and, indeed, this trick, which seems peculiar to Ravel (Debussy never practised it), is disconcerting even to our ears today. But the rich, bold harmonic texture which so imaginatively underlines the irony, and at the same time the poetic insight of Renard's magically evocative miniatures, lift the whole thing to the level of great art; and today it is difficult to think of Ravel without thinking of the *Histoires Naturelles*.

The actual composition of the *Histoires Naturelles* dates from 1906, and in the same year Ravel completed his *Introduction and Allegro* for harp, string quartet, and flute and clarinet, as well as a little-known setting of Henri de Régnier's *Les Grands Vents venus d'Outre-mer* for voice and piano. He had also started to work feverishly at a projected opera which he later abandoned altogether, although the subject had fired his imagination at the time. It was to be a setting of Gerhardt Hauptmann's fantastic fairy play *Die versunkene Glocke* (1896), which he had come across in the French translation of A. F. Hérold. In June 1906 Ravel wrote to his great friend, Maurice Delage, to tell him that for two weeks he had been completely absorbed in the composition of *La Cloche Engloutie*, and in August of the same year he was still working hard on his new opera in Switzerland, where he had gone to be with his father, whose health was then failing (he died in 1908), at Hermance on the Lake of Geneva.

" You can already imagine a great part of the second act," he writes, " in addition to what you know of the first. (Are you anxious to have an opera in 5 acts? You'll have it in a week!) "

But the project came to nothing. Like Debussy, the number of whose projected but never completed works is considerable, Ravel too, from time to time, had planned to write, and even in some cases begun to sketch some half-dozen works of which no trace has remained, including a full-length opera, *à la* Meyerbeer, on the subject of Joan of Arc.* It was not, however, until 1914 that *La Cloche Engloutie* was definitely abandoned, although, according to M. Roland-Manuel, the composer used some of the material in *La Cloche* for *L'Enfant et les Sortilèges*, notably the theme of the Tree and the chorus of Frogs.

The year 1907 was a particularly fruitful one and saw the creation not only of the *Cinq mélodies populaires grecques* but also of two of Ravel's major works—both of Iberian inspiration—the *Rapsodie Espagnole* for orchestra, and the one-act opera *L'Heure Espagnole*. The first of these was his first important symphonic work, the second his first opera. The *Rapsodie* had also the distinction of being one of the few works, together with *La Valse* and *Boléro*, which were scored directly for orchestra and not, as was the case with many of his other works, orchestrated later from the original piano version.

The *Rhapsody* was a perfect vehicle for his virtuosity, and revealed him as a master of the modern orchestra. Manuel de Falla, writing in *La Revue Musicale* in 1939, has recorded his opinion of the *Rhapsody* in the following words: " It surprises one by its (genuinely) Spanish character. In absolute agreement with my own intentions (and diametrically opposed to Rimsky-Korsakov in his *Capriccio*) this ' Hispanization ' is not achieved merely by drawing upon popular or ' folk ' sources (except in the Jota in *Feria*) but rather through the free use of the modal rhythms and melodies and ornamental figures of our ' popular ' music, none of which has altered in any way the natural style of the composer." It is interesting to recall in this context that Falla had expressed the same opinion on

* For further details of these projects, see Appendix IV.

Debussy's *Iberia*, and also on his *Soirée dans Grenade* (one of the three *Estampes* for piano) which he described as " characteristically Spanish down to the smallest details ".

The *Rapsodie Espagnole* was first performed by the Colonne orchestra at the Châtelet, under Edouard Colonne, on March 28, 1908, and, unlike many of Ravel's earlier works, was an immediate success. The second section, *Malagueña*, was even encored; and M. Roland-Manuel recalls that when this provoked some ironical protests from the stalls, the voice of Florent Schmitt was heard from the gallery demanding yet another *bis* " for the gentlemen downstairs who haven't been able to understand ".

There are many examples in French nineteenth- and twentieth-century music of a tendency on the part of composers to borrow from beyond the Pyrenees new rhythms and fresh colours with which to enrich their palette; and one has only to think of Bizet, Lalo, Chabrier, Debussy and Ravel to realize with what apparent ease these composers acquired a mastery of the Spanish idiom that, with the possible exception of Bizet, seems no less authentic than that of the Spanish musicians themselves. Ravel and Debussy, indeed, as we have seen, won the unstinted praise of such a master as Falla, testifying to the absolute authenticity of their " Iberianism ". In Ravel's case, it is true, there was at any rate a partially hereditary explanation for this although, in spite of his Basque origin, there are few, if any, traces of Basque influences in his music. On the contrary, it was, we are told, with the music of the South, the typical dance rhythms of Andalucia and even the Italianized melodies of the nineteenth-century *zarzuelas* sung to him by his mother from which Ravel as a child gained his first impressions of a Spain which later he was to embody in so masterly a fashion in the *Rapsodie*, in *Boléro* and in his brilliant one-act opera *L'Heure Espagnole* which followed closely on the *Rapsodie*.

The opera gave Ravel fresh opportunities to develop the vocal style inaugurated in the settings of Jules Renard's *Histoires Naturelles*, which, in the composer's own words,

" prepared me for the composition of *L'Heure Espagnole*, a lyric comedy by Franc-Nohain which itself is a sort of musical conversation. This work bears witness to my intention of continuing in the tradition of *opéra-bouffe* ". (B.S.)

This idea, expressed so briefly in the biographical sketch written in after years, had, however, been elaborated by the composer at the time of composition in the following statement, addressed apparently to Jean Godebski (and quoted by René Chalupt in his *Ravel au Miroir de ses Lettres*):

> What I have tried to do is rather ambitious—namely, to regenerate the Italian *opera-bouffe*: I mean only the *principle*. This work is not conceived in the traditional form, like its ancestor—its only ancestor—Mussorgsky's *Marriage*, which is a faithful interpretation of Gogol's play. *L'Heure Espagnole* is a musical comedy; apart from a few cuts, I have not altered anything in Franc-Nohain's text. Only the quintet at the end might, by its general " layout ", its *vocalises* and vocal effects, recall the typical repertory " ensemble ". But except for this quintet, it is mostly ordinary declamation rather than singing; for the French language, like any other, has its own accents and musical inflexions. And I do not see why one should not take advantage of these qualities in order to arrive at correct prosody. The spirit of the work is frankly humoristic. It is through the music above all—the harmony, rhythm and orchestration—that I have tried to express irony, and not, as in an operetta, by an arbitrary and comical accumulation of words. I have long been dreaming of a humorous musical work, and the modern orchestra seemed perfectly adapted to underline and exaggerate comic effects. On reading Franc-Nohain's *L'Heure Espagnole*, I formed the opinion that this droll fantasy was just what I was looking for. A whole lot of things in this work attracted me—the mixture of familiar conversation and intentionally absurd lyricism, and the atmosphere of unusual and amusing noises by which the characters are surrounded in this clockmaker's shop. Also, the opportunities for making use of the picturesque rhythms of Spanish music."

These remarks throw an interesting light on Ravel's views on a work which is a landmark, not only in his own production, but also in the history of the French lyric stage. Moreover, in choosing as a subject for his first operatic work this **highly** artificial and somewhat *risqué* comedy by Franc-

Nohain, a contemporary French poet and writer* noted for his dry and caustic wit and sarcastic humour, Ravel was also affirming, as we have seen, his intention of carrying a step farther his ideas on the treatment of the human voice and the possibilities of setting to music a text of a kind which to most composers would have seemed refractory and essentially unmusical. The truth is, Ravel was instinctively attracted by the non-human element in both Renard's ironical sketches of birds and insects and Franc-Nohain's cynically detached presentation of the slightly licentious story of the clockmaker's wife and her lovers. By dehumanizing the passions and emotions of the principals in this lightest of comedies Ravel turned the whole thing into a kind of puppet show, which gave him every opportunity for accentuating the artificiality of the subject and the décor. Indeed, nothing could have delighted him more than the setting of the clockmaker's shop with its whirring and ticking clocks of all sizes and descriptions, the stylized Spanish costumes and the hot noonday sun filtering through the shutters to heighten the sultry atmosphere of heartless passions and libertinage.

In vivid and precise terms Roland-Manuel has described exactly how Ravel has treated the personages in this cynical comedy of amorous intrigue: " Instead of humanizing the characters and softening the passions that inflamed them, he ruthlessly lays bare the elementary mechanism of their instincts . . . uncompromisingly cuts out the guileless or lascivious attraction each one possesses and then, by grafting a cylinder in place of a heart, changes them into marionettes with cunning, but frozen reflexes. But, by a weird substitution, the hearts he tore from them come to beat tenderly in the breasts of clocks and automata, lending to these little steel bodies the semblance of a soul and the sweet warmth of life."†

Although *L'Heure Espagnole* was written in the space of five months in 1907, while Ravel was living with his brother at Levallois, the Parisian suburb where many of his works were

---

* A contributor to *La Revue Blanche* and author of *Poèmes amorphes, Chansons des trains et des gares, Flûtes* and *La nouvelle cuisinière bourgeoise.*

† *Ravel.* Nouvelle Revue Critique, 1938. English translation, Dobson, London, 1947.

composed, it was not until May 19, 1911, that the work was finally staged at the Opéra-Comique, with Geneviève Vix and Jean Périer in the leading roles, under the direction of François Ruhlmann.

In the meantime Ravel continued to pour out in quick succession a number of his best-known compositions: two important piano works, namely the fairy-tale suite for four hands, *Ma Mère l'Oye*, and *Gaspard de la Nuit* (both 1908); the *Minuet on the name of Haydn* (1909); the settings of seven *Folk-Songs* of different nations for voice and piano (1910); and the *Valses Nobles et Sentimentales* (1911).

Two of the above-mentioned works, *Ma Mère l'Oye* and the *Valses Nobles et Sentimentales*, were first performed under the auspices of the newly formed Société Musicale Indépendante (S.M.I.), of which Ravel was one of the founder members. The S.M.I. had been constituted in the spring of 1910 by a group of composers, mostly pupils of Fauré, in opposition to the more conservative Société Nationale de Musique, which was still largely under the influence of the Schola Cantorum, the stronghold of the Franckist tradition.

Ma Mère l'Oye had its first public performance at the S.M.I.'s inaugural concert on April 20, 1910. Ravel had originally intended that it should be played by the two Godebski children, for whom it was written, but this proved to be impracticable and the work was finally entrusted to two small girls, one of whom, a pupil of Mme Marguerite Long, was Mlle Jeanne Leleu, a future Grand Prix de Rome. After the concert Ravel wrote to thank and congratulate her on the performance, as follows:

Mademoiselle,

When you are a great virtuoso and I an old fogey, covered with honours or else completely forgotten, you will perhaps have pleasant memories of having given an artist the rare satisfaction of hearing a work of his, of a rather unusual nature, interpreted exactly as it should be. Thank you a thousand times for your child-like and sensitive performance of *Ma Mère l'Oye*.

Your devoted, etc.

Maurice Ravel.   21/4/10.

The following year the *Valses Nobles et Sentimentales* were performed at another S.M.I. concert under rather special circumstances. It was decided to introduce the work anonymously, and the audience were invited to guess the identity of the composer. Ravel records that his authorship was recognized by only a small majority, and that the *Valses* were received with boos and protests by the public. (B.S.) They were played by Louis Aubert, to whom they are dedicated, but seem to have completely mystified the audience. Although a large proportion of those present were professional musicians or critics, the unfamiliar idiom of the *Valses* led to the strangest attributions of authorship being made—ranging from Kodaly to Erik Satie.

The work seems to us today to represent the quintessence of Ravel's genius, and although he may have written for the piano pages of greater brilliance and perhaps more effective from the purely virtuoso point of view, the *Valses Nobles et Sentimentales* are especially remarkable for their epigrammatic concision combined with a certain subtly sensuous, but rather acid fragrance that no other work of his possesses in quite the same degree. They are, in fact, a little microcosm in which the whole of Ravel's formidable musical equipment, both technical and emotional, and especially his very personal harmonic sense, can be studied to the very best advantage. Roland-Manuel finds in them an echo of Baudelaire, and speaks of the " sensualité un peu sèche ", the " frissons électriques ", the " souplesses de chat " which the music evokes for him, as well as the " malédiction " which seems to have overtaken the work in so far as it is shunned by pianists and generally underrated by the public, who mistakenly prefer that other embodiment of the spirit of the waltz, *La Valse*.*

The music made a more favourable impression the following year when Ravel orchestrated it to accompany a ballet called *Adélaïde, ou le Langage des Fleurs* in which the leading part was danced by Mlle Trouhanova at the Châtelet in April 1912. The ballet only had four (gala) performances altogether, and

* Roland-Manuel: *Maurice Ravel*. Gallimard, 1948.

except for a single representation at the Opéra in 1916, in the middle of the war, *Adélaïde* was never put on again. At its first performace at the Châtelet it was directed by Ravel, making one of his rare appearances as conductor, in a programme in which the other ballets, also conducted by their respective composers, were d'Indy's *Istar*, Florent Schmitt's *Salomé*, and *Le Péri* of Paul Dukas. In music, as in other spheres of life, this was, indeed, France's *belle époque*.

1912 could be said to have been Ravel's " ballet year ", for it also saw the production of *Daphnis et Chloë* by the Ballets Russes of Serge de Diaghilev at the Châtelet on June 8. It was, however, as far back as 1909 that Ravel had first been approached by Diaghilev, then as always on the look-out for new talent. The subject was suggested by Fokine. Ravel accepted, but it took him three years to complete the score. Arrangements for the production and choreography gave rise to endless disputes, and it was only after a major quarrel between Diaghilev and Fokine, which ended in their parting company for good, that the ballet was finally produced. Nijinsky and Karsavina danced the leading roles, the scenery was painted by Léon Bakst, and the first performance was conducted by Pierre Monteux. The press on the whole was favourable. Robert Brussel in the *Figaro* June 9, 1912, had nothing but praise for Ravel's latest major work, which he declared was " the most accomplished and most poetic work yet produced by the artistic enterprise of M. Serge de Diaghilev ". Emile Vuillermoz in the journal *S.I.M.*, June 15, 1912, praised the " firm design, surprising dynamic force and irrestible *élan* " of the music, which showed that Ravel was now completely a master of his art. The last part of the work, he thought, showed " a kind of happy *laisser-aller* and nonchalant mastery which could not fail to delight those musicians who had been sorry to see a certain stiffness and affectation in the ironic Muse of *L'Heure Espagnole* ". The only dissident notes were struck by the two critics generally hostile to Ravel, Pierre Lalo of *Le Temps* and Gaston Carraud of *La Liberté*, both of whom, rather surprisingly, found the music lacking in rhythm. The ballet had only two performances in Paris that year, but was revived with success during the next year's season of Russian Ballet.

For the London production in 1914 Diaghilev had prepared, apparently without obtaining Ravel's consent, an abridged version of the ballet, which caused the composer to address the following letter of protest to the London press, sending copies to *The Times*, *Morning Post*, *Daily Mail* and *Daily Telegraph*:

June 7, 1914.
Sir,

My most important work, *Daphnis et Chloë*, is to be produced at the Drury Lane Theatre on Tuesday, June 9. I was overjoyed; and, fully appreciating the great honour done to me, considered the event as one of the weightiest in my artistic career. Now I learn that what will be produced before the London public is not my work in its original form, but a makeshift arrangement which I had accepted to write at M. Diaghilev's special request in order to facilitate production in certain minor centres. M. Diaghilev probably considers London as one of the aforesaid " minor centres ", since he is about to produce at Drury Lane, in spite of his positive word, the new version without chorus. I am deeply surprised and grieved, and I consider the proceedings as disrespectful towards the London public as well as towards the composer. I shall therefore be extremely thankful to offering you [*sic*] my thanks in anticipation.

I remain, dear Sir,
Faithfully yours,
Maurice Ravel.

In a letter to Vaughan Williams, enclosing a copy of this letter, Ravel is careful to make it clear that the English is not his own, his original letter having been translated by some friend, unspecified.

Before passing on to consider the events of the last year of peace before the cataclysm of 1914, mention should be made of another occasion on which Ravel again played a leading part at a memorable concert of the S.M.I. We have already referred to the composer's admiration for Erik Satie. Now, when he himself was at the height of his fame, he decided the time had come to make the music of Satie more widely known. Accordingly he arranged for the inclusion in the programme of one of the S.M.I.'s concerts a number of Satie's piano works which he played himself. The date was January 16, 1911. Ravel had chosen the second *Sarabande*, the third *Gymnopédie* and the *Prélude du Fils des Etoiles* (which he later orchestrated, but left unpublished). The public was delighted, and the more progressive critics now began to " write up " Satie. In the programme note of this concert reference is made to " the surprising manner in which certain works of Satie anticipated the modernist vocabulary ", and to the " almost prophetic character of certain harmonic inventions they contain ". The writer goes on to say: " M. Claude Debussy paid a striking tribute to this subtle explorer by orchestrating two of his *Gymnopédies*: and now, M. Ravel, by playing today the second *Sarabande*, which bears the astonishing date of 1887, bears witness to the esteem which is felt by the most ' advanced ' composers for the creator who, a quarter of a century ago, was already speaking the musical jargon of tomorrow."

Ravel, indeed, had never concealed his admiration for the older composer, who was well aware of it. In a characteristic letter to his brother Conrad, written only two days before the S.M.I. concert, Satie comments as follows on Ravel's attitude towards him: " Ravel est un Prix de Rome* [*sic*] d'un très grand talent. Un Debussy plus épatant. Il me certifie toutes les fois que je le rencontre qu'il me doit beaucoup. Moi, je veux bien." (" Ravel is a very talented ' Prix de Rome '. A kind of super-Debussy. He assures me every time we meet that he is greatly indebted to me. That's all right by me.") Nevertheless Satie was delighted at this public recognition of him as a serious composer, but, while grateful to Ravel, he could not help regretting the absence of Debussy on this important occasion. Unfortunately Debussy and Ravel were

---

* In 1901, as we have seen, Ravel obtained a second prize, but, unlike Debussy, was never awarded the Grand Prix. How this caused a major scandal has been related in Chapter II.

not on the best of terms at the time, and Debussy may have been jealous of Ravel's patronage of Satie, whom he looked upon rather as his own *protégé*. In any event Ravel's gesture, it is clear, was entirely disinterested, and in paying a public tribute to Satie, whom he genuinely admired, he certainly had no *arrière-pensée* of any kind.

CHAPTER FOUR

1913–1920

ONE of the results of Ravel's collaboration with Diaghilev and his Ballets Russes was the opportunity it gave him to see more of Igor Stravinsky, with whom he was now on very friendly terms. Early in 1913 the two composers were brought even closer together when they were commissioned by Diaghilev to undertake the completion and reorchestration of Mussorgsky's opera *Khovantschina* which, encouraged by the triumphant success of *Boris Godounov*, Diaghilev was anxious to produce in Paris at the earliest opportunity.* Stravinsky was then living at Clarens on the Lake of Geneva, and Ravel went to join him there in April.

In addition to their work on the opera, it so happened that both were engaged at the time in writing works for the same combination of voice and instruments, for Stravinsky was composing his *Japanese Lyrics* and Ravel his settings of three poems by Mallarmé, the scoring in both instances being for voice, piano, string quartet, two flutes and two clarinets. This may have been due less to coincidence than to the fact that both composers were at the time intensely interested in the latest experiments of Schoenberg, whose *Pierrot Lunaire* had just had its first performance in Berlin a few months previously. From Clarens Ravel wrote to the committee of the S.M.I. (of which Alfred Casella was then secretary-general) with suggestions for what he called a " concert scandaleux ", the programme to consist of *Pierrot Lunaire*, Stravinsky's *Japanese Lyrics* and two of his own Mallarmé poems (*Soupir*

* The Ravel-Stravinsky version was never used because Chaliapin declined to sing it and, according to Stravinsky (*Conversations with Robert Craft*), the MS., which he took with him on his last visit to Russia, has been lost or destroyed.

and *Placet futile*). The concert did take place the following year, but not quite as planned; *Pierrot Lunaire* had to be omitted, its place being taken by *Quatre Poèmes Hindous* by Maurice Delage. It was not until after the 1914 war that Schoenberg's famous song-cycle was heard in Paris. Commenting in later years on his *Trois Poèmes de Mallarmé* Ravel admits that he had Schoenberg in mind when writing them, at least as regards their instrumentation, which, he says, is almost exactly the same as that of *Pierrot Lunaire*. (B.S.)

It was at Clarens, too, that Ravel first saw the score of Stravinsky's newly composed *Sacre du Printemps* which was to have its stormy *première* in Paris on May 29 that same year. Enormously impressed, he realized at once the implications of this (as it seemed at the time) revolutionary work and the impact it was bound to have on the course of musical history; and on March 3 he wrote to his friend Lucien Garban urging him not to miss the first performance of the *Sacre*, adding: " I think this will be as important an event as the *première* of *Pelléas*."*

After completing the *Trois Poèmes* Ravel began to plan a Piano Concerto to be based on Basque themes under the title of *Zaspiak-Bat*, but soon came to the conclusion that this would be impracticable as he would find it impossible to adapt folk tunes to the exigencies of his own style and of the form he was contemplating. It is true he had already tried his hand with complete success at harmonizing folk melodies of various nationalities in his *Cinq mélodies populaires grecques* (1907) and in the *Chants Populaires* of 1910, a collection of seven songs— Spanish, French, Italian, Hebrew, Scottish, Flemish and

---

* Ravel's esteem for Stravinsky did not, however, prevent him later from expressing openly his dislike of *Mavra* (1922), which led to a cooling off in the hitherto friendly relations between the two composers. Nor did this temporary estrangement prevent him from expressing with equal frankness his admiration of *Noces*, which Diaghilev produced the following year. In a letter dated June 26, 1923, he wrote as follows to his friend Roland-Manuel (cited in *Revue de Musicologie*, Vol. XXXVIII, July 1956):

Dear Friend,

" I heard *Noces* last Thursday. . . You were right: it is a splendid work. I even think it is Stravinsky's masterpiece to date, and its presentation is also one of the masterpieces of the Russian season. I am indebted to you; had you not insisted, I might perhaps have been deprived of this great joy. . ."

Russian—which he had set for a competition arranged by the *Maison du Lied* in Moscow. But, as Ravel saw, it is one thing to bend your art to meet the requirements of the folk idiom, and another to use that idiom as a basis for more sophisticated forms of music. Hence his decision to proceed no further with *Zaspiak-Bat*.

In the summer of 1913 Ravel retired to St. Jean-de-Luz to work at the *Trio* for violin, violoncello and piano which he had been contemplating since 1908. By March 1914 he had finished the first movement, but the work was not completed until August of that year. In the meantime he had travelled to Geneva and Lyons to be present at concerts of his works. In a letter to Mme Godebski, written after his return to St. Jean-de-Luz in April 1914, Ravel relates with amusement how he heard two ladies discussing his *Histoires Naturelles*, one of them remarking, after the work had been very warmly received: "... tout de même, ce n'était pas du Beethoven." Although the concert was a success, Ravel comments ironically that of course there wasn't the same enthusiasm as he had met with in London—" mais il faut compter avec la froideur méridionale "!

A spirit of mockery was never far beneath the surface of Ravel's habitual detachment, and often coloured his comments on current affairs. Thus the banning of the tango, which was all the rage in 1914, by the Archbishop of Paris caused him to write from St. Jean-de-Luz to his friend Godebski: " I am now slaving away for the benefit of the Pope. You know that this august personage, for whom Redfern is preparing the appropriate costume, has just launched a new dance, the Forlane "—an attempt had been made to substitute this for the tango in polite society—" and I'm now transcribing one by Couperin. I'm going to get Mistinguett and Colette Willy to dance it in fancy dress at the Vatican. Don't be surprised at this return to religion, due, no doubt, to the atmosphere of my birthplace. Ah, there's the Angelus ringing; I'm off now to dinner."

But he was soon to be writing and thinking of more serious

things, for on August 2 general mobilization was ordered, and France found herself at war.   This came as great shock to Ravel; the little world in which he had been living surrounded by his chosen friends was suddenly shattered, and he was obsessed by the thought of all the horrors that war would inevitably bring to those around him and to the world.   The day after war was declared he wrote in a great state of agitation to his friend Godebski: " God knows if this will ever reach you.   I can only hope it will, and in any case I feel it will relieve my feelings to write to a friend. . .   I'm absolutely all in; this perpetual nightmare is too atrocious.   I feel I shall go mad or yield to the obsession.   You think I am no longer working? I have never worked so hard, so madly, so heroically.   You don't know what a lot of that sort of heroism I need so as to hold out against the other kind, which is perhaps more natural. Just think of the horror of this fighting which never stops for a second.   Who will win?   Write to me so that I can hear the voice of a friend.   Love to you all."

His inaptitude for military service was another of Ravel's worries.   Having been rejected in peace time on account of his small stature and light weight, he was now determined to get himself accepted as a volunteer.   To remain inactive when all his friends had gone to join their regiments was something he could not tolerate.   So, after hastening to finish the *Trio*, which, as he confided to his friends, he was prepared to look on as a posthumous work, he lost no time in trying to persuade the military authorities to change their ruling and accept him for some form of service with the Army.   While in this anxious state of mind he wrote on September 26, 1914, to Stravinsky: " Do let me have news of you.   What is happening to you in the middle of all this?   Edouard [his brother] has joined up as a dispatch-rider.   I haven't been so lucky; they don't want me, but I am pinning my hopes on the new medical examination that all those who have been rejected will have to pass and on the strings I may be able to pull when I get to Paris. . . The idea that I should be leaving at once made me get through five months' work in five weeks!   My *Trio* is finished.   But

I have had to abandon the works I hoped to finish this winter: *La Cloche Engloutie*!! and a symphonic poem *Wien*!!!—hardly appropriate at the moment... How are your wife and the children? Write to me very soon; if you only knew how hard it is to be away from everything! Best remembrances to all, Maurice Ravel."

Meeting with no success at his second attempt to join the armed forces, Ravel then turned his attention to the air force, thinking that here his light weight would be, if anything, an advantage. Again he was unsuccessful, the doctors having diagnosed a heart condition which would render him unfit for flying. He therefore had to resign himself to doing orderly work as a civilian among the wounded who were being sent to St. Jean-de-Luz, and it was not until the following year that he finally succeeded in getting himself accepted as a lorry-driver in the Army. By 1916 he was at the front, somewhere near Verdun.

He accepted philosophically and good-humouredly the conditions of life in which he found himself and, although not normally a prolific letter-writer, kept up a steady correspondence with all his friends. He wrote in March to Jacques Durand, his friend and publisher, apologizing for not having called on him to say good-bye: "You probably guessed how it was; I hadn't a moment in the few days before leaving to say good-bye to my friends... After a frightful journey—7 trains, 36 hours travelling and being obliged to spend the second night in the station because of a Zeppelin alert—I had the pleasant surprise of having to pass a sleepless night on guard duty. At the moment I am at ——, some way away from the front and not yet in danger, but very busy with guard and fatigue duties. A lorry which had been assigned to me was in such a bad state that it was taken away from me almost immediately, but I expect to get another soon. My duties will perhaps be more dangerous, but more interesting than what I am doing now. For more than a week I have not heard a word from anyone."

Probably Ravel suffered more from being cut off from his

friends than from any of the hardships and discomforts of life
at the front, for underneath his habitual reserve he was sociably
inclined.   Certainly the tone of his wartime correspondence is
far more extrovert and unsophisticated than was usual with
him; for the first time things happening round him seemed
more important than things happening inside him.   He even
developed a taste for adventure: " it has such an attraction ",
he wrote to Roland-Manuel, " that it becomes necessary.
And yet I am a peace-loving creature; I have never been
brave. What shall I do, what will so many others do after the
war? "

One of his main preoccupations was his mother's health
(he was devoted to her) and the necessity of keeping from her
any news about himself that might alarm her, and his letters
are full of variations on this theme.   " Thank you for your
news about Mamma ", he wrote to Roland-Manuel, " you
know what a joy, what a comfort it is to me to hear about her.
Poor Mamma! If only she suspects nothing and can go on
thinking I am out of harm's way. . ."

But there was another thing he had not forgotten, and that
was his music.   " I thought I had forgotten it ", he wrote
(again to Roland-Manuel), " but since the last few days it has
come back to me again in an overpowering way. I can think
of nothing else."   And again (July 4, 1916): " I have never
been so full of music; I am overflowing with inspiration, plans
of every kind for chamber music, symphonies, ballets. I tell
you, there's only one solution—the end of the war, or else
my return to the front."   It was the inactivity of life behind the
lines that irked him most, for a few days later he returns to the
charge: " I don't care a damn about anything except music. . .
An artist, no doubt, may perhaps be fit to fight, but certainly
not to live the life one leads in barracks."

Unlike Debussy, Ravel had no strong " nationalist " feelings
where music was concerned, and so had little sympathy with
the *Ligue nationale pour la défense de la musique française* which
advocated the banning of all public performances in France of
any German and Austrian music still subject to copyright.

His first impulse was to publish a protest against this policy, believing as he did that French musicians had nothing to gain by ignoring Bartók, Schoenberg and Kodály; but on second thoughts he refrained from doing so, since while he remained in the Army he had no right to publish anything under his own name.* But he wrote to Jean Marnold (music critic of the *Mercure de France*) apropos the League: " All this controversy only strengthens my conviction: all the idiocies uttered by Wagner, Saint-Saëns and Poueigh (a well-known music critic) are of no importance; it's only their music that matters. And the best thing we can do to defend French music is to try to write good French music."

In spite of Ravel's efforts to adjust himself to army life and army food, his physical powers of resistance were gradually undermined until, in September 1916, he fell ill with dysentery and spent some time in hospital at Châlons-sur-Marne. Returning to Paris on convalescent leave he found his mother seriously ill, and in January 1917 she died. Ravel was overcome with grief, and for a long time remained in a kind of trance. On rejoining his depot he felt more alone in the world than ever before, and he speaks in his letters of " cet horrible désespoir " which lay on him like a cloud. Another breakdown in his health resulted in his temporary discharge from the Army, and he was glad to accept the hospitality of his " *marraine de guerre* ", Mme Fernand Dreyfus, in the country not far from Paris, at Lyons-la-Forêt where he spent the summer of 1917. At last he was able to work again, and it was here that he began the composition of *Le Tombeau de Couperin* which had begun to occupy his thoughts at the beginning of the war when he was still at St. Jean de Luz. As he explained later, the work was conceived as a tribute, not so much to Couperin himself as to French music of the eighteenth century in general, and each of its six movements was dedicated to a friend who had lost his life in the war. Thus the *Toccata* was inscribed to Captain Joseph de Marliave, the husband of Mme

---

* For the text of the letter he wrote privately to the committee of the League, see Appendix II.

Marguerite Long who was to give the first public performance of *Le Tombeau*, but not until after the war.

Ravel had not yet recovered from the effects of his experiences at the front or from the shock and feeling of deprivation caused by the death of his mother. The *Tombeau de Couperin* was the last important work he was to undertake for the next year or so, and after finishing it at Lyons-la-Forêt he joined his brother and went to live in a villa at St. Cloud. As his health did not improve—he suffered from insomnia and depression— he was advised to try the effect of mountain air and went for a time, alone, to Mégève, where he spent some rather unhappy weeks early in 1919. In those days Mégève was not the fashionable resort that it has now become; it was, in fact, extremely primitive, and Ravel complained of the absence of every commodity. On January 22 he wrote to his doctor (Dr. Raymond Geiger, who was also his personal friend): " I'm not getting any better. I sleep little, and badly. No improvement as regards the glands... Do you think that cacodylate would do me any good? I can't find anyone here who could handle the instrument [syringe] and I'm afraid of sticking it into a bone; if necessary, I'll try and do it myself... Of course there's no such thing as a chemist in Mégève, nor a barber. You can't imagine how isolated one is. Even the newspapers don't arrive every day, but I don't mind—I don't read them. All that wouldn't matter if only I could sleep properly. Valerian has no effect..."

All his letters written from Mégève reveal the same preoccupation with his health and evident dislike of solitude; they contain few references to musical affairs. The *Tombeau de Couperin* was, however, still very much in his mind, and in a letter to Mme Florent Schmitt he expressed his disappointment that the first performace had had to be postponed again owing to the illness of Mme Marguerite Long. To the latter he wrote on February 23 congratulating her on her recovery and urging her to lose no time in preparing for the concert at which she was to give the first public performance of the *Tombeau*. One of his reasons for treating the matter as urgent was that he had heard that the pianist Edouard Risler, whom he had asked to postpone the performance he was planning of the work, was studying it, and he was afraid that Risler might not consult him again before playing it. But for one reason or another the long-awaited first performance was postponed again, and it was not until nearly a year later, in January 1920, that Mme Long was at last able to present the work at a concert of the S.M.I. at the Salle Gaveau, where it was enthusiastically received, by public and press alike. Almost the only dissentient voice was that of his old enemy, Pierre Lalo of *Le Temps*, who could not resist the temptation to poke fun at the *Tombeau* and its author (with acknowledgments to Rossini) in the following terms: " *Le Tombeau de Couperin* par Monsieur Ravel, c'est gentil. Mais combien plus gentil serait un *Tombeau* de Monsieur Ravel par Couperin! "

Before leaving Mégève Ravel received a communication from Diaghilev offering to produce as a ballet the symphonic poem later to be known as *La Valse*, but which at that time was taking shape in the composer's mind under the title of *Wien* and was intended to be a kind of apotheosis of the Viennese waltz. The idea had come to him as early as 1906, but had never been put into execution. The offer came at a propitious moment and provided Ravel with a fresh incentive to work as well as an opportunity to carry out a project which he had been meditating for many years. Diaghilev had intended to produce *La Valse* at his next Paris season in the summer of 1920, where it would have shared the bill with Stravinsky's new ballet, *Pulcinella*. Ravel accordingly set to work and, after a brief stay at St. Cloud, retired once more to the country the following winter to complete his score. This time he exchanged the mountains of Savoie for the Cevennes, where he had been lent a house at a place called Lapras, in the Ardèche, by his friend Ferdinand Hérold, translator of Hauptmann's *La Cloche Engloutie*,* one of the composer's operatic projects which never came to fruition. Here, once again, he suffered from his self-imposed solitude and was haunted again by memories of his

---

* See Appendix IV.

mother, whom he had never ceased to mourn. In a letter he wrote to his " marraine ", Mme Dreyfus, we seem to hear the cry of an abandoned child—evidence, if need be, that Ravel was not the cold, heartless individual, devoid of human feelings, that he is sometimes made out to be. " Je suis affreusement triste," he writes on December 26, 1919; " she is no longer at my side as she used to be when I was working far away from Paris. And to think of those charming Christmas Eve gatherings in the Avenue Carnot! At any rate I am working now, and that is something." To Roland-Manuel at about the same time he wrote:

" I'm working again at *Wien*. The motor is turning at full speed, and at last I've been able to get into top gear." And again a few weeks later: " I'm waltzing madly; I began to orchestrate on December 31." By the spring of 1920 the orchestration was completed, and in December that year Chevillard conducted the first performance with the Lamoureux orchestra. There was only one fly in the ointment: Diaghilev unaccountably failed to implement his offer, and *La Valse* was never danced by the Ballets Russes.

It was during his stay at Lapras that Ravel was once again the centre of an " affaire " which created some commotion at the time. This was the famous incident of the Légion d'Honneur conferred upon him without his consent by Léon Bérard, then Minister of L'Instruction Publique, at the instigation of some friends of the composer who had not foreseen what his reaction would be. Papers had been sent him, but as no reply had been received, his friends took it upon themselves to inform the Minister that Ravel would accept the honour. However, on reading the news in the papers (January 16, 1920) Ravel was horrified and lost no time in telegraphing to Roland-Manuel: " *Merci vivement prière démentir refuse.*" In the letter that followed he exclaims: " What an absurd affair! Who could have played this trick on me? . . . And I must finish *Wien* by the end of this month. If it hadn't been for that, I would have left this evening." When he had heard the whole story Ravel wrote again: " You can imagine the state I've been in. It has had a disastrous effect on my orchestration all through the day. . . Have you noticed that people who have got the Légion are like mor-phinomaniacs who will go to any lengths to make others share their passion, perhaps in order to justify it in their own eyes? The solution I proposed would be the neatest: ' for Maurice Ravel, read Maurice Rostand. Readers of *L'Officiel* will have already made the correction '."

The scandal would not perhaps have become public had Ravel listened to his friends, who advised him to " put the ribbon in his pocket and keep quiet about it ". It is true he did not make public his refusal at first, but only when he was invited to pay the necessary fees, which he flatly refused to do. This put an end to the matter, and the removal of his name from the promotion list was published in the *Journal Officiel*.

Opinions were divided in musical circles. At that time Ravel was out of favour with Les Six, whose sponsors were Jean Cocteau and Erik Satie, and in one of the issues of *Le Coq*, a series of broadsheets which under Cocteau's direction served as publicity for the Group, Satie made his celebrated but rather malicious jibe at the expense of his erstwhile admirer and bene-factor: " Ravel refuse la Légion d'Honneur, mais toute sa musique l'accepte "; adding: " L'essentiel n'est pas de refuser la Légion d'Honneur, encore faut-il ne pas l'avoir méritée."*

By the spring and summer of 1920 Ravel had started work on two important compositions: *L'Enfant et les Sortilèges* and the *Duo Sonata* for violin and violoncello. The suggestion that he should provide music for a kind of *divertissement* that Colette had written in 1916 under the title *Ballet pour ma fille* was put to Ravel during the war by Jacques Rouché, who was then Director of the Paris Opéra. A copy was even dispatched to him at the front, but failed to reach him. As soon as Ravel was demobilized Rouché sent him a second copy of the scenario. The unusual and rather fantastic subject appealed

---

* " Ravel refuses the Legion of Honour, but all his music accepts it. What is essential is not so much to refuse the Honour, as not to have deserved it."

to him in many ways, but he foresaw difficulties in the handling of such a theme and suggested various alterations. It seemed to him that the best solution would be to make Colette's fantasia into a kind of American-style musical comedy, or operetta, and after agreement had been reached on this point the title was changed to *L'Enfant et les Sortilèges*. It is interesting to note that when Rouché first suggested to Colette a list of composers who might be suitable for the work, the only one she found acceptable was Ravel.

Their collaboration was a curious one: as Roland-Manuel has pointed out, " It would be impossible to find two more original geniuses or two that were more incompatible. . . An enchantress collaborating with an illusionist." Once agreement had been reached they rarely exchanged a letter, rarely even saw each other. Colette has left this account of their first meeting, when Ravel was still a young man. It was at one of Mme de Saint-Marceaux's famous " vendredis ": " It was here that I met for the first time Maurice Ravel. He was young—below the age when people acquire simplicity. . . He wore side-whiskers! Yes, side-whiskers! and a thick crop of hair accentuated the contrast between his large head and tiny body. He had a taste for conspicuous ties and shirt-frills. While anxious to attract attention, he was afraid of criticism; Henry Gauthier-Villars (' Willy ') was always very harsh to him. Secretly, he was probably shy; his manner was aloof and his way of speaking somewhat curt. Apart from the fact that I listened to his music and that I was drawn to it first by curiosity and then by an attraction enhanced by a slightly disturbing element of surprise and the insidiously sensual allurement of novelty, that was all I knew about Ravel for many years. I can't remember any conversation with him or any sort of friendly relationship."*

Even after Ravel's acceptance of Rouché's commission, it was three years before Colette heard from him, and then only to learn that he had not even begun to write the opera. It was on February 27, 1919, that he wrote to her as follows:

* Hélène Jourdan-Morhange: *Ravel et Nous*. Geneva, 1945.

Dear Madame,

   While you were conveying to Rouché your disappointment at
not having heard from me, I was thinking, in my snowbound retreat, of asking you whether you still wanted to go on with such
an unsatisfactory collaborator. The state of my health is my only
excuse; for a long time I was really afraid I should never be able
to do anything again. It looks now as if I were getting better because
I think I want to start work again. I can't do anything here, but
as soon as I get back, at the beginning of April, I intend to begin
working again, starting with our opera. As a matter of fact, I'm
working at it already; I'm making notes, but not writing a single
one! I'm even thinking of making some alterations. . . Don't be
afraid; they won't be cuts: on the contrary. For example: don't
you think the squirrel's narration could be expanded? Just think
of all the things a squirrel could say about the forest, and how that
would lend itself to music!*

After that letter, five years were to elapse. Then, one day,
Ravel called on Colette to tell her the work was finished; but
he seemed distrait and aloof, and never even thought of playing
her something from the score. " The only thing he seemed to
care about ", Colette has recorded, " was the duet of the two
cats; and he asked me very gravely whether I would mind if
he changed ' Mouâo ' to ' Mouain '—or maybe the other way
round. . .†

There was, however, one other point on which he consulted
the author of L'Enfant, and that was the kind of dance to be
danced by the teapot and cup. Colette had originally made
them come from Auvergne, but Ravel had no desire to write
a bourrée. He therefore wrote to Colette asking her to change
the teapot's nationality so that he could write a foxtrot instead. This meant a change in the language too, with the
result that the dialogue between the Chinese porcelain cup
and the black Wedgwood teapot became a fantastic mixture
of Chinese and English(?)-sounding exclamations.

   Ravel broached this delicate subject in the following characteristic terms: " Would you like to have the cup and the old
black Wedgwood teapot singing a ragtime? I must confess

* Op. cit.   † Ed. du Tambourinaire, quoted by H. Jourdan-Morhange.

the idea of making two negroes sing a ragtime in our ' National Academy of Music ' fills me with joy. Note that the form—a single couplet with a refrain—is perfectly suited to the movement in this scene: complaints, recriminations, rage, pursuit. Perhaps you will object that you are not conversant with American-negro slang! I don't know a word of English, but I will do as you do and manage it somehow. I would be grateful if you would let me know how you feel about this, and remain, etc. . . Maurice Ravel."

Colette, as we know, agreed to the change and the opera was finally produced at Monte Carlo in March 1925, with Victor de Sabata conducting; and, according to the few critics who were present, it was very well received. When it reached Paris, nearly a year later, it had a stormy *première* at the Opéra-Comique on February 1, 1926, under the direction of Albert Wolff, although the critics were on the whole more favourably disposed towards it than they had been to any previous work of Ravel's. What shocked the *petit bourgeois* public of the Opéra-Comique was its music-hall atmosphere and apparent frivolity; people either laughed uproariously at, or where shocked by, the famous cats' duet and the foxtrotting teapot, but failed to perceive the tenderness and pathos of much of the music and, above all, its exquisite texture and quality.

We have now to go back six years to the time when we left Ravel just beginning to compose his score for *L'Enfant et les Sortilèges*, the slow gestation of which has been recorded in the foregoing pages—to the spring, that is to say, of 1920. It was in this year that he took an important decision that was to change his manner of life in many respects and provide him with fresh interests. Since the death of their mother, Maurice and Edouard Ravel had given up the apartment in the Avenue Carnot, and when his brother went to live near his business at Levallois Maurice found himself without a fixed abode. The ideal solution appeared to him to be a small house in the country, not too far from Paris, but far enough to enable him to enjoy the peace and quiet he needed for his work. Finally his choice fell upon the charming village of Montfort-L'Amaury, in Seine-et-Oise, about fifty kilometres west of the capital; and it was here that he acquired the property with which his name will always be associated, and which for many years was to be the rendezvous of the artistic, literary and musical *élite* of Paris. "Le Belvédère" is so situated on the side of a steep hill that what is the ground floor when you enter from the street becomes an upper story when seen from the garden on the other side; and a staircase leading downwards gives access to the other rooms opening on to a veranda-terrace commanding an uninterrupted view over a typically harmonious and beautiful landscape of L'Île-de-France. This little house with its tiny rooms and quaint conformation seemed admirably suited to its occupant, and Ravel lost no time filling it with his collection of *bibelots* of all kinds, china and glass ornaments, musical boxes, *chinoiserie* and mechanical toys, to which were added before long a pair of Siamese cats which were to be his cherished companions for many years. It was a year before he had finished decorating and furnishing his new home, but he was at last able to move in in May 1921, a date which marked the beginning of a new creative period in his life.

CHAPTER FIVE

1920—1927

THE first important work to be completed during Ravel's first year at Montfort was the *Sonata* for violin and violoncello of which the composer himself said that it " marked a turning-point in the evolution of my career. Economy of means [*dépouillement*] is here carried to its extreme limits; there are no harmonies to please the ear, but a pronounced reaction in favour of melody." (B.S.) The work is, however, not " melodious " in any accepted sense of the word; what Ravel intended to convey no doubt was that its main interest is linear, rather than harmonic. The writing for the two instruments is stark and uncompromising and the whole thing suggests a deliberate experiment in harshness which may have been inspired by certain works of Bartók. In any case it cost him a great effort to compose, and he was working at it on and off for the best part of two years. " This confounded *Duo* is giving me a lot of trouble," he wrote to Roland-Manuel on September 22, 1921. A week later: "I am beginning to see my way through the *Duo* ", and on February 3, 1922: " The *Duo* was finished, but I then saw that the *Scherzo* was much too long, so I am beginning it again with some new material."

At last the work was finished and given its first performance in May of that year by the violinist Hélène Jourdan-Morhange (a great friend of Ravel's and an accredited interpreter of his works) and the 'cellist Maurice Maréchal. The public and critics were disconcerted by a work that bore so little resemblance to the Ravel of *Daphnis* or *L'Heure Espagnole*, and many deplored what appeared to be his conversion to the "wrong-note " school that was then becoming fashionable. Others attributed the unaccustomed sounds to a lack of skill on the part of the performers. Ravel had evidently heard these criticisms and even reports that he himself had said that the performance had been a " massacre ", for he wrote to Mme Jourdan-Morhange to tell her this, adding ironically: " Everybody, of course, knows my opinion, even you and no doubt Maréchal as well. I imagine this revelation has not worried either of you too much! I also heard at the same time that I was leaving for Africa and about to get married! I don't know which of these events will come first! "

In spite of everything, a second performance was arranged very shortly afterwards at which Ravel promised to be present. " But if it's going to be as bad as the first time ", he wrote mockingly, " I shall applaud—which will be an American way of protesting*—and we'll go and make it up at *Le Bœuf sur le Toit*† afterwards."

Among those who had not found the *Sonata* (the term " Duo " had now been dropped) to their liking was Ravel's old friend Cipa Godebski, and this prompted the composer to write to him as follows: " I hear that you did not care for my *Sonata* for violin and 'cello and that you had the courage to say so. I am very glad to hear it, because that proves, as indeed I already suspected, that it's not only for reasons of friendship or ' snobisme ' that you like my works. And I much prefer this spontaneous impression to that of the good lady who, after congratulating me on my ' modesty ', found my work ' original ' and ' witty '—which is exactly what she said about my Trio. . ."

Ravel's reputation as one of the leading composers of the day was by now well established and, as a result, a great deal more of his time was spent in travelling, as he was continually being invited to appear and to perform at concerts of his works in the various European capitals. Vienna, Amsterdam, Venice,

* An allusion to the American fashion of hissing to express approval.
† The fashionable *boîte* of the 'twenties where the pianists Wiener and Doucet played the latest American blues and ragtimes nightly before a mixed audience of artists, writers and the " Tout Paris ". Much frequented by Cocteau and " Les Six ", and a favourite haunt of Ravel's.

London acclaimed him in turn. He was in London in the summer of 1922 at the invitation of G. Jean-Aubry (then editing *The Chesterian*), who introduced him to Joseph Conrad. Jean-Aubry was Conrad's French translator and had apparently lent Ravel a copy of *Within the Tides* (*En marge des Marées*), as Ravel, in a letter dated July 26, 1922, written after his London visit, alludes to this and also to his meeting with the author. " If you see Conrad ", he wrote, " tell him how touched I was by his present of cigarettes; one doesn't forget such things. I even intend to send him a card to thank him, if you would give me his address and let me know whether one ought to call him 'cher maître '. . ."

Ravel on this occasion appeared in person to play some of his piano pieces at a concert of his works which was given at Lord Rothermere's house. This was reported in *The Times* of July 10, 1922, as follows:

> The programme consisted of the Quartet, played by the Allied Quartet, two pieces from *Miroirs* and the *Sonatine* by the composer, the new *Sonata* for violin and 'cello played by Miss Jelly d'Aranyi and Mr. Hans Kindler, four songs sung by Mme Alvar, and the *Septet* conducted by the composer. . . Put thus close to the quartet, the *Sonata* showed itself to be a true development as regards technical resource. Many of the devices are the same, but pushed a little further; but one hardly expects the one to turn out to be the equal of the other in inspiration.
>
> M. Ravel's own playing was the best thing in the evening— not as playing, exactly, for we have heard more effective performances, but as showing what the printed notes never can, how he came to think it so and what he puts in the foreground or the background and, most of all, that there was nothing novel or outrageous about it; it was simply the old music taken hold of by a new handle.

Ravel visited London again the following year, when he conducted at a Queen's Hall Symphony concert *La Valse* and *Ma Mère l'Oye*. He wrote on April 16, 1923, from Holland Park, W.11, where he was staying with Mrs. Harding, the singer (known professionally as Mme Alvar), to Hélène Jourdan-Morhange: " *Ma Mère l'Oye* and *La Valse* went very

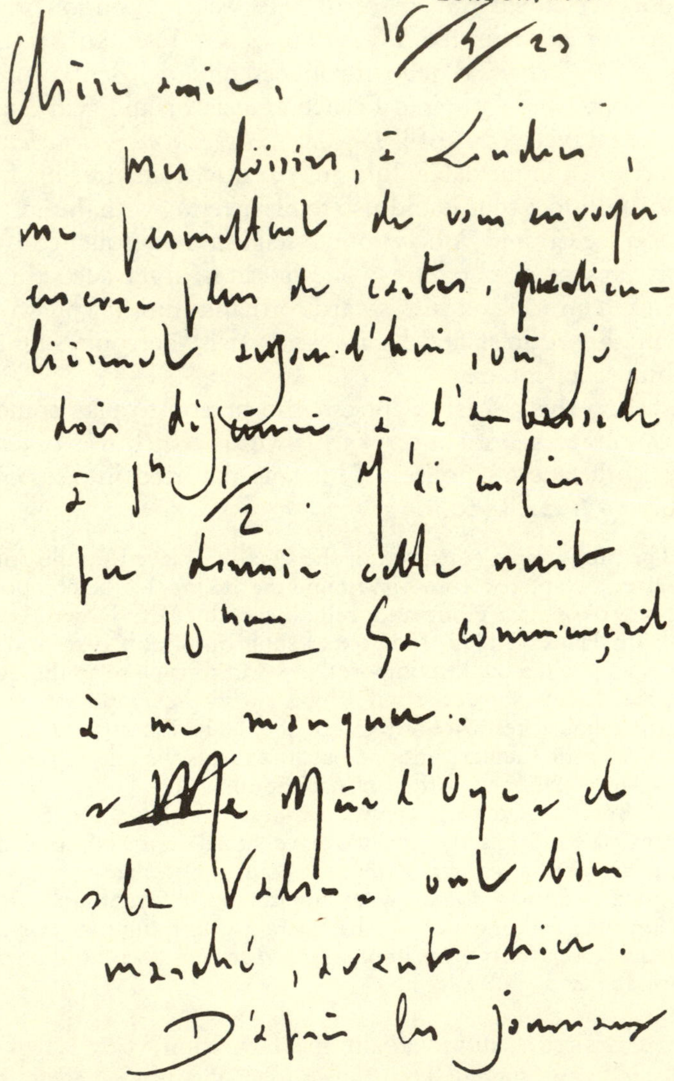

16/4/23

[handwritten letter]

Chère amie,

    Mes loisirs, à Londres, me permettent de vous envoyer encore plus de cartes, particulièrement aujourd'hui, ou je dois déjeuner à l'ambassade à 1h½. J'ai enfin pu dormir cette nuit—10h^{rs}—Ca commençait à me manquer—

    " Ma Mère l'Oye " et " La Valse " ont bien marché avant-hier. D'après les journaux je suis, sinon un grand, au moins un bon chef d'orchestre. Je n'en attendais pas tant . . . Le temps est maussade; pas plus qu'à Rome.

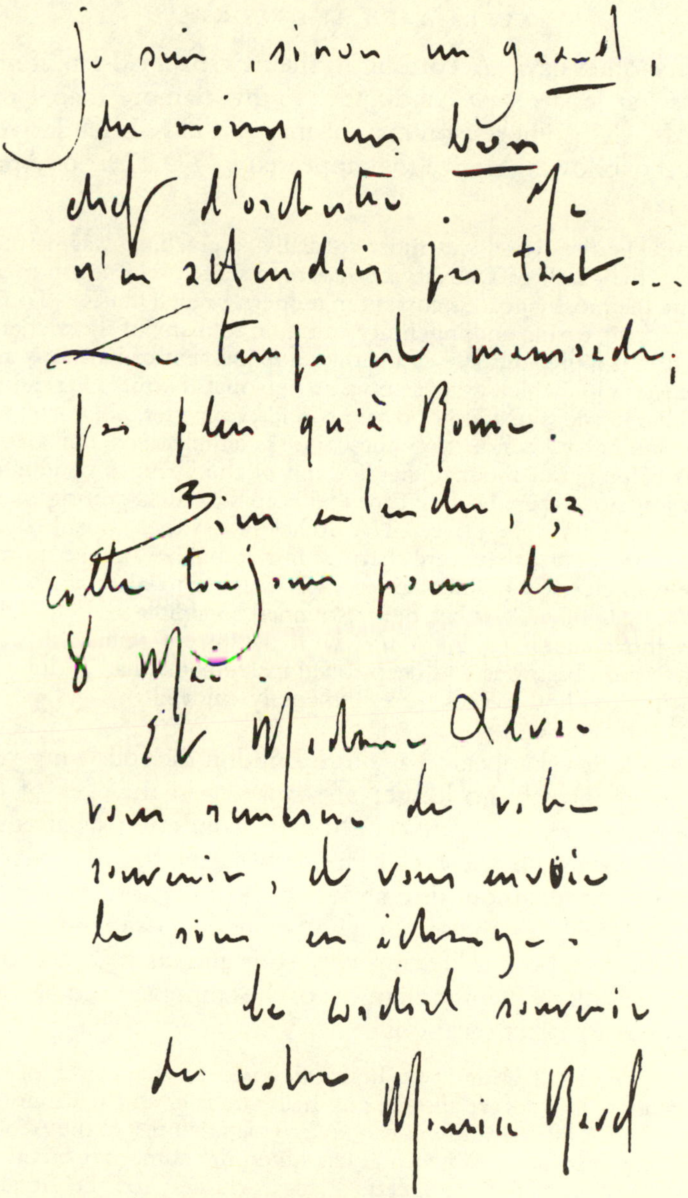

[handwritten letter reproduced as image]

je suis, sinon un grand,
du moins un bon
chef d'orchestre. Me
n'en attendais pas tant...
Le temps est maussade;
pas plus qu'à Rome.

Bien entendu, ça
colle toujours pour le
8 Mai.

Et Madame Alvar
vous remercie de votre
souvenir, et vous envoie
le sien en échange.
Le cordial souvenir
de votre   Maurice Ravel

Bien entendu, ça colle toujours pour le 8 mai.
Et Madame Alvar vous remercie de votre souvenir, et vous envoire le sien en échange.
Le cordial souvenir de votre
Maurice Ravel

well the other day. According to the newspapers 1 am, if not
a great, at least a *good* conductor . . . this is more than I expected." This impression may or may not have been derived
from the following notice that appeared in *The Times* of April
16, 1923:

> M. Maurice Ravel was most cordially received, as was natural.
> Since the death of Debussy he has represented to English musi-
> cians the most vigorous current in modern French music. To the
> enterprise, daring and ingenuity common to many of the moderns
> he brings a preciousness of melody, a refinement of harmony and
> orchestration which give his music a personal charm. He reminds
> us that music is just as good as it sounds, no better, no worse, and
> his manner of conducting these works emphasized the axiom.
> His bâton is not the magician's wand of the virtuoso conductor.
> He just stood there beating time and keeping watch, getting every-
> thing into its right place. The orchestra did their very best for
> him, not because they were charmed into it, but because he showed
> them so clearly what he wanted each member to play, when, and
> how. *Ma Mère l'Oye* has never sounded so simple and childlike;
> the introduction to *La Valse*, with its flitting scraps of waltz
> rhythm on bassoons and deep-toned instruments, had an unusual
> clarity, and both pieces were immensely enjoyed.

But when Ravel appeared again in London the following year
he was apparently no longer *persona grata* in the eyes of the
same newspaper, and one cannot help wondering what could
have happened in the meantime to account for the marked
change of tone, amounting almost to hostility, on the part of
the *Times* critic (if the same) who wrote in those columns on
April 28, 1924, the following very sour and, as it seems to us
today, singularly inept indictment of the composer and of some
of his most perfect creations:

> A concert of about two hours devoted to the works of one
> composer is a severe test of any man's music, and it cannot be
> said that M. Maurice Ravel was able to pass that test at the Aeolian
> Hall on Saturday. When one has given the composer credit for
> his refinement, for the nicety of his form and for the frequent
> prettiness of his effects, there is little more to add in the way of
> praise. To hear a whole programme of his works is like watching
> some midget or pygmy doing clever, but very small things,

within a limited scope. Moreover, the almost reptilian cold-bloodedness, which one suspects of having been consciously cultivated, of most of M. Ravel's music is almost repulsive when heard in bulk; even its beauties are like the markings on snakes and lizards.

The pianoforte works included the *Tombeau de Couperin*, *Gaspard de la Nuit* and *Ma Mère l'Oye* in its original form of a piano duet, played by the composer and M. Gil-Marchex rather like a child and his teacher at a lesson. M. Gil-Marchex gave excellent performances of the solo pieces. Mlle Marcelle Gérar sang a group of songs with great intelligence but a rather thin tone. The songs themselves, which included the *Shéhérazade* set, two of the *Histoires Naturelles* and a new one, *Ronsard à son âme*, proved monotonous. M. Ravel's skill in setting his text carries with it a number of mannerisms, the worst of which is his inconclusive way of ending every song and, indeed, most of his phrases. This trick, when heard again and again, is exceedingly tiresome and no less mannered than the old convention of finishing on a major chord. The *Histoires Naturelles* were the most effective, but they are really matter for a super-refined music-hall programme. The new song, which was repeated, proved very jejune.

The other new work, which had been completed only just in time for the performance, was the *Tzigane* for violin and piano. It is rhapsodical in the literal meaning of the word, being a series of episodes in the Hungarian manner strung together. One is puzzled to understand what M. Ravel is at. Either the work is a parody of all the Liszt-Hubay-Brahms-Joachim school of Hungarian violin music and falls into the class of *La Valse*, or it is an attempt to get away from the limited sphere of his previous compositions to infuse into his work a little of the warm blood it needs. But in neither case does it greatly matter. Miss Jelly d'Aranyi played the work, which is full of great technical difficulties, with such amazing assurance that one could hardly believe that she had had only two days in which to learn it.

The almost total failure to grasp even the rudiments of Ravel's subtle and highly original art as shown in the above quotation (especially the consigning of the *Histoires Naturelles* to the category of a music-hall number) is a painful example of the aberrations to which music critics are prone, although it must be admitted that a similar incomprehension existed in certain circles, as we have seen, the other side of the Channel.

Two stories are told in connexion with this concert of Ravel's music at the Aeolian Hall. One is that Miss Jelly d'Aranyi, on presenting her copy of *Tzigane* to the composer in the hope that he would inscribe thereon some complimentary dedication was disappointed to read only the words: " A Jelly d'Aranyi—Maurice Ravel." " Is that all? " she asked. " Yes, that's all ", replied Ravel. " But it's for posterity." The other story is that at an elegant reception given for the composer by Mrs. Harding, Ravel, who was ordinarily so particular about his dress and appearance, astonished the assembled company by turning up (though otherwise impeccably dressed) in red carpet slippers. [This may, of course, have been a subtle tribute to the reputation for eccentricity which is traditionally the prerogative of English upper-class society. The fact is Ravel could generally be relied upon not to say or do what he thought might be expected of him and took pleasure in disconcerting in this way those he came in contact with outside his immediate circle of friends. On one occasion after a concert of his works in Barcelona he was recognized in a café by the leader of the orchestra who thereupon started to play the *Habanera*, only to be told by the composer that he would much rather hear some jazz.]

Apart from *Tzigane* and the *Sonata* for violin and 'cello, the only other major work belonging to this period was the orchestral version of Mussorgsky's *Pictures from an Exhibition* commissioned by Kussevitzky—a masterly example of Ravel's virtuosity as an orchestrator as well as of his ability to identify himself so completely with the spirit and style of another composer's music as to make it difficult to believe that it could ever have been intended to sound otherwise. Minor works were the *Berceuse* on the name of Gabriel Fauré for violin and piano, composed in 1922 as a supplement to a special number of *La Revue Musicale* in memory of Fauré, and a setting for voice and piano of *Ronsard à son âme*, issued as a supplement to another special number of *La Revue Musicale*, *Le Tombeau de Ronsard*, published in 1924. Ravel had also started to compose his *Violin and Piano Sonata* in 1923, but four years were to elapse before this work, which he had great difficulty in completing, was ready for publication. Nor must it be forgotten that throughout these years he was working on and off, as we have already seen above, at *L'Enfant et les Sortilèges*.

During the first years of his installation at Montfort L'Amaury his social life had taken on a new pattern. While his appearances in Paris were less frequent, it became the custom for his friends to visit him at " Le Belvédère ", where his informal Sunday lunch parties soon became an institution and were attended regularly by a little band of faithful friends and colleagues, including his favourite interpreters, such as the violinist Hélène Jourdan-Morhange, the singers Marcelle Gérar and Madeleine Grey, his great friend and pupil Maurice Delage and his wife Nelly, Germaine Tailleferre, the painter Luc-Albert Moreau, the sculptor Léon Leyritz, author of the well-known bust of Ravel in the foyer of the Paris Opéra, his friends and neighbours M. and Mme Jacques de Zogheb, Dr. Robert Le Masle and the conductor and composer Manuel Rosenthal.

Ravel had few pupils, but among those who profited from his advice and example were Roland-Manuel, Delage and for a short time Vaughan Williams, a little group whom it pleased Ravel to refer to as " L'Ecole de Montfort ". Thus, in a letter to the singer Marcelle Gérar, who was inviting friends to hear the first performance of *Ronsard à son âme*, Ravel wrote: " ' L'Ecole de Montfort ' will be almost complete with Roland; but Vaughan Williams will not be with us—it is too late to get him to come over from London."

The two composers had known each other since 1908, the year in which Vaughan Williams decided to ask Ravel whether he would be willing to give him some lessons and guidance in composition and orchestration; it was on the recommendation of M. D. Calvocoressi that Vaughan Williams chose Ravel rather than Vincent d'Indy, who had been suggested by Edwin Evans. There is no doubt, as we shall see later, that the choice was the right one.

Calvocoressi* records that the matter was discussed over dinner at the Savage Club with Vaughan Williams, Edwin Evans and himself, although Evans was by no means convinced that Ravel would be able to give Vaughan Williams what he was looking for. Indeed, so sceptical was he that, according to Calvocoressi, he later actually stated in print that Calvocoressi was waiting at the Gare du Nord to meet Vaughan Williams to make sure he did not go straight to the *Schola* after all! This the author of *Musicians' Gallery* denies, producing, as evidence that Vaughan Williams certainly had not regretted his decision, the following letter written soon after his arrival in Paris from the quaintly named Hôtel de l'Univers et du Portugal (which still exists): " Ravel is exactly the man I was looking for. As far as I know my own faults, he hit on them exactly, and is telling me to do exactly what I half felt in my mind I ought to do—but it just wanted saying." Again: " I am getting a lot out of Ravel. Only I feel that ten years with him would teach me all I want."

Vaughan Williams makes no reference here to what he told friends in England in after years, namely that the first thing Ravel gave him to do was to orchestrate a Mozart Minuet, which he flatly refused to do, saying he hadn't come to him for that sort of thing of which he had had quite enough in London.

How long the actual lessons lasted is not clear, but the two composers corresponded from time to time between 1908 and 1919, during which period Ravel was on more than one occasion the guest of Vaughan Williams and his first wife in their London house. I am greatly indebted to Mrs. Ursula Vaughan Williams for her courtesy in allowing me to reproduce extracts from some of the hitherto unpublished letters from Ravel which her husband had preserved. The earliest, discussing the possibility of performing one of Vaughan Williams' works in Paris, is dated March 3, 1908, and was written from Valvins, where Ravel was staying at the time: " First of all, forgive me for not having written before. I have had a fearful lot of work lately. My *Rapsodie Espagnole*

* *Musicians' Gallery.* Faber, 1933.

is being performed at a Colonne concert on March 15 and only the fourth section was orchestrated! Now let us talk about your own works. When you get this letter send off your score and the transcription to M. Marcel Labey, c/o Maison Pleyel, rue Rochechouart. If the *Société Nationale* can give two orchestral concerts, we will do your *Fantasia*. If not, it will be more difficult, as French composers must naturally take priority in a *National* society. In any case, I need not tell you I shall do my best to encourage a performance of the work of a pupil of whom I have reason to be proud. . .''

As it turned out, Vaughan Williams sent in his score too late for the committee to consider it, and Ravel wrote again explaining what had occurred, adding: " You have nothing to regret in any case, as they changed the programme too radically, and your work would have been insufficiently rehearsed and badly presented. You will be able to have your revenge next season. Let me know how your work is going. . .''

In 1909 Ravel went to stay with the Vaughan Williams in Cheyne Walk. In accepting their invitation he expressed his " apprehension " about visiting a country whose language he didn't know, and he was characteristically vague about time of arrival. However, he evidently enjoyed his visit, as can be seen from the " thank-you " letter he wrote on his return to France, dated May 5, 1909. " Here I am, a Parisian once more. But a Parisian who is homesick for London. This is the first time I have ever regretted leaving a foreign country. And yet I left France feeling somewhat apprehensive about venturing into the unknown. . . Only after the cordial and attentive welcome which was extended to me at Cheyne Walk did I begin to feel at home in an unfamiliar atmosphere and to appreciate the charm and magnificence of London, almost as if I were a Londoner. . . I would like now to convey to you and Mrs. Williams all the gratitude I feel."

Two years later he was again the guest of the Vaughan Williams in London, and again felt apprehension, as " thanks to my laziness my knowledge of English has not improved ". Ravel was notoriously unpractical, but his travel arrangements

on this occasion seem to have been more than usually hap-
hazard, for he writes: " As I arrive at Charing Cross at 11.30
p.m. I thought this would be an inconvenient hour for you, so
in prevision of this a room has been reserved for me for the
night of Tuesday–Wednesday, but in what hotel I do not
know. . ."

After an unsuccessful attempt to arrange a performance at
the S.M.I. of Vaughan Williams' Quartet in A minor early
in 1911, Ravel wrote in January 1912 to say that the S.M.I.
hoped next season to do *On Wenlock Edge*—" les mélodies
avec accompagnement du quintette que je trouve tout-à-fait
remarquables "—and in February he was able to announce
that a performance had definitely been arranged. " The concert will be exceptionally brilliant. Fauré will accompany
Jeanne Raunay. I am trying to persuade Cyril Scott to come
himself and play his *Suite* which is included in the programme.
And no doubt the British Embassy will be represented and
leading members of the English colony will also be present.
We thought of engaging as your interpreter Plamondon, a
well-known tenor and excellent musician who sings in English.
The Wuillaume Quartet will accompany him. If you would
consent to play the piano part yourself, that would be splendid. If not, I offer you my services. I hope in any case to
have the pleasure of seeing you again. Your presence will be
necessary, if only to indicate the tempo. Please reply by
return—it is important for the publicity we intend to organize
for this exceptional occasion. . ."

The work evidently was well received, for Ravel writes from
St. Jean-de-Luz later in the year congratulating Vaughan
Williams on the success of his " *poèmes lyriques,* which, from
all accounts, were a revelation. I hope to say this very soon in
an article which will be largely devoted to you ". [I have
been unable to trace this article, but Ravel was constantly
forming projects that were never carried out.] " The various
works of mine which were produced last season, and especially
Daphnis et Chloë, have left me in a sorry state. They had to
pack me off to the country to ward off an incipient neuras-

thenia. I have now nearly recovered, here in my native country. . ."

When war came in 1914 Ravel, as we have seen, was eventually sent to the front after several unsuccessful attempts to get himself accepted for the Army, and in June 1916 Vaughan Williams received a postcard from " conducteur Ravel, 15e. section de parc automobile " (he was in charge of a lorry), which ran as follows: " Mon cher ami, if this reaches you I would be very pleased to have news of you. Are you still in England? I have been at the front for some months now—and a very lively part of the front, too! It seems years since I left Paris. I have had some exciting, not to say painful, experiences, and dangerous enough to make me feel astonished at having come out of them alive. And yet I am longing to get back again to that life of adventure. For nearly a month I have been enjoying enforced leisure—my lorry is being repaired and I myself am very exhausted. And the kind of life one leads in these *dépôts* couldn't be more boring. I hope Mme Vaughan Williams is in good health. . ."

The last letter of this correspondence, dated September 18, 1919, shows the state of Ravel's health after the war. " I ought to have answered your letter before," he writes. " I haven't even the excuse of work—I haven't been able to start working again. And yet my stay in the mountains did me a lot of good. It is the *moral* now that needs looking after, and I don't know how to set about it. Make my excuses to Fox Strangways—I was imprudent enough to promise to contribute to a paper. They are still waiting for my first article! Won't you be coming to Paris again soon? I should be very pleased to see you after all these terrible years. I ought to be going to England next season, but on reflection I think it would be better for me to do some work, if I am still able to. . ."

And on that rather pathetic note the correspondence ends. He did, as we have seen, go to England in 1922 and 1923 and again in the spring of 1926, when he also had concert engagements in Scandinavia. He was in Edinburgh in February the following year for a performance of his *Trio*. While there he visited Loch Lomond, and sent a picture postcard to Mme Casella bearing the words " un souvenir affectueux de ces beaux lacs 1830 ".   His Scandinavian tour prevented him from being present at the *première* of *L'Enfant et les Sortilèges* at the Opéra-Comique, but on his return to Montfort he had important work to do.   For the composition on which he was then engaged was none other than the *Chansons Madécasses*, which had been commissioned the previous year by Mrs. Elizabeth Sprague Coolidge, the well-known American patroness of music.   Strictly speaking, what had been commissioned was not any specific work, but " a cycle of songs on poems of his own choosing, scored, if possible, for voice with accompaniment of flute, 'cello and piano ".   These were the only specifications laid down in the cable he received from the 'cellist Hans Kindler, acting on Mrs. Coolidge's behalf.

Ravel was always ready to work to a predetermined plan, and accepted the challenge gladly.   It only remained for him to choose his text.   He had in his library among other works dating from his favourite eighteenth century a volume bearing the following title: " Chansons madécasses traduites en français suivies de poésies fugitives par M. le Chevalier de P. . .   Se vend à Paris chez Hardouin et Gattey Libraires du Palais Royal et chez les marchands de nouveautés.   CMDCCLXXXVII." A modern edition, published by the N.R.F. in 1920, gives the author's name: Evariste Parny.

Parny, whose full name and title was Evariste Désiré de Forges, Vicomte de Parny (1753–1814) was a Creole born at St. Paul de Bourbon in La Réunion, a member of one of the earliest French colonial families.   He had been called by the Marquis de Fontanes, one of Napoleon's protégés, poet and politician and Grand Master of the University of Paris, " the first French elegiac poet ".   He was also known to Voltaire, who on his deathbed addressed him as " Mon cher Tibulle ", thus consecrating his poetic standing. Parny is said to have written these poems, based on original Madagascan sources, in France at a place called Feuillancourt between Marly and

Saint-Germain. In his preface he points out that verse is un-known to the natives of Madagascar; their " poetry " is merely rhythmic prose, and their music invariably melancholy.

Ravel felt instinctively attracted by this author, and the exotic subject and setting appealed to his inborn love for the strange and unfamiliar. He chose three poems—*Nahandove*, *Aoua!* and *Il est doux*, the first and third voluptuous and melan-choly, the second a cry of revolt; and in his settings these moods are faithfully reflected. The work had its first per-formance at the Salle Erard in Paris on June 13, 1926; the singer was Jane Bathori. Curiously enough, the work was criticized in some quarters on political grounds, especially the second song *Aoua!* with its defiant: " Méfiez-vous des blancs, habitants du rivage " which was considered provoca-tive and most inopportune at a time when Frenchmen were engaged in fighting the Moroccan rebel Abd-el-Krim. This attitude was confined to a few right-wing musicians such as Pierre de Bréville, but was apparently not shared by the Minister for War, who applauded heartily, we are told, at the first performance of the songs.

Commenting on the *Chansons* later Ravel wrote that they " seem to introduce a new element, dramatic and even erotic, arising out of the actual subject of Parny's poems. The work is a sort of quartet in which the voice is the principal instru-ment. The keynote is simplicity. The independence of the individual parts will be found again, still more pronounced, in the violin and piano *Sonata*." (B.S.)

This *Sonata*, begun in 1923, is musically not unlike the *Chansons Madécasses*. As to the independence of the part-writing, Ravel stated that he had imposed this on himself " when writing a Sonata for piano and violin, two essentially incompatible instruments which, far from balancing their contrasting characters, emphasize in this work this very in-compatibility ". (B.S.) Hélène Jourdan-Morhange, to whom the work is dedicated, describes it as being very difficult to play, despite the composer's assurances to the contrary, on account of its very simplicity. The second movement is a blues, another instance of Ravel's predilection for the exotic rhythms of New Orleans jazz, which was at that time proving so irresistible to the more sophisticated among Continental composers. It was to receive its final consecration in his hands in the magnificent " jazz " section of the *Concerto for the Left Hand*, very far removed from the trifling foxtrot it amused him to introduce into *L'Enfant et les Sortilèges*. As it turned out, Mme Jourdan-Morhange was unable to play the *Sonata* at the first performance owing to the first onslaught of the rheumatism which was unhappily to put a premature end to her brilliant career as a violinist. It was given its first public hearing at the Salle Erard on May 30, 1927, by Georges Enesco with the composer at the piano.

The only other works of any significance dating from this year were a setting of a poem by Léon-Paul Fargue, Ravel's favourite poet, entitled *Rêves*, and a little *Fanfare* which was written as a prelude to a children's ballet, *L'Eventail de Jeanne*, for which Mme René Dubost had commissioned music from seven composers: Ferroud, Ibert, Poulenc, Roland-Manuel, Delannoy, Auric and Milhaud.

Preparations for his American tour, first mooted some five years previously, were now complete and, after a flying visit to Amsterdam in September, Ravel embarked at the end of November 1927 for the United States.

CHAPTER SIX

1928—1937

His four-months concert tour across America and Canada was for Ravel a veritable voyage of discovery. Everything astonished or delighted him—the enthusiasm of his audiences, the skyscrapers of New York, the scenery, the comfort of the long-distance trains in which he found it possible to rest and sleep. His first letter was for his brother Edouard, written in the train between New York and Chicago on January 16, 1928: " I am writing from an armchair in the Chicago express. I arrive tomorrow at 9.45 in the morning; it is now 8 p.m. The concert in New York went well. Very flattering articles, sometimes a whole page. Only the French paper in New York did not mention me. . ."

A few days later he wrote again from Chicago: " The chamber music concert was the day before yesterday. Today everything went well. When I came on to bow I was greeted with a fanfare from all the brass. It was like spring when I arrived in Chicago, but yesterday it turned icy cold with a fiendish wind that nearly blows your head off, and the water and ice smell of Eau de Javel. The town is extraordinary, much more so than New York. Tomorrow is the second symphony concert, after which I leave for Cleveland."

Cleveland January 26: " The second concert went well; 3,500 people standing up, and another fanfare. . ."

From Los Angeles he went to Hollywood, where he met Douglas Fairbanks " who luckily speaks French ". He adds that he should have lunched with Charlie Chaplin, " but I thought it wouldn't be any more amusing for him than for me. He doesn't speak a word of French."

The itinerary he had to follow was a complicated one involving two return journeys to New York so that the route he covered was as follows: Chicago, San Francisco, Los Angeles, Seattle, Vancouver, Minneapolis, New York, New Orleans, Houston, Colorado (the Grand Canyon), Buffalo, New York, Montreal, with short visits to Boston, Cambridge and Cleveland thrown in. He wrote on February 10 to Hélène Jourdan-Morhange: "I am seeing some magnificent cities and enchanting country, but triumphs are very exhausting. At Los Angeles I ran away from everybody; besides, I was dying of hunger."

Ravel was always something of a gourmet and had a healthy appetite; American food, however, was not much to his liking, nor apparently did he always get enough to eat, even in the houses of the rich who entertained him, for he wrote to his brother from Cleveland: "Dined the other day in Chicago with Mrs. Rockefeller McCormic, the millionairess. Got back to my hotel as quickly as possible and ordered a beefsteak. I dined here with Mme Cim, who has some fine Lautrec, Gauguin, Degas, etc., good wines and a famous cognac... While I think of it, would you mind changing the Hoover for a stronger one (like the one we have at the Hôtel d'Athènes)..."

This preoccupation with small domestic details and creature comforts is typical of Ravel, who was never, as some artists are, oblivious of or indifferent to his surroundings and personal comfort. A remark made by his friend Delage intended as a comment on his musical aesthetic applies also to his attitude towards the things of everyday life: "Ravel reduces the universe to the scale of the field of vision imposed upon him by events." Small things could be for him of the first importance; thus, for example, he very nearly declined the offer of the concert tour in the United States for fear lest he should be deprived of his favourite Caporal cigarettes. Finally it was arranged for supplies to be sent out to him through diplomatic channels. He was also, as we have seen, extremely particular about his dress, and on one occasion during the tour he refused to go on to the platform to conduct an important orchestral concert in Chicago when he found he had left his evening shoes in one of his trunks at the railway station. In the end it was the lady who was to sing for him who had to go to the station to collect the shoes, with the result that the concert started half an hour late.

He was greatly impressed by the Grand Canyon and the " splendid ' painted desert ' where the plesiosaurus and the pterodactyls have left their footmarks ", remarking that it would have been worth crossing the Atlantic if only to see this fantastic landscape.

Somehow or other his health did not suffer from the strain imposed by incessant travelling and concert-giving, and to friends who were apprehensive on this account he wrote: " I have never been so well as during this mad tour, and I have now discovered the reason: it is because I have never before led such an orderly life."

Ravel disliked appearing in public, especially as a pianist. " I am not a pianist," he used to say, " and I don't like being exhibited as if I were in a circus." However, he played his *Sonatine* to the Americans, accompanied his songs and played with Szigeti in New York the *Violin Sonata*. The public were astonished at his use of the blues rhythm in the *Sonata* and found it difficult to understand his own astonishment that American musicians had not drawn more freely on jazz sources, although they welcomed and assimilated the charac- teristic features of all other countries. Gershwin was an exception, and Ravel admired his *Rhapsody in Blue*; but when the two composers met and Gershwin, who greatly admired Ravel, asked if he could study with him, Ravel refused, saying: " You would only lose the spontaneous quality of your melody and end by writing bad Ravel."

The last lap of his journey—what Ravel called " la petite balade finale "—took him to New Orleans (" only to have a glimpse of this old French colony and taste a ' pompano en papillotes ' accompanied by French wines "), Houston, Grand Canyon, Buffalo (this stage being the equivalent, as he pointed out, to Paris–Constantinople–Stockholm), Montreal and, finally, New York, which he reached on April 21 in time to join the *Paris*, which was sailing at midnight for France.

He reached Le Havre on April 27, 1928, and was met by a group of friends who had come down from Paris to welcome him. He was now a famous composer, and commissions and social engagements of all kinds awaited him. He was ready now to settle down to work again, and in a letter to Hélène Jourdan-Morhange written soon after his return he outlined his immediate programme: " You know I had intended to dine with you? But I can't budge from here and shall be hard at work until mid-October. After that I shall have to be simultaneously at Oxford to assume the gown of a ' Doctor honoris causa ', in Spain and at the Opéra where Ida Rubinstein will be giving *La Valse* and a new work which will perhaps be finished by then. All that will no doubt sort itself out in the end! "

The " new work " was a ballet which Ida Rubinstein had commissioned him to write before he left for America, leaving to him the choice of subject. At first Ravel had intended merely to orchestrate some pieces from the *Iberia* of Albeniz, as he did not feel like undertaking any important composition at that moment. He was therefore considerably put out when he heard that the orchestration rights in respect of all works by Albeniz had been granted by his heirs exclusively to the Madrid composer and conductor Fernandez Arbos. This did not, however, alter his determination to make this ballet a pretext for an essay in orchestration rather than write an entirely new work, especially as the date for the first performance was already fixed and time was running out. The simplest solution would be to orchestrate one of his own works, but as nothing suitable existed, Ravel decided to compose a piece which would simply be a vehicle for an experiment in instrumentation, the character and scope of which he defined as follows, in the driest and most characteristically impersonal terms: " In 1928, at the request of Mme Ida Rubinstein I composed a *boléro* for orchestra. It is a rather slow dance, uniform throughout in its melody, harmony and rhythm, the latter being tapped out continuously on the drum. The only element of variety is supplied by the orchestral *crescendo*." (B.S.)

Thus there came into existence a work which, although inseparably associated with the name of Ravel and whistled, sung and played all over the world, yet represents only a particular and limited aspect of his genius. Technically it is a masterpiece, but, as Ravel said of it himself: " Malheureusement il est vide de musique ". It is true that a piece of music that depends for its effect on the skilful use of contrasting orchestral timbres, an implacable rhythm and a long and meticulously controlled *crescendo* with no variation at all in the theme, repeated over and over again from the first bar to the last, must necessarily appeal to the senses rather than to the mind or spirit; and that is no doubt what Ravel had in mind when he decried its purely musical content. And yet the actual musical material, such as it is, is handled in so masterly a fashion that *Boléro*, in the last resort, must be considered as something a little more exalted than a mere orchestral *tour de force*, even if its essential musicality resides in its matter rather than in its meaning.

No one was more surprised than Ravel at its instant success and popularity; he had been for a long time convinced it would never find its way into the concert room, thinking that, when divorced from its choreographic context, which alone provided the element of variety that was absent from the music, it would prove unpalatable to the ordinary symphony concert audience.

Gustave Samazeuilh has related how one morning at St. Jean-de-Luz Ravel, dressed in a yellow dressing-gown and a scarlet bathing cap, picked out the tune on his piano with one finger, saying: " Mme Rubinstein has asked me for a ballet; don't you think this theme has an insistent quality about it? I shall try and repeat it a number of times without any development whatsoever, graduating my orchestra as best I can." And thus was *Boléro* born. One of the most surprising things about it is its title. It is hard to see why Ravel, whose knowledge of Spain and things Spanish was particularly extensive and had already been manifested in such things as the *Rapsodie Espagnole* and *L'Heure Espagnole*, should have described as a " bolero " a work which, in form, tempo and rhythm, bears only the slightest resemblance to the authentic Spanish dance of that name. When this was pointed out to the composer by his friend and colleague Joaquin Nin, among others, he merely replied: " Cela n'a aucune importance." It has nevertheless made it difficult for the work to be accepted by Spanish audiences.

When the time came for the work to be presented as a ballet, Ravel had decided ideas as to the décor and interpretation. Ida Rubinstein and Alexandre Benois had imagined a vast room in some squalid cabaret in Barcelona's " Paralelo ", with a platform in the middle on which a woman danced alone, surrounded by a crowd of men. Ravel would have preferred an open-air setting with a factory in the background and a crowd of workmen and women emerging to take part in the general dance. In addition he suggested a romantic intrigue involving a *torero* and a jealous lover. However, for the first performances he agreed to Benois' décor, but in the meantime asked his friend Léon Leyritz to prepare a *maquette* embodying his ideas; this was, in fact, used in Rouché's revival of *Boléro* at the Opéra after the composer's death, in spite of some opposition on the part of the conductor Philippe Gaubert and Serge Lifar. The factory which served as a model was one which Ravel often passed on his way to the Parisian suburb of Le Vésinet and which he used to refer to as " l'usine de *Boléro* ".

The first performance was given at the Opéra on November 22, 1928, by the Ballet Rubinstein, under the direction of Walter Straram, with choreography by Nijinska. It was sandwiched between two other new ballets—*Les Noces de l'Amour et de Psyché* by Honegger, and Bach, after *La Bien-Aimée* by Milhaud, after Schubert—but they were completely overshadowed by *Boléro*, which was received with wild enthusiasm. And, in spite of Ravel's prediction that the " Sunday concerts " would never dare to include it in their programmes, no sooner had the work fallen into the public domain (in 1930) than it was immediately taken up by all the leading symphony orchestras, both in Paris and abroad.

Ravel conducted it himself, beating time with metronome-like regularity, holding back the *crescendo* and avoiding any suspicion of an *accelerando* from beginning to end. He felt very strongly about this, and did not hesitate to point out to Toscanini, who was rehearsing it with the New York Phil-harmonic, that he was (*a*) playing it too fast and (*b*) accelerating before the end. To which the maestro is said to have replied, with his formidable transalpine accent: " Vous né connaissez rien à votre mousique. C'était la seule façon de la faire passer." (" You don't understand your own music. That was the only way to put it over.") Ravel said nothing more, but after the concert, when Toscanini had again made an *accelerando*, Ravel was furious and was unwilling even to shake hands with the conductor after the performance. Only on the insistence of Freitas Branco did he finally consent to do so, remarking: " You! but no one else! " Ravel was no respecter of persons, still less of hierarchies or exalted reputations, and he was just as ready to criticize Toscanini, if necessary, as he would have been to find fault with a musician in the orchestra.

He described the incident in the following terms in a letter to Mme Casella of May 6, 1930: " It's a pity you didn't come back stage; there was quite a little scene. People were horri-fied because I had the audacity to tell the great virtuoso that he had played it twice as fast as it should go. I only came for that . . . all the same, he's a wonderful virtuoso, as wonderful as his orchestra. . ." And to Mme Godebski he tells the same story: " If I was seen at the Opéra it is because I knew Toscanini was taking *Boléro* at a ridiculous speed and wanted to tell him so—which seems to have horrified everybody, including the great virtuoso himself."

But for Ravel precision in everything, especially in music, was all-important, and all his scores are marked in such a way as to leave no room for doubt about his intentions. As one of his contemporaries remarked: " There are several ways of playing Debussy but only one way to play Ravel."

October 1928 marked another phase in Ravel's rise to fame, as it brought him for the first time academic recognition when Oxford University announced its intention of conferring upon him the degree of Doctor of Music, *honoris causa*. The ceremony and the donning of academic robes must have appealed to Ravel's feeling for tradition; at the same time he was, no doubt, amused at finding himself in such an unaccustomed role and being addressed as follows by the Public Orator: " Itaque missis ambagibus praesento vobis musarum interpretem modorum daedalum Mauricium Ravel, ut admittatur ad gradum doctoris in arte musica honoris causa."

In the autumn of 1929 Ravel left Montfort for St. Jean-de-Luz where a festival was being held in his honour, while at nearby Ciboure, his birthplace, the name of the street in which stands the house where he was born was changed, at a ceremony at which he was present, from Quai de la Nivelle to Quai Maurice Ravel. From Ciboure to Biarritz the Basque coast was *en fête*, with *pelota* matches and *fandangos* danced in the streets. Ravel was touched by these demonstrations, but embarrassed at being the object of them. The games and dancing certainly appealed to him more than the official ceremonies, and we find him writing to Leyritz on his return: " The festivities went off very well—the *pelota* match especially was splendid."

Ravel was now at work on two important compositions: a piano concerto, which he had originally intended to play himself on his concert tour in the United States, and a piano concerto for the left hand alone which he was writing for the one-armed Austrian pianist Wittgenstein, whom he met in Vienna in 1930. In an interview he gave to the *Daily Telegraph*, which has often been quoted, he described the essential differences between the two concertos. The first, in G major for two hands, a concerto in the strict sense of the word, follows the model of Mozart and Saint-Saëns, for " a concerto can be gay and brilliant and need not try to be profound or strive after dramatic effects. It has been said of some of the great

classic composers that their concertos were written, not *for*
but *against* the piano, and I think this is perfectly correct. . .
In some respects my *Concerto* resembles my *Violin Sonata*; it
contains some elements borrowed from jazz, but in modera-
tion. The *Concerto for the Left Hand* is quite different and in
one movement with a lot of jazz effects, and the writing is not
so simple ".

This concerto is one of Ravel's greatest and most original
works; in it he strikes a new note of almost tragic foreboding
scarcely discernible in any of his previous works. The writing
is masterly and the emotional content far nearer the surface
than in any other work from his pen.

Both concertos were completed by the autumn of 1931.
In Vienna the Left Hand Concerto was performed for the first
time on November 27, and on January 14, 1933, Marguerite
Long, with Ravel conducting, played the G major at the Salle
Pleyel in Paris. The *Concerto in D* was not heard in Paris
until March 1937, when it was played by Jacques Février, who
had studied the work with the composer and from then on was
looked upon as its accredited interpreter.

Shortly after the *première* of the Piano Concerto in G
Ravel embarked on an extensive concert tour in Central
Europe with Marguerite Long. That same year he was involved in a motor accident when his taxi collided with another
car, and although he suffered no visible injury his friends were
apprehensive as to the possible effect of the shock on his
nervous system. His health had no doubt been impaired
during the war; all his life he suffered from insomnia; in 1920
he spoke of his " tristesse affreuse " which may have been an
attack of neurasthenia; in 1926 there was a threat of cerebral
anaemia and in 1928 the first signs of amnesia. It may well
be that the illness which was to prove fatal five years later was
hastened by this slight accident, but this can only be a matter
for speculation.

Before the end of the year Ravel, along with several other
composers, was approached by a film company with an invitation to write the music for a film on the theme of Don Quixote

with Chaliapin in the title role.   The offer was made simultaneously to Ravel, Milhaud, Marcel Delannoy and Jacques
Ibert, none of whom, of course, had any reason to suspect
that the others had been approached.   Ravel as usual was dila-
tory, and finally the music was commissioned from Jacques
Ibert.   The whole project, however, came to nothing in the
end, but only after Ravel had written the three *Chansons de Don
Quichotte à Dulcinée*, with words by Paul Morand, which proved
to be his swan song.   The last of the three songs, a drinking
song, ends with the words: " Je bois à la joie."   On this note
and with these words Ravel put down his pen for the last
time.   He was never to compose another note of music.
Before him lay the Valley of the Shadows through which he
was to grope his way in a misty semi-trance, yet with intellect
and sensibility unimpaired, until death released him after
five years of mental suffering.

The real tragedy of his condition was that while his brain
was perfectly clear, it was unable to transmit its impulses
through the usual channels, so that ideas could no longer be
transferred to paper through a hand that could not write, and
only with difficulty by word of mouth owing to an impedi-
ment of speech.   " Apraxia ", " dysphasia "—these are the
words the doctors use to describe this painful state in which the
sufferer, fully conscious and even intellectually alert, is, as it
were, the helpless spectator of his own misfortune.   It was
not that Ravel's musical imagination was any less active; on
the contrary, he used to say: " I've still so much to say, so
many ideas in my head."   The tragedy was his total inability
to give tangible shape to his ideas by committing them to
paper, for by now he was unable even to sign his name.   To
write a letter cost him, even in the early stages of his illness,
untold efforts; for although the spelling of the words was clear
in his mind, he could not remember how the letters were
formed, and had to look each word up in a dictionary.   Thus
it took him eight days, on his own confession, " with the aid
of Larousse " to write a letter of some fifty words to condole
with his great friend Maurice Delage on the death of his

mother. The date was March 22, 1934, and the letter was the last he ever wrote. Already in January of that year Dr. Valléry-Radot, who had attended Debussy during his last years and had been with him when he died, had examined Ravel and found his condition disquieting. He wrote in these terms to Hélène Jourdan-Morhange: " If you see Maurice Ravel's brother, tell him, without alarming him, because he seems to me to be very sensitive, that I am very worried about his brother. I have examined him very thoroughly so as to be sure not to overlook a lesion of some kind, but there is none. However, he shows signs of great intellectual fatigue which I find very alarming. It is absolutely necessary—and you must impress this upon him—that he should have a complete rest for a very considerable time, and for that it would be best if he could go to friends in the Midi or else to some mountain resort."

Ravel did, in fact, go to Switzerland for a time, but his condition did not improve. He even lost the sense of touch, and seemed to retreat farther and farther away into some nebulous region into which his friends were unable to penetrate, although it was obvious to them that his mind was as lucid as ever behind the veil which had descended to cut him off from the warm contacts and simple pleasures he had so much appreciated, and above all from the creative activities which were his life.

But there was one thing that still gave him pleasure, apart from the company of his friends, and that was travel. It was accordingly arranged, largely owing to the generosity behind the scenes of Mme Ida Rubinstein, that his great friend, Léon Leyritz, the sculptor, should accompany him on a voyage to Spain and Morocco, a country which Ravel had for long wanted to visit. Travelling across Spain via Madrid to Algeciras, they crossed from there to Tangiers, where Ravel was enchanted by the oriental atmosphere: the sights and sounds and vivid colours; the camels and the snake-charmers; the bright costumes and exotic fruits piled high in the bazaars; the scenery, and types who seemed to have stepped straight out of the pages of *The Arabian Nights*. He was very " eastern-minded " at the time, and in spite of his illness was still dreaming of the ballet-opera he wanted to write—*Morgiane*, the story of Ali Baba. It seems that the score and general plan of the work were already taking shape in his head, but now it was too late; he was quite incapable of writing it down. By a cruel irony of fate, just when circumstances might have been especially favourable for the carrying out of this project and when to find himself in such surroundings might well have stimulated his inspiration, he was less than ever in a position to profit by the situation in which he found himself.

After Tangiers came Marrakech, where the travellers spent three weeks at the Mamounia Hotel and were invited to a memorable *soirée* at the palace of one of the sons of " El Glaoui " in the Atlas Mountains. Ravel was enchanted by the oriental splendour of the pageant arranged in his honour, with a hundred dancing girls, a native orchestra and Arab warriors leading magnificent black deerhounds. At Fez he was received by the Director of Fine Arts, who showed him over the château and magnificent gardens of the Residence. To the suggestion that this marvellous décor might inspire him to compose a work with a truly Arab atmosphere Ravel retorted: " If I wrote anything Arab it would be far more Arab than all this ! "

It was in Fez, too, that Ravel was the guest of honour at a reception given by a group of young European doctors in an old Arab palace where there were as many cats as guests. He had always been a great cat-lover and was devoted to his Siamese companions in the villa at Montfort; so he was willing enough to submit to the caresses and attentions of the dozen or more cats who perched on his shoulders or sat on his knees, saying: " You see, they know how much I love them." This was one of Ravel's happiest recollections of his Moroccan tour, which he used to refer to as " la soirée des chats ".

On the return journey a halt was made at Seville, where Ravel heard the authentic " Cante Jondo " sung by the famous Niña de los Peines, went to a bullfight, and spent hours sitting

in the cafés of the town watching or mingling with the picturesque crowd of passers-by. Here he met Ernesto Halffter,
the Spanish composer, and many young Spanish musicians who
came to pay their respects. Ravel felt at home in Spain, and
eagerly absorbed the atmosphere, responding emotionally not
only to the austere beauty of its landscape, the grandeur of its
art and architecture, but to impressions such as those aroused
by hearing a peasant singing in the fields at night a perfect
malagueña.

From Seville the travellers made their way back to France
through Sórdoba, Vitoria, Burgos and Pamplona. A second
visit to Cdain in the summer of that year, this time to the
Cantabrian coast, was Ravel's farewell to the country he loved
best after France, and after that he travelled no more.

These journeys provided him with the only distraction
possible since his dreadful malady had paralysed his creative
impulses and made it difficult for him to communicate with
those around him. His friends did all in their power to help
him and relieve his solitude, and he now had a pied-à-terre in
his brother's house at Levallois where he could stay when he
came up from the country. At " Le Belvédère " he was looked
after by his faithful housekeeper, Mme Révelot (who had
been with Marcel Proust) and visited daily by his neighbours,
especially by his devoted friend de Zogheb, who has left an
account of some of his last meetings with Ravel. "From now
on ", he wrote, " until his death Ravel was slowly descending
into the shadows of night, into an agony in which he was both
the actor and the principal spectator. He was able, with his
clear vision and pitiless faculty of self-criticism, to observe
day by day, and hour by hour, this disintegration and diminu-
tion of himself which persisted until the end. . . He was
writing the music, as it were, but this time in silence, of his
living death, and in his still lucid mind he could hear his
Requiem, with its invisible orchestra—that he alone could
perceive—of muted fifes and muffled drums."

The full pathos of his condition was revealed on the last
occasion when he was taken by his friends to a concert at which

his own works were being played. His eyes filled with tears.
" C'était beau, tout de même. Et puis, j'avais encore tant de
musique dans la tête. Maintenant, c'est fini pour moi."

It was, indeed, the end. By the autumn of 1937 his condition had become so much worse that it was decided to risk
an operation. On December 17 he entered the clinic at the
Centre Français de Médecine et de Chirurgie in the Rue
Boileau at Auteuil, and two days later the operation was performed by the famous surgeon, Professor Clovis Vincent.
At first it was believed that Ravel would recover. He rallied
after the operation, asked to see his brother, then relapsed
for eight days into a state of semi-coma. At dawn on December 28 his sufferings were over. The cause of death was
discovered to be not, as was at first supposed, a tumour on the
brain, but the hardening and consequent obstruction of an
important blood-vessel that supplies the brain.

He was buried in the cemetery at Levallois (*Division 16,
allée centrale*) on December 30, in the presence of many of his
peers, including Igor Stravinsky, and laid to rest in the family
tomb which now bears the following three inscriptions:

JOSEPH RAVEL
1832–1908

———

MME VEUVE RAVEL
NÉE DELOUART
1840–1917

———

MAURICE RAVEL
COMPOSITEUR
1875–1937

A funeral oration was pronounced by the Minister of
Education, M. Jean Zay, who, in speaking of Ravel's genius,
showed a degree of discernment and understanding not often
found in official tributes. " If I call to mind ", he said, " the
greatest names in our moral and artistic tradition and ask
myself what was characteristic of all those men of genius, and

especially of the genius of Ravel, I believe I should be right in saying that it was in every case a supremely intelligent way of looking at things, whether the most passionate or the most pathetic, and subjecting them to the discipline of style. There is a place in our French spiritual universe for every manifestation of the human heart, which is in no way demeaned by submission to rule."

But it was perhaps Colette who found the words that best express the loss that music suffered by the death of Maurice Ravel: " We can never forget that he was deprived of the gift of memory, lost the power of speech and the ability to write, and died stifled, but fully conscious, while there still surged within him so many harmonies, so many memories of birdsong and guitars, of dancing and melodious nights. . ."

In every country of the world, particularly in England, Germany and the United States, the death of Ravel called forth countless expressions of regret at the passing of a master musician, and innumerable tributes to his genius. The French critic, Emile Vuillermoz, assessed the loss that music had suffered through his death in the following words: " With Maurice Ravel has disappeared the greatest French composer of our age. Since the deaths of Gabriel Fauré and Claude Debussy, it was in his hands that the torch of our national art was kept alight. . . He dominated from afar all the musicians of his time."

PART II

THE WORKS

CHAPTER SEVEN

GENERAL CHARACTERISTICS

RAVEL was in no sense a revolutionary musician. He did not seek to disrupt either the grammar or the syntax of music, but was content to work in classical forms and on the basis of the generally accepted harmonic system of his day, still firmly rooted in tonality. But this is not to say that he did not considerably extend that basis and enrich the harmonic language derived from it in a manner that seemed at the time both original and bold. It could almost be said that he created a language of his own, so very personal and individual was his adaptation and manipulation of the traditional nineteenth-century musical idiom as taught in the conservatories when he was a young man. He was not an iconoclast, but rather an emancipator. He saw what diatonic harmony was potentially capable of, and being endowed with an extremely acute ear and an ultra-sensitive harmonic sense he was able to build on existing foundations a wonderfully rare and subtle sonorous edifice which bears the stamp of his personality as unmistakably as any page of Bach or Chopin. His principal biographer, Roland-Manuel, was probably thinking of this when he remarked that: " Ravel is one of the very rare French composers who have left so strong an imprint on their art that music after them can never be the same as it was before they appeared on the scene."*

This is true in the sense that Ravelian harmonies have now been accepted and incorporated into twentieth-century harmony, but the remark is one that could more properly have been applied to Debussy, who has undoubtedly had a far

* " Le génie de Maurice Ravel ". *Temps Present*, Paris, January 7, 1938.

greater influence on twentieth-century music than Ravel, and who was indeed far more of a pioneer. Debussy cut the swaddling-bands of diatonic harmony; Ravel merely loosened them. It is not surprising that during their lifetime the two composers were for long the centre of a controversy of which we must now give an account.

It was no doubt inevitable that the co-existence of two such outstanding musicians should have led to misunderstandings and rivalries, not so much between the protagonists themselves as among the lesser fry who followed in their wake, and among rival schools of musical thought and their respective mouthpieces, the critics. A great deal of unnecessary confusion was caused by the initial error, widely committed, of dubbing both composers as " Impressionists ". Debussy's earlier works were undoubtedly influenced by the Symbolist movement in painting and literature, and it would not be fanciful to see a Whistlerian influence, both in the choice of title and in the style of, for example, the *Nocturnes* scarcely less obvious than that of Mallarmé in the *Prélude à l'Après-midi d'un Faune*.

These influences were in the air at the turn of the century, and it so happened that both composers (although Ravel was by thirteen years Debussy's junior) had the same kind of literary preferences—for example an admiration for Baudelaire, Mallarmé and E. A. Poe, and a taste for rare and precious sensations, so that their aesthetic outlook was very similar. They were also united in their opposition to the Franckist school and to what they considered to be the deadening influence of academic teaching in France; and both, of course, were alive to the necessity of protecting French music against the danger of Wagnerian influences.

But there the resemblance ended. In methods and technique, and above all in temperament, they were very different. Where Debussy's music is wrapped in a kind of sensuous haze, Ravel's outlines are hard and clear-cut; where one shimmers, the other glitters. Debussy's pantheism coloured everything he wrote; he vibrated in sympathy with the forces of nature—

the sun, the sea, the wind—whereas Ravel would have been more likely to vibrate in the presence of some stylized imitation of sun or sea; a forest oak would have stirred his imagination far less than a Japanese dwarf tree with all its artificial implications. He would never have said, as Debussy did, that he was guided only by " the counsels of the wind that passes and tells us the story of the world ". Nor would he have endorsed Debussy's well-known remark that it was " more useful to see the dawn rise than to hear the Pastoral Symphony; musicians who only know music will never get anywhere ".

Yet in spite of these fundamental differences of outlook, people persisted in confusing the two composers, and it became the fashion to accuse Ravel of plagiarizing his elder, although it should have been obvious that their styles and tendencies were really very different. The classicism of Ravel's form alone was in marked contrast with Debussy's much more fluid construction, and whereas the former made a point of stressing the clarity of his formal design, the latter was especially anxious that his music should sound like an improvisation. Ravel did not mind if his scaffolding was visible, but Debussy was always careful to conceal any traces of the mechanics of his art. It was this firm adherence on Ravel's part to the principles of classical form that prompted his friend M. D. Calvocoressi to sum up the situation as follows: " This music [Ravel's] which helped to preserve a feeling for classical form throughout the entire period of musical impressionism constitutes, by virtue of that very quality, a link between Debussy's generation and those of the post-war period [1918]."

Relations between the two composers were never very cordial, though each had a genuine respect and admiration for the other. We have already referred to Debussy's advice to Ravel in 1902 not to alter a note of his quartet " in the name of the gods of music and in mine ", advice which must have been singularly encouraging to the young Ravel; and we know that Ravel all his life deeply admired Debussy. He was a fervent *Pelléas* enthusiast from the very first, and never missed a performance in the early days when the success of the opera depended largely on support from the young *avant-garde* musicians. And we must not forget the tribute he paid to Debussy late in life when, on hearing a record of the *Prélude à l'Après-midi d'un Faune* he turned to his friend de Zogheb with tears in his eyes and said: " It was when I first heard that many years ago that I understood what music is."* But his admiration for Debussy did not prevent Ravel from developing his own personality and style in so unmistakable a fashion that it is difficult for us today to see how he could have been accused of " imitating " Debussy. There is, on the contrary, some evidence that if any plagiarism had been committed, it was by Debussy himself, whose *Soirées dans Grenade* (Estampes) published in 1903 bore a certain resemblance to Ravel's early *Habanera*, composed in 1895, the manuscript score of which had been lent to Debussy at the time by the composer. Subsequently Ravel incorporated his *Habanera* in the *Rapsodie Espagnole* of 1907, but added a note to indicate the date of its composition.

This was the beginning of the Ravel-Debussy controversy which was further aggravated when Pierre Lalo gave Debussy the credit of having inaugurated an entirely new pianistic style in his *L'Île Joyeuse* and *Reflets dans l'Eau*. This caused Ravel to emerge from his usual position of aloof detachment and make a statement to the effect that when he composed *Jeux d'Eau* in 1902 Debussy had then written for the piano nothing more important than *Pour le Piano*, " a work which ", said Ravel, " I need hardly say I passionately admire, but which, from a purely pianistic point of view, conveyed nothing really new ".

In spite of these two episodes, there was no real rivalry between the two composers, and what there was was encouraged far more by their supporters than by themselves. If they eventually became estranged, they had only their friends to thank for this—" those stupid meddlers ", as Laloy† called them, " who seemed to take pleasure in making it inevitable . . .

* Ravel's arrangement of *L'Après-midi d'un Faune* for two pianos (four hands) was published by Jobert, Paris.
† Louis Laloy, Debussy's friend and biographer.

though I can vouch for the fact that they [Debussy and Ravel] both regretted the rupture ". But, as Ravel remarked later, " It's probably better for us, after all, to be on frigid terms for illogical reasons ".

From the evidence available it seems that Pierre Lalo, music critic of *Le Temps*, was largely responsible for, or at least played a leading part in, the anti-Ravel campaign, and it is instructive to examine the arguments he used to establish his case. The controversy came to a head with the publication in *Le Temps* of March 19, 1907, of an article from Lalo's pen entitled " Ravel et le Debussysme ".

He begins by referring to the " dangerous and disturbing publicity to which Ravel has been subjected by his imprudent friends; he would be better served by more discreet enemies ". Then, after criticizing severely both the *Histoires Naturelles* and the orchestral version of *Une Barque sur l'Océan*, proceeds as follows: " In both these works one hears continually a very distinct echo of the music of M. Debussy. You are, of course, aware that Ravel is not the only one of his kind; it is an indisputable fact that a very large number of young French composers are writing ' Debussyist ' music. ' Debussysme ' in recent years has taken the place of the now superannuated ' Massenetism ' and nearly extinct Wagnerism."

He then develops the argument that, in order to avoid the accusation of Debussysme the younger school invented a doctrine to protect themselves which was welcomed by all composers whose music resembled Debussy's. This, he says, can be summarized as follows: " M. Debussy has not created out of nothing an entirely new art; he was only the most eloquent spokesman for a whole generation of musicians who, inspired by the same ideals, have for a long time past been composing in silence and obscurity all his most admired discoveries. In other words, M. Debussy has invented nothing. It must be said straight away that their theory, in my opinion, is nothing but an impudent joke and cannot be sustained either by the dates of the works concerned, or by their nature, or on historical or aesthetic grounds." [Here follows a list of the

dates of Debussy's works.]   " The eldest of these young men,
M. Ravel, is barely thirty.   Fifteen years ago what had he
produced? . . .   It is really carrying the joke too far, this
attempt to hoodwink the public into believing that Debussy-
ism is a collective phenomenon in which Debussy himself is
no more important than anyone else; the dates are there and
speak for themselves."

To this attack Ravel replied in the following terms in a
letter published in *Le Temps* on April 9, 1907:

> To the Editor
> Dear Sir,
>   I have had brought to my notice an article published in *Le
> Temps* of March 19 in which there are many references to myself.
> M. Pierre Lalo, with all his accustomed and consummate in-
> genuity, attempts once again to prove that I am devoid of person-
> ality.   That may well be.   What is more serious is that he puts
> into the mouth of " certain musicians " some very strange re-
> marks with regard to an artist of genius, Claude Debussy.   In
> accordance with modern usage, M. Lalo does not name the
> "young musicians " whom he accuses in this casual way.   But
> as my name is frequently mentioned in the course of the article
> this might create a regrettable confusion and lead the uninformed
> reader to suppose that the writer was alluding to me.   It is a pity
> that he was not a little more explicit.   I consider it my duty to
> repudiate M. Lalo's insinuation and to challenge him to produce
> a single witness who has heard me utter any such absurdities.
> It is a matter of indifference to me if I am looked upon, by those
> who only know my works through the critics, as an impudent
> plagiarist; but I object to being made to appear, even in their eyes,
> as an imbecile.

Commenting on this letter, Lalo made the point that Ravel
once said to him in conversation that any likeness between his
music and Debussy's was due, not to any " influence ", but to
an " innate resemblance " (*similitude innée*).

Ravel takes up the cudgels again in defence of Debussy six
years later in an article published in *Les Cahiers d'Aujourd'hui*,
of February 1913, after the first performance of the orchestral
Images.   Once again he was tilting at those critics who, like
Pierre Lalo and Gaston Carraud (critic of *La Liberté*), were

trying to diminish Debussy. Carraud had written, in his notice of this new work of Debussy's: " It must be confessed that everything that M. Debussy has written since *Pelléas et Mélisande* has been a disappointment to many of his former admirers. A few, it is true, are becoming increasingly enthusiastic, and even go so far as to assert that it is only now that he is entering upon a period of fully conscious maturity . . . thus we have on the one hand the musicians and really sensitive people, and on the other the painters and littérateurs."

Ravel proceeds to demolish this point of view, classing himself, sarcastically, with the " painters and littérateurs " in company with Igor Stravinsky, Florent Schmitt, Roger Ducasse and Albert Roussel—" the only ' musicians and sensitive people' being, of course, MM. Camille Mauclair, Pierre Lalo and Gaston Carraud. It only remains for these ' sensitive people ' to indulge in the harmless mania of closing their eyes in the face of the rising sun and proclaiming loudly that night is falling ".

That musical opinion was very much concerned with the question of the alleged influence of Debussy on so many contemporary composers is shown by the fact that the files of *Le Temps* are full of references to this subject, especially during the years 1907–1910. The " Debussystes ", among whom Ravel was wrongly included at that time by such critics as Lalo, were reproached with imitating the mannerisms of their model and nothing else. Thus, in another article on this theme that appeared in *Le Temps* of August 18, 1909, the writer refers to " these young men who have three or four tricks up their sleeve and are then at the end of their resources. And the tricks are not even their own; it is M. Debussy who invented them and showed them the way; and all that they can do is to go on repeating them. But don't ask them for ideas or feeling; they have only got the recipes and are, in fact, exactly the opposite of the musician to whom they owe their existence. . . The Debussystes have neither the intelligence nor the sensibility of M. Debussy; they only copy his technique, which is nothing, or at least not important. . . It would

not be a bad thing if the public showed them in no uncertain manner that their little tricks are already out of date and that they have ceased to give pleasure. . ."

The following year Lalo returned to the charge (*Le Temps*, February 26, 1910): " The worst of it is that although M. Debussy is undoubtedly skilful (in his pursuit of rare sonorities) there are others who are just as, if not more, skilful than he is. . . When it is a question of inventing and combining special little ' effects ' of an unusual kind and of ' dosing ' this sort of pharmaceutical product—a pinch of sonorities here and a drop of harmony there—the young men who imitate M. Debussy, for example, M. Ravel, are as good and even better at the game than he is himself. . . M. Debussy, however, is a magician and not a chemist."

Enough has been said to show that the error of imagining that Ravel had anything in common with Debussy apart from certain quite superficial features persisted in some quarters for a considerable time. Even their harmonic language showed fundamental points of difference, Debussy's being characterized by a preference for chords of the ninth and the hexaphonic or whole-tone scale, while Ravel cultivated the eleventh harmonic and never employed the whole-tone scale. His melodies are almost invariably modal, and the modes he used most frequently were the (medieval) Dorian (d–d') and Phrygian (e–e'), the latter being characteristic of Andalucian folk-music and the former of Basque music, although it is also found frequently in old French songs. Ravel rarely uses the ordinary classical major scale and, if he does, avoids the leading note; there are no instances at all in his music, I think, of the classical minor scale. Chords of the seventh, ninth and eleventh based on the two modes mentioned above are the foundation of Ravel's harmony, but appear variously disguised, often with unresolved appoggiaturas in major sevenths:

Ex. 2

and sometimes with an augmented fifth in a chord of the eleventh:

Ex.3

very characteristic. A great deal of his sometimes very complex-looking harmony can be analysed and reduced to simpler terms, almost always in relation to conventional harmony with a definitely tonal basis or core.

The *Valses Nobles et Sentimentales* contain in essence all the main features of Ravel's harmonic language stripped bare of inessentials and revealing the framework of ninths and elevenths, seconds, and unresolved appoggiaturas which impart a peculiarly acid flavour to so much of this music. The opening bars of the first waltz are a good example of this and have been the subject of much discussion among analysts and commentators:

Ex.4

But it was left to Alfredo Casella, in a penetrating study of Ravel's harmony in *La Revue Musicale* of April 1, 1925, to reduce this passage to its bare bones, as follows:

Ex. 5

I do not propose to enter here upon an exhaustive study of the ingredients from which Ravel brewed his very individual and potent brand of harmonic spice; examples as they occur will be dealt with when we come to examine individual works in the next section. I would mention, however, that a very complete analysis of Ravel's style and technique is to be found in M. Jules van Ackere's *Maurice Ravel* (Editions Elsevier, Brussels, 1957), a book in which the student will find everything he needs to know about the actual mechanics of Ravel's art. He was, of course, a superb craftsman and handled his musical material with an astonishing mastery and precision only equalled in our day by Stravinsky. However, it is interesting to hear what Ravel himself had to say about the vexed question of *métier*, which he possessed to a supreme degree. Rather unexpectedly, he takes into account in his evaluation of the importance of *métier* pure and simple in musical composition the part played by " inspiration ", expressing his thought in the following terms: " There are rules to ensure that a building remains upright, but none that govern a series of modulations. Yes, there is one—inspiration. The essence of genius, that is to say the essence of artistic *invention*, can only be found in instinct or sensibility. In art there can be no such thing as *métier* in the absolute sense of the word. The part played by inspiration in ensuring the harmonious proportions and elegant fashioning of a work is almost unlimited, while the deliberate cultivation of ' development ' can only be sterile in its results."

It is difficult to speak of a definite evolution in Ravel's harmonic style, the essential features of which are already present in his earliest works, as for example in the astonishing *Habanera*, written when he was only twenty. Unlike most composers, he seems to have acquired in his student days a technical mastery which remained constant throughout his career; his touch was no less sure in the *Quartet* of 1902 than in the *Tombeau de Couperin* of 1917 or, for that matter, the piano concertos of 1931. At the same time, his harmonic language underwent some modifications; the " rich " period culminating in *Daphnis et Chloë* was succeeded by one in which the style became more chastened, as in the *Tombeau*, and even austere as in the *Sonatas* for violin and 'cello and violin and piano. During this period [1922–1927] he also wrote the remarkable *Chansons Madécasses*. *Boléro* represents a deliberate *tour de force* of simplification, while the two *Piano Concertos* incorporate, in a final résumé as it were, all the most characteristic aspects of Ravel's genius—the gay, ingeniously wrought, almost frivolous (apart from the slow movement) G major work forming a striking contrast to the sombre and tragic pathos of the powerful *Concerto for the Left Hand*.

His music is often accused of being soulless, cold and artificial. It is true it is for the most part impersonal, passionless and highly polished, but it frequently rises to heights of eloquence, if not emotion, as in *Daphnis*, *La Valse* and above all in the *Concerto for the Left Hand* or the slow movement of the *Piano Concerto in G*. As to its artificiality, did not the composer once protest to Calvocoressi: " How do they know that I am not artificial by nature? " A profound remark, and one that may provide the key to an understanding of his music. Put differently, it might be said that Ravel, perhaps more than any other composer, approached his art from outside, as it were, self-consciously and at the same time objectively. He deliberately refrained, in fact, from trying to express " himself ". The music he created had an independent, objective existence of its own, its shape and form and content being determined solely by extraneous circumstances: if dramatic, by the nature of the text and subject-matter: if purely instrumental, by the nature of the technical problems to be surmounted as, for example, in the *Trio*, the violin and 'cello *Sonata* and, pre-eminently, *Boléro*.

Roland-Manuel in a penetrating analysis of Ravel's aesthetic, which he calls " L'Esthétique de l'Imposture "* remarks: " It is not necessary to know Maurice Ravel personally, nor to have penetrated deeply into his fundamental way of thinking, to be convinced that his whole art, methods of procedure and technique are the result of deliberate research and a distrust of inspiration. . . It is difficult to imagine Ravel in a suppliant

* *La Revue Musicale*, April 1925.

posture, urging his heart to bring forth the genius within. Should ever his skill fail him, he can never plead sincerity as an excuse. Art for him is not an obligation, as it is for the Romantics. It is not, in his eyes, the supreme truth, but rather the most dazzling lie—a marvellous imposture. For does not all music lie that abjures the expression of feeling and relies instead on artifice? And what more astonishing artifice is there than this art, of all the least faithful and bearing the least resemblance to the objects it evokes? If this music pleases you or moves you to tears, know that it is made by a man who did not go on his knees ' before and after ', who wept no tears in writing it and who agrees with a great poet who said: ' he who wishes to write down his dream must himself be very wide awake '."

There is no doubt that Ravel's art fulfils this last condition. No composer could ever have been more fully conscious of what he was doing. He did not claim to have invented anything new; perfection rather than innovation was his aim. Roland-Manuel has said that there is no single work of his that is not at bottom a pastiche. He will take as his model a sonata by Mozart, a concerto by Saint-Saëns; but when his work is finished, all trace of the original will generally have disappeared. By a super-refinement, or perversion, of taste he even preferred the pastiche to the original when seeking a model, so that the finished product, his own pastiche of that pastiche, would be at two removes from the real thing.

Jankélévitch, in his study of Ravel,* suggests that his choice of the title *Miroirs*, for example, is significant; for does it not seem to depreciate the original and glorify the reflection? " Ravel ", he remarks very aptly, " plays hide-and-seek with himself; he has three alibis to protect his ' pudeur ': naturalism, which serves to hide his real self; exoticism to mask this naturalism, and pastiche to mask the exoticism." Thus he would see ancient Greece or China preferably through eighteenth-century eyes (*Daphnis et Chloë*, *Empress of the Pagodas*), that century being for him the mirror through which all previous

* Paris, 1956.

epochs or cultures were reflected. It has been said, indeed, that he saw antiquity through the eyes of the painters of the Revolution, and Couperin through Marie-Antoinette! The exotic element in Ravel's music, however, is not the result of any nostalgic longings or of "escapism" in any form, but rather the reflection of his extraordinary aptitude to assume a role and, having assumed it, to ensure that every detail, every inflexion of voice and accent will be perfect.

He was, in fact, a great musical traveller and polyglot, equally at home in the East, from Damascus to Pekin (cf. *Asie* in *Shéhérazade*, or the *Chansons Hébraïques*); in the South (*Chansons Madécasses*); in the steppes of Central Europe (*Tzigane*); and in Spain (*Rapsodie Espagnole, Pavane, Alborada, Habanera, L'Heure Espagnole, Don Quichotte à Dulcinée*). But in every case, be it noted, he drew his inspiration from the copy rather than from the original; his Orient is the Orient of the *Arabian Nights*, his Spain the Spain of the nineteenth-century romantics (Jankélévitch compares the *Pavane* to "a Velasquez seen through the eyes of Liszt");* his Madagascar a re-creation of the impression of an eighteenth-century French poet; his Hungarian gipsy the conventional romantic Lisztian *Zigeuner* rather than the Bartókian peasant-fiddler, and so on and so forth. This passion for the inauthentic found further expression in his collection of "fake" works of art and *objets d'art* with which he surrounded himself in his house and took pleasure in showing to mystified visitors. There was, for instance, a fake Monticelli of which he was especially proud. This delight in *faux*, incidentally, was a trait he shared with Erik Satie, who, in his *Mémoires d'un Amnésique* speaks lovingly of his "*faux Rembrandt*", "imitation Teniers" and "a delightful portrait attributed to an unknown painter"; though in Satie's case these things existed probably only in his imagination.

There remain the poets and writers to whom he later turned when seeking texts to set to music. The naïve and childlike

---

* An exception is the *Rapsodie Espagnole* whose authenticity is vouched for by Falla, whose own *Nuits dans les Jardins d'Espagne* is said to have been inspired by the *Rapsodie*.

side to his nature (and this was more positive than might have been supposed) was drawn irresistibly to the world of sprites and fairies, and so we find him in due course setting tales by Perrault (*La Belle au Bois Dormant* and *Petit Poucet*), his female counterpart, the Comtesse d'Aulnoy (*Laideronette, Impératrice des Pagodes*), Mme Leprince de Beaumont (*La Belle et la Bête*), and Colette (*L'Enfant et les Sortilèges*).

Going farther back to the pure fountain of Renaissance poetry we are not surprised to see Ravel turning to the chief poets of the *Pléiade*, Ronsard and Clément Marot, in such exquisite small lyrics as *Ronsard à son âme* and the two by Marot, *D'Anne qui me jecta de la neige*, and *D'Anne jouant de l'espinette*. Here we see displayed the typical French qualities of grace and polish in a medium offering a piquant combination of archaism and modernism which suited Ravel's style to perfection. The Romantic poets in general did not appeal to him, but he made an exception in favour of that curious personage Louis, known as Aloysius, Bertrand, who was in some respects a precursor of the modern movement, but who might well have been forgotten had it not been for Ravel's setting of the fantastic triptych, *Gaspard de la Nuit*.

Of the nineteenth-century poets his favourites, as we have seen, were such contemporaries as Mallarmé, Henri de Régnier, Emile Verhaeren, Franc-Nohain and Tristan Klingsor, who supplied him, respectively, with the texts for his settings of *Sainte* (1896) and the *Trois Poèmes* (1913); *Les Grands Vents venus d'Outre-mer* (1906); *Si Morne* (1899); *L'Heure Espagnole* (1907); and *Shéhérazade* (1903).

Another aspect of his sophisticated, " artificial " tastes is to be seen in his preference for non-human subjects as material for musical treatment, such as fairy-tales and fantasies (*Ma Mère l'Oye*, *L'Enfant et les Sortilèges*); sprites and supernatural creatures (*Scarbo*, *Ondine*); birds and animals (*Oiseaux Tristes*, *Histoires Naturelles*, *L'Enfant*); stylized pictorial evocations (*Pavane pour une Infante défunte*); or puppet-like stage characters in artificial comedy as in *L'Heure Espagnole*. Archaistic pastiche, too, was a source of inspiration, as in the *Menuet Antique*,

Tombeau de Couperin, Epigrammes (Clément Marot) and *Ronsard à son âme*.

Almost the only work in which flesh-and-blood emotions are depicted is the *Chansons Madécasses*, where, for the first time, in his *œuvre*, as Ravel himself points out, an erotic element is introduced. Did he, then, imply that this element was not present in Franc-Nohain's highly spiced comedy *L'Heure Espagnole*? In the biographical sketch in which he comments briefly on his own production he describes this work merely as " a kind of conversation in music "; and it must be admitted that in his handling of this slightly libertine story he somehow manages to dehumanize completely the principal actors in it and reduce them to the level of puppets. For human passions and dramatic situations have no place in his artistic universe, from which all " personal " emotions or impressions are excluded and artifice reigns supreme. His art is, in fact, a perfect example of the old nineteenth-century aesthetic slogan " art for art's sake ". On this plane, and within these limitations, he aimed at, and achieved, a degree of perfection in sheer craftsmanship which has rarely been equalled. He was, as Léon-Paul Fargue expressed it, " fou de perfection ". This explains, I think, why he was content to work within the limits of classical form and was always ready to accept restrictions imposed from without, e.g. the challenge of some particularly technical problem or the conditions attaching to some specially commissioned work or *pièce d'occasion*, such as the writing of a test piece for the Conservatoire (the piano *Prelude* of 1913) or for a prescribed combination of instruments (*Chansons Madécasses*). Ravel, indeed, would have heartily endorsed the famous saying of Leonardo da Vinci: " Strength is born of constraint and dies of liberty."

What appears in all this to be sophistication and artificiality springs essentially from the composer's determination not to identify himself in any way with the objects or characters he depicts. The French critic André Suarès has stressed this extreme temperamental reserve and detachment as being one of Ravel's fundamental characteristics. The passage is worth quoting in full. "Nothing", he says, "could be more objective than the art of Ravel, or more deliberately intended to be so. If music is capable of painting an object without first revealing the painter's feeling towards it, then Ravel's music achieves this more than any other. We have to go back to the eighteenth century, to the *divertissements* of Couperin and Rameau, to encounter a similar inclination. Moreover, Couperin is far from excluding the expression of feeling or from distrusting it so ferociously in a manner that seems at first sight to be derisive, but which is really very serious, if we come to think about it. Stravinsky, too, is closely attached to objects, but identifies himself with them, as with some natural element, almost unconsciously; whereas Ravel is always a more or less ironical spectator, even when he is moved; for when his feelings are aroused he disguises them in order, as it were, to throw the hearer off the scent. Such cunning in self-concealment, such a penchant for deception, are rare in music. Berlioz would certainly not have understood this attitude. Everything in Ravel's music indicates deliberate self-effacement, a determination to indulge in no confidences. His harmonies, his search for and discovery of new effects, the nervous tension and surreptitious smile, the trembling of the lips in his melodies, the hidden fever and agitation of his rhythms are sufficient proof of his sensibility; but he conceals it; he covers it with a veil that allows nothing to appear; he is not only ashamed of it but almost hates it; he denies its existence; and so he abjures all rhetoric and, from fear of excess, he is capable of putting up with what might seem to be indigence. He prefers dryness to abundance. In short, he is so reticent with regard to his feelings that he would prefer to appear to have none at all rather than reveal them. . . Like Baudelaire, he is ashamed to have a heart; and if his heart shows in his art, he would consider that to be a betrayal of his art. . . His music often gives the impression of being a marvellous machine—a watch regulated to the tenth of a second, its mechanism adjusted to a hundredth of a millimetre. A celebrated musician is credited with having said that ' Ravel is the most perfect of Swiss watchmakers '. . . And yet the intuition of this musical engineer remains intact. Nothing can alter his taste, his powers of invention in sound, the exquisite refinement of his ear. He lives, thinks and, so to speak, sees through his sense of hearing. . ."*

Ravel himself would have endorsed this last statement. For did he not remark that: " My ambition is to say with notes what a poet expresses in words; I think and feel in music." He also said†—and this seems to be in contradiction to the views expressed above and indeed to the general opinion of most students of Ravel: ". . . there are two kinds of music: intellectual music, like d'Indy's, and sentimental, instinctive music, like mine." Here again it is difficult to reconcile this statement with another often-quoted saying of Ravel's to the effect that music is a product of the brain. But perhaps after all the contradiction is not so complete as it sounds; the composition of music is an intellectual exercise, whatever its emotive origin may be. In any case Ravel would never admit that he was devoid of feeling merely because he did not wear his heart on his sleeve. His friend de Zogheb records that on one occasion Ravel confided in him—and there were few to whom he would have opened his heart in this way: " People are always talking about my having no heart (sécheresse de cœur). It's not true. But I am a Basque, and the Basques feel very deeply but seldom show it, and then only to a very few." As we remarked above, Ravel was full of contradictions and, to set against this confession, we must remember the *cri de cœur* already quoted: " Has it never occurred to them that I may be artificial by nature? "

We can only conclude that his was a highly complex nature in which the dichotomy between the man and the artist was complete, in the sense that he was determined not to use his art as a vehicle for the expression of private and personal sentiments. There remain for our consideration two main influences, or rather poles of attraction, on which we have not

---

* *La Revue Musicale.* April, 1925.
† Or is reported to have said—but see p. 126.

yet touched but which played an important part in the general orientation of his *œuvre*. The first is what we may call the Iberian influence as revealed in some of his key works, such as the *Rapsodie Espagnole*, the *Habanera*, *L'Heure Espagnole* and the *Alborada*. The second is his predilection for dance rhythms of all species and nationalities which recur again and again in so many of his works, in which examples can be found of the minuet, the pavane, the forlane, the rigaudon, the czardas, the habanera, the passacaglia, the bolero, the waltz, the foxtrot and the blues.

His attachments to Spain can no doubt be ascribed partly to racial affinities, for he was after all a Pyrenean born, and had a Spanish mother. Curiously enough, his music shows no traces of Basque influences, and when he is deliberately evoking Spain it is from *flamenco* and Andalucian sources, in rhythm, accent and colour, that he clearly derives his inspiration. But his mastery of the Spanish idiom was complete and authentic and vouched for by Spanish musicians, notably Manuel de Falla, who paid tribute to its accuracy. This makes it all the more surprising that in one instance he should have departed from his usual high standards of accuracy by conferring the title " Boléro " on a piece which has none of the characteristics of that particular dance-form.

With regard to his preference for dance-forms in general, he is here, of course, reverting to type and proclaiming his affinities with the seventeenth- and eighteenth-century clavecinists to whom he paid tribute in *Le Tombeau de Couperin*. It is also in keeping with his conception of music as being primarily a *divertissement*. The dance is an anti-romantic, objective form, strictly impersonal and, at the same time, the foundation of all music; here Ravel felt on safe ground and could be emotionally disengaged. In this context, it is perhaps not without significance that he never attempted to write a symphony—the one musical form *par excellence* that depends on inner conflict, dramatic development, contrast and at least some degree of emotional and nervous tension. *La Valse* is perhaps the nearest Ravel ever came to the expression of an inner tension, amounting almost to disequilibrium, in quasi-symphonic form. The same note of some sort of *personal* tragedy can be detected here as in the great *Concerto for the Left Hand*, due, perhaps, to a premonition of the mental darkness in which the composer was doomed to spend the last years of his life. *La Valse*, in fact, in spite of the purely pictorial and objective character ascribed to it by its author, may more properly be looked upon as a kind of *danse macabre*. As Roland-Manuel has pointed out, " the drama here is not in the picture, but in the painter . . . the real tragedy is in the artist's soul. . . In the course of this work the musician touched at several points the limits of his empire. . . Prisoner of his own perfection, he tries vainly to break the chains he has forged so patiently, and in doing so stains his hands with blood. . . He weaves his spells with less detachment than of yore . . . in fact, he is chafing at the bit, and if, like Ramiro in *L'Heure Espagnole*, he still has ' a smile on his lips ', the smile is now a wry one."

Ravel was a supreme master of the orchestra, and possessed an infallible ear for the precise and accurate dosage of instrumental sonorities, delicate adjustments of tone-colour and the balance of opposing timbres. He had a fondness for using instruments in unusual registers, and took pleasure sometimes in making them play out of character, so that, for example, the horn would be made to impersonate the trumpet, or vice versa. All his effects are minutely calculated, nothing is left to chance. And Ravel expected his interpreters to carry out his instructions to the letter, and would not tolerate any " personal " interpretations. The conductor has only to observe strictly the minute indications with which Ravel covered his scores and " play what is written ". The dosage is as precise as in a doctor's prescription. Coming as he did at a time when Debussy had already perfected the Impressionist technique and Stravinsky was preparing the charge of dynamite with which to blow up the old traditional fabric of the nineteenth-century orchestra, it is amazing that Ravel was able to make his very individual contribution to the art of instrumentation without plagiarizing either of the great masters who were his contemporaries. And he was no less successful in his orchestrations of the works of other composers, a signal example being his masterly orchestration of Mussorgsky's *Pictures from an Exhibition*, in which, one feels, he identifies himself completely with the spirit of the original in a way that is quite uncanny.

Ravel also made a distinctive contribution to the literature and technique of the piano—in *Jeux d'Eau, Gaspard de la Nuit, Le Tombeau de Couperin* and the two *Concertos*, to name only the most significant; to vocal music, notably in the song-cycle *Shéhérazade*, the *Histoires Naturelles* and the *Chansons Madécasses*; to chamber music in the *Quartet*, *Trio* and *Sonatas* for violin and 'cello and to the theatre with the operas *L'Heure Espagnole* and *L'Enfant et les Sortilèges* and the ballet *Daphnis et Chloë*. We shall be considering all these works in detail in the next section; for the moment we are concerned only with the general characteristics of Ravel's style and musical imprint as revealed in the different domains to which these works belong. His writing for the voice is characterized by a meticulous respect for the inflexions of natural speech and vocal *tessitura*; in chamber music he broke new ground in his search for new sonorities in the combination of strings and piano, as in the *Trio* and violin and violin and 'cello *Sonatas*; he inaugurated a new pianistic technique and considerably extended the possibilities of that instrument; and, finally, he enriched the lyric stage with two completely original and in some ways revolutionary musical comedies, which, although intensely French, were yet held to violate the French operatic tradition in more respects than one.

In everything he wrote style, perfection of form and attention to detail are conspicuous. And although Ravel was by no means, as we have seen, chauvinistic or even particularly patriotic in his views on art and politics, yet his music is quintessentially French, not only on the surface, but in its undertones. His contemporary, the French author and critic Benjamin Crémieux, indeed finds in his music an echo of each of the following: Marot, Ronsard, La Fontaine, Racine, La Bruyère, Diderot, Chénier, Nerval, Baudelaire, Mallarmé, Valéry, Giraudoux; Clouet, Poussin, Claude Lorrain, Watteau, Ingres, Courbet, Renoir, Degas, Cézanne; but no foreign influences at all, save perhaps Goya. Even allowing for a certain amount of fanciful exaggeration in this appraisal of Ravel's musical " aura ", it is possible, even for a foreigner, to see that there is a good deal of truth in it. Wit and grace and elegance; clarity, flexibility and firmness; probity, fantasy and irony; humour, and even tenderness—such are the qualities reflected in the music of Ravel. But even if we feel it has no mystery, no secret undertones; even if in our eyes its bright light seems to cast no shadows; even if it can fairly be said to have poise without passion and sensibility without sentiment, it is still the work of a great stylist, a master of understatement, the subtlest of craftsmen, a poet of the rarer delights of the mind and senses. Ravel will always be a musician for the minority; there was no place in his aesthetic for outward manifestations of ordinary human feelings or emotions. For him music was a craft; it lived and moved and had its being in a sphere where every artifice, every refinement of technique, every perfection of form had to be cultivated for their own sakes alone. And it is by these standards that Ravel's music must ultimately be judged.

CHAPTER EIGHT

THE MUSIC

1. Vocal; 2. Piano; 3. Chamber Music; 4. Orchestral; 5. Operatic

1. VOCAL

THE solo song, or *mélodie*, to borrow the more appropriate French term, occupies an important place in Ravel's *œuvre*. He responded readily to the stimulus of poetic imagery, and in his settings of both verse and prose he often achieved a rare fusion of musical and poetic values which lends great distinction to all his vocal writing. His choice of texts is evidence of a fastidious literary taste, and his treatment of the words shows that he had a keen ear for verbal as well as tonal niceties.

There are seventeen (published) titles for a solo voice with piano or instrumental accompaniment, consisting of either single songs or sets of two or more (including two sets of arrangements of *chants populaires* from other lands), and one set of three songs for mixed *a cappella* chorus. Ravel also wrote, but did not publish, the following songs: *Ballade de la Reine morte d'aimer* (Roland de Marès), 1894; *Le Rouet* (Leconte de Lisle), 1894; *Un grand sommeil noir* (Verlaine), 1895; *Si morne . . .* (Verhaeren), 1899; as well as three cantatas which failed to win the Prix de Rome: *Myrrha* (Fernand Beissier), 1901; *Alcyone* (Eugène and Ed. Adenis), 1902; and *Alyssa* (Marguerite Coiffier), 1903.

As we saw in the preceding chapter, his preferences in literature had been from an early age for the rare and esoteric, so it is not surprising that his first published song was a setting of a poem by Stéphane Mallarmé, the poet whose influence on

116

young *avant-garde* artists at that time was very considerable and, in the case of Ravel, particularly marked.

TITLE: *Sainte*.
DEDICATION: à Madame Edmond Bonniot, *née* Mallarmé (the poet's daughter).
PUBLISHER: Durand.   DATE: 1896.   VOICE AND PIANO.

> A la fenêtre, recélant
> Le santal vieux qui se dédore
> De la viole étincelant
> Jadis avec flûte ou mandore,
>
> Est la sainte pâle, étalant
> Le livre vieux qui se déplie
> Du Magnificat ruisselant
> Jadis, selon messe ou complie.
>
> A ce vitrage d'ostensoir
> Que frôle une harpe par l'Ange
> Formée, avec son vol du soir,
> Pour la délicate phalange
>
> Du doigt que, sans le vieux santal
> Ni le vieux livre, elle balance
> Sur le plumage instrumental:
> Musicienne du silence.

The composer's indications are: *Liturgiquement, sans aucune nuance jusqu'à la fin, très calme*.   The accompaniment, with its detached chords, four crotchets to a bar, mostly sevenths and ninths, recalls Erik Satie's *Sonneries de la Rose-Croix* written a few years earlier, and the solemn, hieratic progressions admirably reflect the poet's vision of the saint in the stained-glass window.

Two years later came the settings of *Deux Epigrammes* by Clément Marot (1495–1544).

TITLE: 1. *D'Anne qui me jecta de la neige.*
        2. *D'Anne jouant de l'espinette.*
DEDICATION: 1. à M. Hardy-Thé. 2. à M. Hardy-Thé.
PUBLISHER: Demets (Eschig).   DATE: 1898.   VOICE AND PIANO

1.

Anne par jeu me jecta de la neige
Que je cuidoys froide certainement:
Mais c'estoit feu, l'expérience en ay-je
Car embrasé je fuz soubdainement
Puisque le feu loge secrètement
Dedans la neige, où trouveray-je place
Pour n'ardre point? Anne, ta seule grâce
Estaindre peut le feu que je sens bien
Non point par eau, par neige, ne par glace
Mais par sentir ung feu pareil au mien.

Ravel here adopts a deliberately archaic style, characterized by consecutive fifths and major sevenths and ninths foreshadowing in a sense the *Pavane pour une Infante défunte* written a year later. The style is thoroughly in keeping with Marot's conceit about the snowball that burnt like fire—a fire that could only be extinguished in the lover's breast if his mistress felt a similar fire in hers.

2.

Lors-que je voy en ordre la brunette
Jeune en bon point, de la ligne des Dieux
Et que sa voix, ses doits et l'espinette
Meinent ung bruyct doulx et mélodieux
J'ay du plaisir, et d'oreilles et d'yeulx
Plus que les sainctz en leur gloire immortelle
Et autant qu'eulx je devien glorieux
Dès que je pense estre ung peu aymé d'elle.

The indication for the accompaniment is " Clavecin ou Piano (en sourdine) " showing the effect the composer had in mind. The writing is crisp and close-knit, in 5/4 time and suggests the tinkling of a spinet. The poet compares himself to the " immortal saints ", so happy is he when he hears and sees his mistress playing the spinet and fancies he may be " loved a little by her ".

Ravel's next important vocal work was the song-cycle *Shéhérazade*, which reveals him in full possession of his powers. This time he turned for his text to a contemporary poet, his friend and fellow " Apache ", Tristan Klingsor. The latter's recently published volume of poems entitled *Shéhérazade* made an immediate appeal to Ravel, whose passion for everything oriental remained with him all his life. " Ravel ", wrote Klingsor, " immediately announced his intention of setting some of my poems to music. His love of difficulty led him to choose, in addition to *l'Indifférent* and *La Flûte Enchantée*, one which, by reason of its length and narrative form, seemed the least suited for his purpose: *Asie*. The fact is that he was just at that time extremely preoccupied with the problem of adapting music to speech, heightening its accents and inflexions and magnifying them by transforming them into melody; and to assist him to carry out his project he asked me to read the poems out loud to him." Speaking of this composition in later life Ravel remarks that " the influence of Debussy is fairly obvious. Here again I yielded to the profound attraction which the East has always held for me since my childhood." (B.S.) The song-cycle had its first performance, with Mme Jane Hatto as the singer and Alfred Cortot conducting, at a concert of the *Société Nationale* on May 17, 1904.

TITLE: *Shéhérazade, Trois Poèmes de Tristan Klingsor.*
  1. Asie.
  2. La Flûte Enchantée.
  3. L'Indifférent.
DEDICATION: 1. à Mademoiselle Jane Hatto (his interpreter).
           2. à Madame René de Saint-Marceaux (Parisian hostess).
           3. à Madame Sigismond Bardac (Debussy's second wife to be).
PUBLISHER: Durand.   DATE: 1903.   VOICE AND ORCHESTRA* (piano arrangement).

1. *Asie*

Asie, Asie, Asie
Vieux pays merveilleux des contes de nourrice
Où dort la fantaisie comme une impératrice

---

* Scored for: 3 fl. (1 picc.), 2 ob., 1 cor anglais, 2 cl. in A, 2 bn., 4 horns in F (chromatic), 2 trp. in C (chromatic), 3 trb., 1 tuba, kettledrums, triangle, tambourine, side drum, bass drum, cymbals, gong, glockenspiel, celesta, 2 harps, usual strings.

En sa forêt emplie de mystère, Asie
Je voudrais m'en aller avec la goëlette
Qui se berce ce soir dans le port
Mystérieuse et solitaire
Et qui déploie enfin ses voiles violettes
Comme un immense oiseau de nuit dans le ciel d'or.

Je voudrais m'en aller vers des îles de fleurs
En écoutant chanter la mer perverse
Sur un vieux rythme ensorceleur
Je voudrais voir Damas et les villes de Perse
Avec les minarets légers dans l'air.
Je voudrais voir de beaux turbans de soie
Sur des visages noirs aux dents claires;
Je voudrais voir des yeux sombres d'amour
Et des prunelles brillantes de joie
En des peaux jaunes comme des oranges;
Je voudrais voir des vêtements de velours
Et des habits à longues franges.
Je voudrais voir des calumets entre des bouches
Tout entourées de barbe blanche;
Je voudrais voir d'âpres marchands aux regards louches,
Et des cadis, et des vizirs
Qui du seul mouvement de leur doigt qui se penche
Accordent vie ou mort au gré de leur désir.
Je voudrais voir la Perse, et l'Inde, et puis la Chine,
Les mandarins ventrus sous les ombrelles,
Et les princesses aux mains fines
Et les lettrés qui se querellent
Sur la poésie et sur la beauté;
Je voudrais m'attarder au palais enchanté
Et comme un voyageur étranger
Contempler à loisir des paysages peints·
Sur des étoffes en des cadres de sapin
Avec un personnage au milieu d'un verger;
Je voudrais voir des assassins souriant
Du bourreau qui coupe un cou d'innocent
Avec son grand sabre courbé d'Orient.
Je voudrais voir des pauvres et des reines;
Je voudrais voir des roses et du sang;
Je voudrais voir mourir d'amour ou bien de haine.
Et puis m'en revenir plus tard
Narrer mon aventure aux curieux de rêves
En élevant comme Sinbad ma vieille tasse arabe

De temps en temps jusqu'à mes levres
Pour interrompre le conte avec art...

Ravel has woven round this rhapsodic invocation of the mysterious and passionate East a sumptuous web of rich orchestral sound. Each phase of the poet's imaginary journey, from his departure in the barque with its " violet sails " through the " flowery islands ", to Damascus, and Persia with its " airy minarets ", then on to India and China and savage lands where " assassins smile to see the executioner cut off an innocent head with his curved scimitar " and where the poet longs to see men " die of love, or else of hate " and then return to tell his tale " to those who have an ear for dreams "—each phase of this fantastic oriental kaleidoscope is underlined with a marvellous musical commentary that changes to fit each passing mood. There is a kind of opulence in this score, showing some Russian influence, that we shall not meet again until the ballet *Daphnis et Chloë*, where this Arabian Nights atmosphere will have been exchanged for that of pagan Greece. The various episodes in the score are organically linked under a freely moving independent vocal line.

2. *La Flute Enchantée*

L'ombre est douce et mon maître dort
Coiffé d'un bonnet conique de soie
Et son long nez jaune en sa barbe blanche.
Mais moi, je suis éveillée encore
Et j'écoute au dehors
Une chanson de flûte où s'épanche
Tour à tour la tristesse ou la joie.
Un air tour à tour langoureux ou frivole
Que mon amoureux chéri joue,
Et quand je m'approche de la croisée
Il me semble que chaque note s'envole
De la flûte vers ma joue
Comme un mystérieux baiser.

Here a flowing counterpoint is maintained between the voice and the flute over muted strings creating a languorous, almost conventionally oriental atmosphere which inevitably invites comparison with the *Scheherazade* of Rimsky-Korsakov. The young woman listens, while her " master " sleeps, to her lover playing on his flute; and when she goes to the window it is as if each note from his flute was leaving on her cheek the imprint of a " mysterious kiss ".

3. *L'Indifférent*

Tes yeux sont doux comme ceux d'une fille,
Jeune étranger,
Et la courbe fine
De ton beau visage de duvet ombragé
Est plus séduisante encor de ligne.
Ta lèvre chante sur le pas de ma porte
Une langue inconnue et charmante
Comme une musique fausse.
Entre !
Et que mon vin te réconforte. . .
Mais non, tu passes
Et de mon seuil je te vois t'éloigner
Me faisant un dernier geste avec grâce
Et la hanche légèrement ployée
Par ta démarche féminine et lasse. . .

A mysterious youth, with eyes like a girl's and speaking " an unknown and charming tongue like music out of tune " passes by, indifferent to the woman who watches him depart with his " languid and feminine walk ". With complete sureness of touch and the simplest means Ravel suggests discreetly the ambiguous charm of the mysterious passer-by.

In the same year, 1903, Ravel accepted a commission from a member of the *Comédie Française*, a certain Paul Gravolet, to set one of his poems to music. The poem, *Manteau de Fleurs*, was one of a collection entitled *Frissons* which a number of distinguished composers had been invited to set to music, each taking a different poem. Among those invited, in addition to Ravel, were Caplet, Chaminade, Debussy, d'Indy, Vidal and Widor, but the only settings that have survived are those of Debussy---*Dans le Jardin*— and Ravel's *Manteau de Fleurs*.

PUBLISHER: Hamelle. DATE: 1903. VOICE AND PIANO.

Toutes les fleurs de mon jardin sont roses,
Le rose sied à sa beauté.
Les primevères sont les premières écloses,
Puis viennent les tulipes et les jacinthes roses,
Les jolis œillets, les si belles roses,
Toute la variété des fleurs si roses
Du printemps et de l'été!
Le rose sied à sa beauté!
Toutes mes pivoines sont roses,
Roses aussi, mes glaieuls,
Roses mes géraniums; seuls,
Dans tout ce rose un peu troublant,
Les lys ont le droit d'être blancs.
Et quand elle passe au milieu des fleurs
Emperlées de rosée en pleurs,
Dans le parfum grisant des roses,
Et sous la caresse des choses
Toute grâce, amour, pureté!
Les fleurs lui font un manteau rose
Dont elle pare sa beauté.

The poet's garden, where all the flowers are roses or rose-tinted and only the lilies are white, enhances the beauty of the lady who walks among them. Ravel's setting of this rather precious little poem is rather over-elaborate, but otherwise calls for no special mention.

In the next song he wrote, after a lapse of two years, Ravel was his own librettist. He believed that music, painting and literature were merely different aspects of art, and that the difference between composers, painters and writers was simply a question of specialization. He used to say that when he looked at a picture it was as a painter, and not as an amateur, and that Manet's *Olympia* had given him as a young man one of his greatest emotional experiences. " If I am not a writer ", he once said, " it is simply through lack of training. But I read with a professional eye."

The *Noël des Jouets* shows him as a considerable craftsman, but the little poem as a whole is rather cold and stilted.

TITLE: *Noël des Jouets.*
DEDICATION: à Madame Jean Cruppi.
PUBLISHER: Mathot.   DATE: 1905.   VOICE AND PIANO (also orchestrated).

> Le troupeau verni des moutons
> Roule en tumulte vers la crèche
> Les lapins tambours, brefs et rêches,
> Couvrent leurs aigres mirlitons.
>
> Vierge Marie, en crinoline,
> Ses yeux d'émail sans cesse ouverts,
> En attendant Bonhomme hiver,
> Veille Jésus qui se dodine,
>
> Car, près de là, sous un sapin,
> Furtif, emmitouflé dans l'ombre
> Du bois, Belzébuth, le chien sombre,
> Guette l'enfant de sucre peint.
>
> Mais les beaux anges incassables
> Suspendus par des fils d'archal
> Du haut de l'arbuste hiémal
> Assurent la paix des étables
>
> Et leur vol de clinquant vermeil
> Qui cliquette en bruits symétriques
> S'accorde au bétail mécanique
> Dont la voix grêle bêle: Noël!

In this little cameo of a *crèche* such as can be seen in the shop windows at Christmas-time, with its toy animals and " unbreakable angels " hanging from tinsel wires over the cradle in which lies an infant Jesus made of coloured sugar and watched over by a Virgin in a crinoline and a fierce dog called Beelzebub, Ravel does not attempt to do more than to envelop his little poem in a simple musical setting in which the voice quietly recites until, in the last quatrain, a *fortissimo* climax is reached in a kind of fanfare on the word *Noël*. Incidentally, it seems strange that the poet-musician's ear could have tolerated the last line of the poem: " *Dont la voix grêle bêle: Noël!* "

We come now to one of the key works in Ravel's production —his settings of five *Histoires Naturelles* by the contemporary French novelist and man of letters, Jules Renard. The composer has related (in a passage quoted in Chapter III) how he was "attracted by the clear, direct language and deep, hidden poetry of these sketches by Jules Renard". The fact that they were in prose did not deter him; on the contrary he welcomed the opportunity of devising a new form of declamation which would follow closely the inflexions of the French language. Renard had written a kind of miniature "bestiaire", consisting of thumbnail sketches of birds and animals, and full of humour and ironic observation expressed in a dry, matter-of-fact style that scarcely seems to invite musical treatment. But Ravel accepted the challenge and out of this superficially unpromising material produced a little masterpiece. Renard, like many men of letters, was totally unmusical and showed no enthusiasm when he heard of Ravel's project. In a passage in his *Journal*, which must be taken with more than a grain of salt because of certain obvious inaccuracies, he records that on November 19, 1906, he received a visit from Thadée Natanson (see Chapter II), who had come to tell him that there was a composer who wanted to set some of his *Histoires Naturelles* to music. "He is an *avant-garde* musician", said Natanson, "who is highly thought of and who looks upon Debussy already as an old bore.* What do you think of that?"

"Nothing at all."

"But surely you must be pleased!"

"Not at all."

"What message must I give him?"

"Anything you like. Just say thank you."

"Wouldn't you like him to let you hear his music?"

"No, no, no. Certainly not."

Another entry in Renard's *Journal* reads as follows:

January 12, 1907. M. Ravel, the composer of the *Histoires Naturelles*, dark, rich and elegant, urges me to go and hear his songs tonight. I told him I knew nothing about music, and asked

---

* This, of course, was quite untrue; Ravel never ceased to admire Debussy.

him what he had been able to add to the *Histoires Naturelles*. He replied:

" I did not intend to add anything, only to interpret them."

" But in what way? "

" I have tried to say in music what you have said in words. . . There are two kinds of music: instinctive, sentimental music, like mine (naturally you must learn your craft first), and intellectual music, like d'Indy's. The audience this evening will consist mainly of d'Indys; they don't recognize feeling and don't wish to explain it. I take the opposite view, but they find my work interesting. This test tonight is very important for me; in any case I can rely on my interpreter; she is quite excellent."

It is impossible to believe that Jules Renard was reporting correctly what Ravel actually said, the views expressed being completely out of character. His description of Ravel as " rich " was, of course, quite unfounded and shows he must have formed an entirely false impression of him. But the passage is worth quoting, if only to show that diaries are not always to be relied upon for impartial and objective description of people or events.

The *Histoires Naturelles* had their first performance at a *Société Nationale* concert at the Salle Erard on January 12, 1907, sung by Mme Jane Bathori, with the composer at the piano. They had a hostile reception from the audience, who found it shocking that a serious composer should attempt to set such trivialities to music, and above all to music that was in itself an outrage. The general feeling was reflected in an article published some weeks later by Pierre Lalo in *Le Temps*, March 19, 1907:

The idea of setting to music the *Histoires Naturelles* is in itself surprising. Nothing could be more foreign to music than these little fragments of arid and precious prose, these little images of animals laboriously constructed that seem as if they had been carved out of boxwood. . . M. Ravel has discovered something lyrical in M. Renard's *Guinea-fowl* and *Peacock*; in my opinion this subtle musician has never been so completely mistaken. . . His music is well fitted to the text—it is just as precious, just as laborious, just as dry and almost as unmusical; a collection of the most out-of-the-way harmonies, industriously contrived, and the most elaborate and complicated sequences of chords . . . all this reminds one rather of the *café-concert*—but a *café-concert* with chords of the ninth! I would almost rather have the *café-concert* without any frills... These songs are totally lacking in good humour, simplicity and spontaneity; they are full of a frigid solemnity and stilted pedantry which never relaxes for an instant. When our good Chabrier made a song about *Turkeys* and *Little Pink Pigs*, he did it with gaiety and let himself go; he treated it as a joke. M. Ravel is solemn all the time with his farmyard animals; he doesn't smile, but reads us a sermon on the Peacock and the Guinea-fowl...

There is plenty of humour in this music for those who have ears to hear, together with acute observation and brilliant characterization of the different creatures as depicted by the author with a wonderful economy of words and the precision and eye for detail of a Chinese artist or Japanese " Hai-Kai " poet. Musically, these songs mark a new development in Ravel's art and break new ground from the point of view of both harmony and vocal declamation in which he was experimenting at the moment to prepare himself, as he stated in his biographical sketch, for the composition of *L'Heure Espagnole*, " itself a kind of conversation in music ".

TITLE: *Histoires Naturelles* (Jules Renard).
    1. Le Paon (The Peacock).
    2. Le Grillon (The Cricket).
    3. Le Cygne (The Swan).
    4. Le Martin-Pêcheur (The Kingfisher).
    5. La Pintade (The Guinea-fowl).
DEDICATION: 1. à Madame Jane Bathori.
             2. à Mademoiselle Madeleine Picard.
             3. à Madame Alfred Edwards, née Godebska.
             4. à Emile Engel.
             5. à Roger Ducasse.
PUBLISHER: Durand. DATE: 1909. VOICE AND PIANO (orchestrated by Manuel Rosenthal).

1. LE PAON

Il va sûrement se marier aujourd'hui. Ce devait être pour hier. En habit de gala il était prêt. Il n'attendait que sa fiancée. Elle n'est pas venue. Elle ne peut tarder. Glorieux, il se promène avec une allure de prince indien et porte sur lui les riches présents d'usage. L'amour avive l'éclat de ses couleurs et son aigrette tremble comme une lyre. La fiancée n'arrive

pas. Il monte au haut du toit et regarde du côté du soleil. Il
jette son cri diabolique : Léon ! Léon ! C'est ainsi qu'il appelle
sa fiancée. Il ne voit rien venir et personne ne répond. Les
volailles habituées ne lèvent même point la tête. Elles sont
lasses de l'admirer. Il redescend dans la cour, si sûr d'être beau
qu'il est incapable de rancune. Son mariage sera pour demain.
Et, ne sachant que faire du reste de la journée, il se dirige vers
le perron. Il gravit les marches, comme des marches de temple,
d'un pas officiel. Il relève sa robe à queue toute lourde des
yeux qui n'ont pu se détacher d'elle. Il répète encore une fois
la cérémonie.

It is the Peacock's wedding day, but his bride never came.
All glorious in his splendid robe, he struts like an Indian
Prince, and from the roof-top utters his diabolical cry : Léon !
Léon ! The other fowls, tired of admiring him, do not even
raise their heads to look at him. His marriage will take place
tomorrow. Not knowing how to spend the rest of the day, he
mounts the steps solemnly and spreads out his tail, resplendent
with the eyes which are imprisoned there, and then goes
through the same ceremony again.

Striding octaves in the bass with bare fourths and fifths
introduce the peacock, the basic rhythm being maintained
throughout the piece. The general indication is : " Sans
hâte et noblement ", and at appropriate places in the score we
read " solennel ", " très expressif " (rarely used by Ravel) and
" avec majesté ". The peacock's piercing cry is strikingly
rendered, thus :

Ex.6

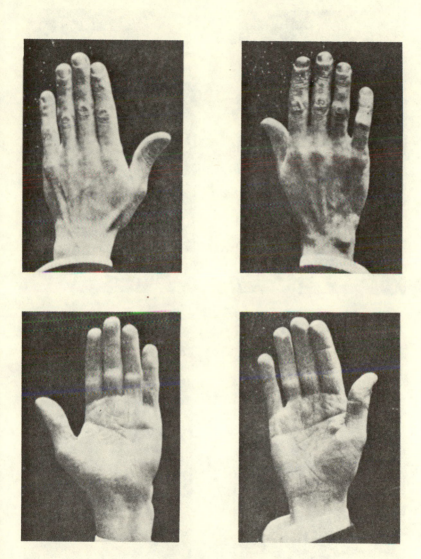

RAVEL'S HANDS

Discussion with Lennox Berkeley   *Degree Day at Oxford*

RAVEL IN ENGLAND IN 1928

[Reproduced by kind permission of Mr. Lennox Berkeley]

and the spreading of his tail by a *glissando* on the black keys in contrary motion—two deliberately descriptive touches in an otherwise purely lyrical presentation of the proud but frustrated peacock. A point to be noted in this, as in all the other *Histoires Naturelles*, is Ravel's disregard of traditional French prosody in his treatment of mute terminal vowels, which he elides mercilessly for the sake of greater concision, as well as sometimes reducing the syllabic value of the word itself, e.g.:

La fian-cée n'ar-rive pas.

This in itself was enough to shock the purists and the generally rather straitlaced and conservative *Société Nationale* audience, quite apart from the unconventional subject, audacious harmonies and novel form of declamation.

2. LE GRILLON

C'est l'heure où, las d'errer, l' insecte nègre revient de promenade et répare avec soin le désordre de son domaine. D'abord il ratisse ses étroites allées de sable. Il fait du bran de scie qu'il écarte au seuil de sa retraite. Il lime la racine de cette grande herbe propre à le harceler. Il se repose. Puis il remonte sa minuscule montre. A-t-il fini? est-elle cassée? Il se repose encore un peu. Il rentre chez lui et ferme sa porte. Longtemps il tourne sa clef dans la serrure délicate. Et il écoute: Point d'alarme dehors. Mais il ne se trouve pas en sûreté. Et comme par une chaînette dont la poulie grince, il descend jusqu'au fond de la terre. On n'entend plus rien. Dans la campagne muette, les peupliers se dressent comme des doigts en l'air et désignent la lune.

One of the best of the set is this delightful vignette of the cricket setting its little house in order; raking the sand outside its door, filing down the root of a tall blade of grass, winding up its tiny watch, turning the key in the lock and then lowering itself, as if by a creaking winch, into safety deep down in the ground. Then silence. " And in the quiet countryside the poplar trees stand erect, like fingers pointing towards the moon."

The mood and tempo are indicated by the one word " *Placide* ", and the dynamic range lies between *p* and *pppp* throughout. The cricket's chirp and the sound that suggests the winding of the tiny watch are rendered by an *appoggiatura* of a G and A natural against an octave A flat in the highest register of the piano, played *ppp*. Every shade and accent in this miniature portrait of an insect is etched in by the composer with incomparable skill and imagination.

3. LE CYGNE

Il glisse sur le bassin, comme un traineau blanc, de nuage en nuage car il n'a faim que des nuages floconneux qu'il voit naître, bouger, et se perdre dans l'eau. C'est l'un d'eux qu'il désire. Il le vise du bec, et il plonge tout à coup son col vêtu de neige. Puis, tel un bras de femme sort d'une manche, il le retire. Il n'a rien. Il regarde: les nuages effarouchés ont disparu. Il ne reste qu'un instant désabusé, car les nuages tardent peu à revenir, et, là-bas, ou meurent les ondulations de l'eau, en voici un qui se reforme. Doucement, sur son léger coussin de plumes, le cygne rame et s'approche... Il s'épuise à pêcher de vains reflets, et peut-être qu'il mourra, victime de cette illusion, avant d'attraper un seul morceau de nuage. Mais qu'est-ce que je dis? Chaque fois qu'il plonge, il fouille du bec la vase nourrissante et ramène un ver. Il engraisse comme une oie.

The swan is pictured as gliding over the water " like a white sledge " pursuing the reflections of the clouds and from time to time plunging his long neck under the water hoping to catch one in his beak. But he never succeeds, " and maybe he will die, the victim of his illusion, without ever having caught a single bit of cloud. But not at all: every time he plunges he brings up a worm from the rich slime at the bottom of the pond. He's getting as fat as a goose."

An undulating arpeggio figure, marked " *très doux et enveloppé de pédales* ", is the basis of the accompaniment over which the voice quietly recites. Once again, every nuance in the text is reflected faithfully in the music, down to the realistic twist at the end " debunking ", as it were, the romantic associations of the conventional " Swan " motif in music and ballet.

4. Le Martin-Pêcheur

Ça n'a pas mordu, ce soir, mais je rapporte une rare émotion. Comme je tenais ma perche de ligne tendue, un martin-pêcheur est venu s'y poser. Nous n'avons pas d'oiseau plus éclatant. Il semblait une grosse fleur bleue au bout d'une longue tige. La perche pliait sous le poids. Je ne respirais plus, tout fier d'être pris pour un arbre par un martin-pêcheur. Et je suis sûr qu'il ne s'est pas envolé de peur, mais qu'il a cru qu'il ne faisait que passer d'une branche à une autre.

Perhaps the gem of the collection. A kingfisher alights on the angler's rod, looking like a big, blue flower at the end of a long stalk. " Of all our birds he is the most brilliant. I held my breath, proud to have been mistaken for a tree by a kingfisher. And I am sure he did not fly away from fright but simply imagined he was passing from one branch to another."

Twenty-three bars of breathless suspense suggesting immobility and the " rare emotion " experienced by the angler, and containing some " rare " Ravelian harmonies. The score is marked " *On ne peut plus lent* " which gives the singer ample time in which to create the atmosphere.

5. La Pintade

C'est la bossue de la cour. Elle ne rêve que plaies à cause de sa bosse. Les poules ne lui disent rien: Brusquement elle se précipite et les harcèle. Puis elle baisse sa tête, penche le corps, et, de toute la vitesse de ses pattes maigres, elle court frapper de son bec dur, juste au centre de la roue d'une dinde. Cette poseuse l'agaçait. Ainsi, la tête bleue, ses barbillons à vif, cocardière, elle rage du matin au soir. Elle se bat sans motif, peut-être parce qu'elle s'imagine toujours qu'on se moque de sa taille, de son crâne chauve et de sa queue basse. Et elle ne cesse de jeter un cri discordant qui perce l'air comme une pointe. Parfois elle quitte la cour et disparaît. Elle laisse aux volailles pacifiques un moment de répit. Mais elle revient plus turbulente et plus criarde. Et, frénétique, elle se vautre par terre. Qu'a-t-elle donc? La sournoise fait une farce. Elle est allée

pondre son œuf à la campagne.   Je peux le chercher si ça
m'amuse.   Et elle se roule dans la poussière comme une bossue.

A vivid portrait of the turbulent, irascible Guinea-fowl, the
" humpback " of the farmyard, harassing the hens and peck-
ing the turkey, angry from morning to night and perpetually
uttering her piercing, discordant cry.   She is always fighting,
perhaps because she thinks the others are making fun of her
on account of her bald head and trailing tail.   Sometimes she
disappears, going off to lay her eggs out in the fields.   Then
she comes back to roll in the dust in a frenzy.

Another vivid farmyard impression in which the guinea-
fowl's " discordant " cry is faithfully reproduced.   It provides
a fitting end to this little " bestiaire ", Ravel's only excursion
into the realm of natural history.

Ravel wrote one other song in the same year as the *Histoires
Naturelles*—a rather tormented and overcharged setting of a
poem by Henri de Régnier, *Les Grands Vents venus d'Outre-mer*.

DEDICATION: à Jacques Durand.
PUBLISHER: Durand.   DATE: 1906.   VOICE AND PIANO.

> Les grands vents venus d'outre-mer
> Passent par la ville, l'hiver,
> Comme des étrangers amers.
>
> Ils se concertent, graves et pâles,
> Sur les places, et leurs sandales
> Ensablent le marbre des dalles.
>
> Comme de crosses à leurs mains fortes,
> Ils heurtent l'auvent et la porte
> Derrière qui l'horloge est morte
>
> Et les adolescents amers
> S'en vont avec eux vers la mer.

A piece of Symbolist poetry in which words play a more important part than ideas.   The great winds from beyond the
seas sweep through the town in winter like a horde of grim
foreign invaders, scattering the sand all over the public

squares and battering at the doors of deserted houses where all the clocks have stopped. And on their return the disillusioned adolescents go back with them towards the sea. The music seems rather laboured and excessively chromatic, which is unusual with Ravel, and does not call for special comment.

This song was followed a year later by Ravel's only setting of a poem by Verlaine, a poet with whom, unlike Debussy, he does not seem to have had any special affinity.

TITLE: *Sur L'Herbe*.
PUBLISHER: Durand. DATE: 1907. VOICE AND PIANO.

> L'abbé divague
> Et toi, Marquis,
> Tu mets de travers ta perruque.
> Ce vieux vin de Chypre est exquis
> Moins, Camergo, que votre nuque.
> Ma flamme... Do, mi, sol, la, si.
> L' abbé, ta noirceur se dévoile
> Que je meure, mesdames, si
> Je ne vous décroche une étoile.
> Je voudrais être petit chien!
> Embrassons nos bergères, l'une
> Après l'autre—Messieurs, eh bien?
> Do, mi, sol. Hé! bonsoir la Lune!

Ravel has succeeded admirably in capturing the very eighteenth-century atmosphere of this amusing trifle in which the Abbé, having shown his appreciation of the wine of Cyprus, indulges in a few rather incoherent *galanteries*. The accompaniment, based on a graceful flowing figure in ternary time, suggests a minuet.

To the same year belongs the *Vocalise en forme d'Habanera*, which seems to have been commissioned for the purpose of initiating students at the Conservatoire into contemporary music. In it Ravel displays his skill in writing for the voice and his knowledge of its potentialities. Over his favourite Habanera rhythm in the piano the vocalist is called on to execute all kinds of trills and rapid scales, with *staccato* and *portamento* effects and other devices providing plenty of material for technical display. (Published by Leduc; date of composition 1907.)

The harmonizations of five Greek folk-songs also date from this period. Folk-song was not one of Ravel's major preoccupations; indeed, he was far from being folk-minded, but it was at the suggestion of his friend and fellow " Apache " Calvocoressi, who had collected the tunes in the island of Chios, that he consented to provide them with accompaniments, performing this task in the incredibly short time of thirty-six hours!

TITLE: *Cinq melodies populaires grecques*:
  1. Le réveil de la mariée.
  2. Là-bas vers l'église.
  3. Quel galant!
  4. Chanson des cueilleuses de lentisques.
  5. Tout gai!
PUBLISHER: Durand. DATE: 1907. VOICE AND PIANO. (Orchestrated).*

  1. The bridegroom greets the bride and offers her a ribbon for her hair.
  2. People have come from far and near to worship the Virgin at the shrine of Agio-Sidero.
  3. What other of your suitors can compare with me? Tell me that, my love, O proud Vassiliki.
  4. The girls are singing as they gather the lentisks but are troubled when the handsome young man appears.
  5. Be gay, Tra-la-la, and come and join the dance.

These little folk-songs are set by Ravel very simply but with an unerring feeling for style and atmosphere.

A sixth song, *Tripatos*, harmonized in 1909, was published in *La Revue Musicale*, December 1938.

It happened that three years later, after having written no more songs in the meantime, Ravel was again called upon to arrange some folk-songs, this time for a competition organized by the *Maison du Lied* in Moscow. Of the seven songs he submitted, four were awarded a prize and published by Jurgenson; these were arrangements of Spanish, French, Italian and

---

* Nos. 1 and 5 by the composer; Nos. 2, 3, 4 by Manuel Rosenthal.

Hebrew melodies, the last of which was orchestrated. The remaining three—the Scottish, Flemish and Russian songs—were never published.

Then, after another lapse of three years, he produced, in circumstances which have already been related in Chapter IV, while staying with Stravinsky in Switzerland, one of his major works—the *Trois Poèmes de Stéphane Mallarmé* for voice and instrumental ensemble. The change in style, and even vocabulary, so noticeable in this work has generally been attributed to the influence of Schoenberg's *Pierrot Lunaire*, which Stravinsky had heard in Berlin in 1912 and had then brought to the notice of Ravel. Both composers were immensely impressed by the work, even if they did not at the time fully grasp all its implications and realize that in it Schoenberg was preparing the way for the complete disintegration of the traditional tonal system on which Western music had been based for several centuries. For an exhaustive analysis of the precise manner in which Stravinsky and Ravel reacted to the impact of Schoenberg I would refer the reader to an interesting article by Pierre Boulez under the title " Trajectoires: Ravel, Stravinsky, Schoenberg ", with special reference to Stravinsky's *Japanese Lyrics* and Ravel's *Trois Poèmes*.*

Briefly, the argument is that Ravel merely assimilated some of Schoenberg's external procedures and devices, especially as regards instrumentation, incorporating them in his own already formed compositional technique, but failing to see that Schoenberg's discoveries were intended to bring about the dissolution of that very elaborate and essentially coherent tonal system to which Ravel was still committed. Boulez, in fact, maintains that Ravel was still only interested in the purely " auditive " effects that this new style of writing, with its novel harmonic and above all instrumental texture, could be made to yield, and was content to borrow from it some of its external features to suit his own ends—which were, in fact, very different from those of Schoenberg. Be that as it may,

---

* *Contrepoints*, Autumn, 1949. Paris, ed. Richard-Masse. Unfortunately this excellent musical review no longer exists.

there is no doubt that *Pierrot Lunaire* was a fertilizing influence that made itself felt, at any rate superficially, in Ravel's settings of Mallarmé's poems. In this context it may be recalled that Ravel's advice to young composers who came to him for guidance was: "If you have nothing to say, you cannot do better, until you decide to give up composing for good, than say again what has already been well said. If you have something to say, that something will never emerge more distinctly than when you are being unwittingly unfaithful to your model." In confirmation of this dictum no better example could be found than Ravel himself.

It was inevitable that, with his love of complexity and instinctive sympathy with the more private and esoteric forms of art, Ravel should have been attracted to Mallarmé, that weaver of magic webs of suggestive sound and elusive symbols where poetry dwells in splendid isolation, yielding her secrets only to those blessed with powers of divination. Nor is it surprising that the same poet should have inspired Debussy, although it is a curious coincidence that both composers should have set, in the same year, three poems by Mallarmé and that each should have chosen the same two poems, differing only in their choice of the third one. Thus after *Soupir* and *Placet futile* Ravel adds *Surgi de la croupe et du bond*, whereas Debussy chooses the less abstruse *Eventail*.

TITLE: *Trois Poèmes de Stéphane Mallarmé.*
    1. Soupir.
    2. Placet Futile.
    3. Surgi de la croupe et du bond.
DEDICATION: 1. à Igor Stravinsky.
           2. à Florent Schmitt.
           3. à Erik Satie.
PUBLISHER: Durand. DATE: 1913. VOICE, 2 FLUTES, 2 CLARINETS (2ND DOUBLING BASS-CLARINET), STRING QUARTET AND PIANO.

1. SOUPIR

Mon âme sur ton front où rêve, O calme sœur,
Un automne jonché de taches de rousseur
Et vers le ciel errant de ton œil angélique

Monte, comme dans un jardin mélancolique,
Fidèle, un blanc jet d'eau soupire vers l'Azur!
Vers l'Azur attendri d'Octobre pâle et pur
Qui mire aux grands bassins sa langueur infinie
Et laisse, sur l'eau morte ou la fauve agonie
Des feuilles erre au vent et creuse un froid sillon,
Se traîner le soleil jaune d'un long rayon.

The poet evokes a vision of a deserted garden in autumn
where a fountain plays under the pale blue October sky and
the dead leaves are blown about, furrowing the surface of the
stagnant water in the marble basins on which a long ray of
yellow sunlight falls.

   The vocal line is more in the nature of a sustained melody
and less declamatory than in previous songs, but the whole
piece depends for its effect on the instrumental accompaniment
which supplies colour, variety and harmonic interest, some of
the harmonic progressions being extremely strange and un-
usually dissonant even for Ravel.

Ex. 8

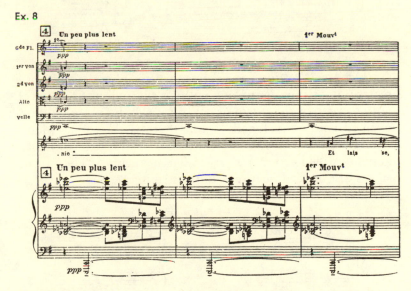

Scintillating arpeggios in harmonics on the muted strings are
a feature of the first part of the accompaniment down to the

words " vers l'Azur "; the movement then dies down and
becomes more static, the voice moving over spaced chords
until the end when the cadence is softly underlined with a
flicker of arpeggios forming an extended *appoggiatura*.

Ex. 9

In Debussy's setting for voice and piano there is perhaps a
greater unity from first to last, with no sharp division between
the two parts of the poem as with Ravel—the mood is more
sustained and " enveloped "—but there is the same evident
desire to match the subtle refinements of the text with harmonies distilled from not dissimilar elements.   The resemblances are, indeed, at times quite striking, e.g.:

Ravel

Debussy

2. Placet Futile

Princesse! à jalouser le destin d'une Hébé
Qui poind sur cette tasse au baiser de vos lèvres
J'use mes feux mais n'ai rang discret que d'abbé
Et ne figurerai même nu sur la Sèvres
Comme je ne suis pas ton bichon embarbé,
—Ni la pastille, ni du rouge, ni jeux mièvres
Et que sur moi je sais ton regard clos tombé,
Blonde dont les coiffeurs divins sont des orfèvres!
Nommez-nous . . . toi de qui tant de ris framboisés
Se joignent en troupeau d'agneaux apprivoisés,
Chez tous broutant les voeux et bêlant aux délires,
Nommez-nous . . . pour qu'Amour ailé d'un éventail
M'y peigne flute aux doigts endormant ce bercail
Princesse, nommez-nous berger de vos sourires.

A gallant Abbé begs the lady to appoint him " shepherd of her smiles ". The following example gives a good idea of the diaphanous texture of the instrumentation, which has a definitely Schoenbergian flavour recalling *Pierrot Lunaire*, even to the *portamento* prescribed for the voice, which throughout is treated instrumentally as a member of the ensemble. There is, however, no suggestion of *sprechstimme*.

Ex. 12

It is interesting to compare the two settings of Ravel and Debussy, which, as regards the vocal line, even show certain resemblances. Both, for example, employ the interval of a sixth for the word " Princesse ", falling in Debussy's setting, rising in Ravel's, while both end with a falling fourth (one of Ravel's favourite intervals) on the word " sourires ". Thus:

Ex. 13

Prin-ces - se   nom-mez   nous ber-ger de vos sou-ri———res

Debussy

Ex. 14

Prin-ces——se,   nom-mez   nous ber-ger— de vos sou-ri—res.

Ravel

While Debussy's setting of *Placet Futile* is perhaps the simpler of the two and employs fewer trappings, it is no less successful than Ravel's in capturing the spirit of the poem and especially that "préciosité pleine de profondeur si spéciale à Mallarmé" to which Ravel specifically refers.

3. SURGI DE LA CROUPE ET DU BOND

Surgi de la croupe et du bond
D'une verrerie éphémère
Sans fleurir la veillée amère
Le col ignoré s'interrompt.
Je crois bien que deux bouches n'ont
Bu, ni son amant ni ma mère
Jamais à la même chimère
Moi, sylphe de ce froid plafond!
Le pur vase d'aucun breuvage
Que l'inexhaustible veuvage
Agonise mais ne consent,
—Naïf baiser des plus funèbres!
A rien expirer annonçant
Une rose dans les ténèbres.

This famous example of Mallarméan obscurity defies translation, but is devoid of any very profound significance, being merely an evocation of a vase empty of flowers.

Its verbal virtuosity is well matched by Ravel's instrumental wizardry and fantastic scoring, of which the following two bars are a typical example:

Ex. 15

Elsewhere the voice has passages of declamation over sustained chords, in harmonics, on the strings and in the lowest register of the piano, punctuated with occasional bare octaves struck with the right hand and left vibrating like accents suspended over the harmonic texture—an anticipation, in fact, of the modern " *pointilliste* " technique. The Mallarmé poems are unique in Ravel's *œuvre* and open up vistas of what he might have done had he ever been able to renounce tonality entirely. For this reason they are extraordinarily interesting to study, and must be considered as one of his most original and remarkable achievements. Unfortunately, being excessively difficult to perform, they are seldom heard.

Ravel's last excursion into the realm of folk-lore took the form of two settings of traditional Hebrew melodies, *Kaddisch* and *L'Enigme Eternelle* which he composed in 1914. The first is a kind of psalmody on a Hebrew text, very impressively treated in a piano accompaniment, sparse in texture but underlining in poignant fashion the fervent and stylized melisma of the original liturgical chant. The second is a simple " tra, la, la " melody which Ravel accompanies with a monotonous *ostinato* figure throughout. There is also an orchestral version.

Ravel composed only one work for chorus *a cappella*—the *Trois Chansons*, for which he wrote the words himself, as he had done once before in the *Noël des Jouets*.

TITLE: *Trois Chansons.*
    1. Nicolette.
    2. Trois beaux oiseaux du Paradis.
    3. Ronde.
DEDICATION: 1. à Tristan Klingsor.
              2. à Paul Painlevé.
              3. à Madame Paul Clemenceau.
PUBLISHER: Durand. DATE: 1916. UNACCOMPANIED MIXED VOICES IN FOUR PARTS.

1. NICOLETTE

Nicolette, à la vesprée,
S'allait promener au pré,
Cueillir la pâquerette, la jonquille et le muguet.
Toute sautillante, toute guillerette.
Lorgnant çi, là, de tous les côtés.
Rencontra vieux loup grognant
Tout hérissé, l'œil brillant:
" Hé là! ma Nicolette, viens-tu pas chez Mère Grand? "
A perte d'haleine s'enfuit Nicolette
Laissant là cornette et socques blancs.
Rencontra page joli,
Chausses bleues et pourpoint gris:
" Hé là! ma Nicolette, veux-tu pas d'un doux ami? "

Sage, s'en retourna
A cœur marri.
Rencontra seigneur chenu,
Tors, laid, puant et ventru:
" Hé là! ma Nicolette, veux-tu pas tous ces écus? "
Vite fut en ses bras bonne Nicolette
Jamais au pré n'est plus revenue.

Nicolette picking flowers meets a wolf who tries to persuade her to visit " Grandmother ", but she runs away in fear. Then she meets a handsome young man, but turns him down, reluctantly. But when a rich and ugly old man offers her his gold she jumps straight into his arms and never comes back.

Adopting a deliberately archaic style to fit his mock-folk words, Ravel produces some amusing effects—for example, the " Ta ka ta ka ta ka " that accompanies Nicolette's flight from the wolf, and the part-writing is lively and piquant with its contrasts of *legato* and *staccato* in the different voices.

2. TROIS BEAUX OISEAUX DU PARADIS

Trois beaux oiseaux du Paradis
(Mon ami z-il est à la guerre)
Trois beaux oiseaux du Paradis
Ont passé par ici.
Le premier était plus bleu que ciel
(Mon ami z-il est à la guerre)
Le second était couleur de neige,
Le troisième rouge vermeil.
" Beaux oiselets du Paradis
(Mon ami z-il est à la guerre)
Beaux oiselets du Paradis qu'apportez par ici? "
" J'apporte un regard couleur d'azur.
(Ton ami z-il est à la guerre)
" Et moi, sur beau front couleur de neige,
Un baiser dois mettre, encor plus pur."
" Oiseau vermeil du Paradis,
(Mon ami z-il est à la guerre)
Oiseau vermeil du Paradis, que portez-vous ainsi? "
" Un joli cœur tout cramoisi
(Ton ami z-il est à la guerre)
" Ah! je sens mon cœur qui froidit. . .
Emportez-le aussi."

While her lover is at the wars the lady is visited by three lovely birds of Paradise, one blue as the sky, the second white as snow and the third vermilion red. Each brings a different gift, but to the third who offers her a crimson heart she yields up her own. Each voice in turn sings the melody while the others weave a simple counterpoint in a wordless accompaniment sung to " Ah ". The writing is limpid and melodious.

3. RONDE

N'allez pas au bois d'Ormonde
Jeunes filles, n'allez pas au bois:
Il y a plein de satyres, de centaures, de malins sorciers
Des farfadets et des incubes,
Des ogres, des lutins
Des faunes, des follets, des lamies
Diables, diablots, diablotins,
Des chèvre-pieds, des gnomes, des démons,
Des loups-garous, des elfes des myrmidons,
Des enchanteurs et des mages, des stryges, des
    moines bourrus, des cyclopes, des djinns, gobelins,
    korrigans, nécromans, kobolds. . .
N'allez pas au bois d'Ormonde
Jeunes garçons, n'allez pas au bois:
Il y a plein de faunesses, de bacchantes et de males fées,
Des satyres, des ogresses
Et des baba-iagas
Des centauresses et des diablesses,
Goules sortant du sabbat,
Des farfadettes et des démones
Des larves, des nymphes, des myrmidones,
Hamadryades, dryades, naïades, ménades, thyades, follettes
    gnomides, succubes, gorgones, gobelines
Ah! n'allez pas au bois d'Ormonde.
N'irons plus au bois d'Ormonde,
Hélas! plus jamais n'irons au bois.
Il n'y a plus de satyres, plus de nymphes, ni de males fées
Plus de farfadets, plus d'incubes,
Plus d'ogres, de lutins
De faunes, de follets, de lamies,
Diables, diablots, diablotins
De chèvre-pieds, de gnomes, de démons,
De loups-garous, ni d'elfes, de myrmidons,

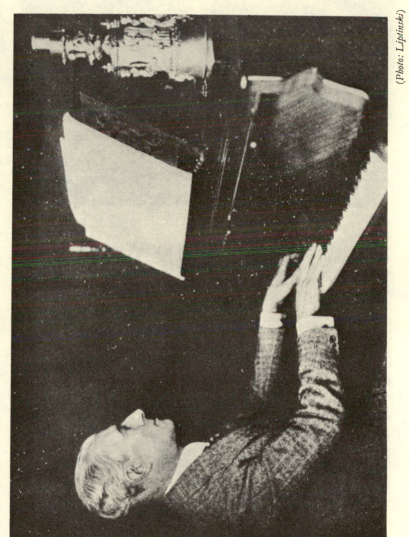

RAVEL AT THE PIANO

(Photo: Lipinski)

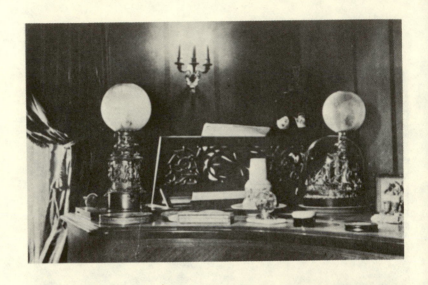

RAVEL'S PIANO AND DESK AT LE BELVEDERE

Plus d'enchanteurs ni de mages, de stryges, de sylphes, de
  moines bourrus, de cyclopes, de djinns, de diabloteaux,
  d'efrits, d'aegypans, de sylvains, gobelins, korrigans,
  nécromans, kobolds. . .
Ah!
N'allez pas au bois d'Ormonde
Les malavisées vieilles,
Les malavisés vieux les ont effarouchés—Ah!

Ravel here gives full rein to his fantasy, and the whole piece,
with its exhaustive catalogue of every sort of hobgoblin,
leprechaun, gnome, satyr, kobold, demon, ogre and devil,
male and female, with which the old women threaten the girls
and young men who would dare to enter the forest of Ormonde
is a *tour de force* of alliteration and brilliant vocal writing which
produces an irresistible effect.

In 1924, in celebration of the four-hundreth anniversary of
the birth of Pierre de Ronsard, Henry Prunières, who was then
editing *La Revue Musicale*, invited a number of composers to
contribute to a special number of the *Revue* settings of some
of Ronsard's poems. Ravel's contribution was *Ronsard à son
âme*.

PUBLISHER: Durand. DATE: 1924. VOICE AND PIANO (has been
orchestrated).

Amelette Ronsardelette,
Mignonnelette, doucelette,
Très chère hôtesse de mon corps,
Tu descends là-bas foiblelette,
Pâle, maigrelette, seulette,
Dans le froid royaume des morts,
Toutesfois simple, sans remords
De meurtre, poison, et rancune,
Méprisant faveurs et trésors
Tant enviés par la commune.
Passant, j'ai dit; sui ta fortune,
Ne trouble mon repos: je dor!

The poet takes leave in affectionate terms of his soul, " dear
hostess of my body ", which is about to descend to the kingdom of the dead. Innocent of all crime or bitterness, and
scorning favours and riches coveted by ordinary mortals, he

only wants to be left in peace: " Passer-by, go thy way, do not disturb my rest: I sleep! "

The accompaniment is of an austere simplicity, consisting entirely of bare open fifths to sustain the voice, suggesting the old medieval *organum*; the effect is very beautiful.

It was in the following year that Ravel was commissioned by the American musical Maecenas, Mrs. Elizabeth Sprague Coolidge, to write a " cycle of melodies on poems of his own choosing, if possible for voice accompanied by piano, 'cello and flute ". The result was the *Chansons Madécasses*, a setting of poems by Evariste Parny, an eighteenth-century Creole poet of whom some account was given in Chapter V. Both in subject-matter and treatment the work occupies a special position in Ravel's *œuvre* and marks a new departure in his technical and aesthetic evolution. The old preciosity has gone and in its place we find not only a greater degree of sensuality, but an uninhibited, almost brutal directness of utterance not hitherto encountered. Ravel himself stresses the work's " simplicity ", and indeed, compared with *Shéhérazade* or the *Trois Poèmes de Mallarmé* the music of the *Chansons Madécasses* certainly seems to spring from a far more primitive and less sophisticated approach to the matter in hand. Parny's poems are described on the title-page as " translations ", but are more probably free adaptations of the Madagascan original texts.

TITLE: *Chansons Madécasses*.
    1. Nahandove.
    2. Aoua!
    3. Il est doux. . .
PUBLISHER: Durand. DATE: 1926. SOPRANO, PIANO, FLUTE AND 'CELLO.

TEXT 1.

Nahandove, O belle Nahandove! l'oiseau nocturne a commencé ses cris, la pleine lune brille sur ma tête, et la rosée naissante humecte mes cheveux. Voici l'heure:—qui peut t'arrêter, Nahandove, O belle Nahandove? Le lit des feuilles est préparé; je l'ai parsemé de fleurs et d'herbes odiferantes, il est digne de tes charmes, Nahandove... Elle vient. J'ai reconnu la respiration précipitée que donne une marche rapide;

j'entends le froissement de la pagne qui l'enveloppe: c'est elle,
c'est elle, c'est elle, Nahandove, le belle Nahandove! O
reprends haleine ma jeune amie; repose-toi sur mes genoux.
Que ton regard est enchanteur, que le mouvement de ton sein
est vif et délicieux sous la main qui le pressure! Tu souris,
Nahandove, O belle Nahandove! Tes baisers pénétrent jusqu'à
l'âme; tes caresses brûlent tous mes sens: arrête, ou je vais
mourir. Meurt-on de volupté, Nahandove, O belle Nahandove?
Le plaisir passe comme un éclair; ta douce haleine s'affaiblit,
tes yeux humides se referment, ta tête se penche mollement, et
tes transports s'éteignent dans la langueur. Jamais tu ne fus si
belle, Nahandove, O belle Nahandove! Tu pars, et je vais
languir, dans les regrets et les désirs; je languirai jusqu'au soir;
tu reviendras ce soir, Nahandove, O belle Nahandove!

Around this passionate love-song Ravel has woven an enchanting piece of musical tapestry in which the voice and
instruments pursue their different ways blending and crossing
and clashing like threads of different coloured silk. The 'cello
alone accompanies the voice at the beginning, the piano join-
ing in when the loved one arrives to the delight of her im-
patient lover. The flute enters at the words: " c'est elle " in
imitation of the restless rhythmic figure on the piano which in
turn is derived from the opening 'cello phrase:

Ex. 16

on which the whole movement is based. The voice is treated,
as it were, instrumentally, as one member of the ensemble
rather than as a solo instrument, and Ravel shows great ingenuity in combining and contrasting the different timbres.
The music remains throughout at a noticeably cooler tempera-
ture than the words.

TEXT 2.

Aoua! Aoua! Méfiez-vous des blancs, habitants du rivage.
Du tems de nos pères, des blancs descendirent dans cette île; on
leur dit: Voilà des terres; que vos femmes les cultivent. Soyez

justes, soyez bons, et devenez nos frères. Les blancs promirent,
et cependant ils faisaient des retranchemens. Un fort menaçant
s'éleva, le tonnerre fut renfermé dans des bouches d'airain;
leurs prêtres voulurent nous donner un Dieu que nous ne con-
naissons pas; ils parlèrent enfin d'obéisance et d'esclavage:
plutôt la mort! Le carnage fut long et terrible; mais, malgré
la foudre qu'ils vomissaient, et qui écrasait des armées entières,
ils furent tous exterminés. Aoua! Aoua! Méfiez-vous des
blancs! Nous avons vu de nouveaux tyrans, plus forts et plus
nombreux, planter leur pavilion sur le rivage: le ciel a com-
battu pour nous; il a fait tomber sur eux les pluies, les tempêtes
et les vents empoisonnés. Ils ne sont plus, et nous vivons, et
nous vivons libres. Aoua! Aoua! Méfiez-vous des blancs,
habitants du rivage.

In this war song, an incitement to revolt against the white
men who came to the island with fair words and promises but
afterwards sought to enslave the inhabitants and destroy them
until they were themselves exterminated, Ravel succeeds in
creating an atmosphere of savage exultation, striking a note of
primitive barbarity that occurs in no other of his works. The
music is largely bi-tonal, and the composer emphasizes this
by endowing, for example, the voice stave and right hand of
the piano with a key-signature of six sharps, while the flute
and 'cello and left hand of the piano staves have no key-
signature at all, or vice versa. The independence of the part-
writing is again a feature of this section, while the piano is
treated as an instrument of percussion and used mainly in its
lower register, marking the beat with hammered strokes consisting of clashing major sevenths. At one place the flute,
also in its lowest register, is directed to play like a trumpet
" *quasi tromba* ". At the end the war-cry, *Aoua!* and the words
" Méfiez-vous des blancs " are repeated *pianissimo*, and the
movement ends quietly and mysteriously on an ambiguous
suspension—a minor seventh played by 'cello and flute—D
sharp–C sharp—over a major seventh—G–F sharp—in the
bass of the piano. With a marked economy of means Ravel
achieves here an effect of stark realism and force which is without a parallel elsewhere in his production.

TEXT 3.

Il est doux de se coucher durant la chaleur sous un arbre touffu, et d'attendre que le vent du soir amène la fraîcheur. Femmes, approchez. Tandis que je me repose ici sous un arbre touffu, occupez mon oreille par vos accents prolongés; répétez la chanson de la jeune fille, lorsque ses doigts tressent la natte, ou lorsqu'assise auprès du riz, elle chasse les oiseaux avides. Le chant plaît à mon âme; la danse est pour moi presqu'aussi douce qu'un baiser. Que vos pas soient lents, qu'ils imitent les attitudes du plaisir et l'abandon de la volupté. Le vent du soir se lève; la lune commence à briller au travers des arbres de la montagne. Allez, et préparez le repas.

How pleasant to lie during the heat of the day under a leafy tree and wait for the cool evening breeze. Let the women come and charm their master's ear with the song of the young girl weaving or chasing away the greedy birds, and let their movements be slow and voluptuous. . . Now the moon is rising behind the trees on the mountain top, and it is time to prepare the evening meal. . .

The setting of this pastoral piece is predominantly atmospheric; a *cantilena* on the flute, harmonics and plucked strings on the 'cello, and softly struck isolated chords—mostly Ravel's favourite major sevenths—on the piano support the voice in its quiet recital of the flowing melodic line which seems, in places, to recall the *Socrate* of Erik Satie. Altogether the triptych of the *Chansons Madécasses* must be reckoned one of Ravel's most original contributions to the music of his time.

After completing the *Chansons Madécasses* Ravel set for the first time a poem by his friend and fellow " Apache " Léon-Paul Fargue, entitled *Rêves*. Published by Durand after making its first appearance in a volume compiled by the poet* it was composed in 1927. For voice and piano.

> Un enfant court
> Autour des marbres. . .
> Une voix sourd
> Des hauts parages. . .
> Les yeux si tendres de ceux qui t'aiment

* *Pour la Musique*. Librairie Gallimard, 1914.

Songent et passent
Entre les arbres. . .
Aux grandes orgues
De quelque gare
Gronde la vague
Des grands départs. . .
Dans un vieux rêve
Au pays vague
Des choses brèves qui meurent sages. . .

A child playing, a voice calling, tender looks from those who pass on, a railway station echoing with the noise and bustle of travellers embarking on long journeys—all these things seen in a dream in the dim land of half-remembered happenings.

This is really only a graceful trifle in Ravel's most *dépouillé* style using a minimum of notes. During the next five years he wrote no more for the voice, and *Rêves* would doubtless have been his last song had he not been offered an entirely unexpected commission in a field of which he had had no previous experience. For in 1932 he was invited by a film company to write some music for a projected film on the story of *Don Quixote* in circumstances which have already been related in Chapter VI. Paul Morand was to be responsible for the script, and wrote the three poems which Ravel set to music. These were his last songs and, indeed, the last music he ever wrote.

TITLE: *Don Quichotte á Dulcinée.*
    1. Chanson romanesque.
    2. Chanson épique.
    3. Chanson à boire.
DEDICATION: 1. à Robert Couzinou.
                2. à Martial Singher.
                3. à Roger Bourdin.
PUBLISHER: Durand. DATE: 1932. VOICE AND PIANO (orchestrated).

1. CHANSON ROMANESQUE

Si vous me disiez que la terre
A tant tourner vous offensa,
Je lui dépêcherais Pança
Vous la verriez fixe et se taire

Si vous me disiez que l'ennui
Vous vient du ciel trop fleuri d'astres,
Déchirant les divins cadastres,
Je faucherais d'un coup la nuit.

Si vous me disiez que l'espace,
Ainsi vidé ne vous plaît point,
Chevalier dieu, la lance au poing,
J'étoilerais le vent qui passe !

Mais si vous disiez que mon sang
Est plus à moi qu'à vous ma Dame,
Je blêmirais dessous le blâme
Et je mourrais, vous bénissant.
O Dulcinée.

To please his mistress Don Quixote is ready to perform all
sorts of prodigies; he would stop the earth from turning, chase
the stars from the sky and, if necessary, put them back again.
But if she were to suggest that his life was not wholly devoted
to her service, he would die of shame, blessing the name of
Dulcinea.

Very simply harmonized, in alternate bars of 6/8 and 3/4
throughout—the characteristic rhythm of the Spanish dance,
the *Quajira*—the song make an immediate appeal.

2. CHANSON EPIQUE

Bon Saint Michel qui me donnez loisir
De voir ma Dame et de l'entendre,
Bon Saint Michel qui me daignez choisir
Pour lui complaire et la défendre,
· Bon Saint Michel veuillez descendre
Avec Saint Georges sur l'autel
De la Madone au bleu mantel.
D'un rayon du ciel bénissez ma lame
Et son égale en pureté
Et son égale en piété
Comme en pudeur et chasteté: Ma Dame,
(O grands Saint Georges et Saint Michel)
L'ange qui veille sur ma veille,

Ma douce Dame si pareille
A vous, Madone au bleu mantel! Amen.

The Knight prays to St. Michael and St. George to bless his
sword before the altar of the Madonna in her blue cloak whom
his Lady so much resembles.

Again the harmonies are simple and the rhythm, in 5/4 time,
is derived from the Basque dance *Zortzico*.

3. CHANSON A BOIRE

Foin du bâtard, illustre Dame,
Qui pour me perdre à vos doux yeux
Dit que l'amour et le vin vieux
Mettent en deuil mon cœur, mon âme!
Ah! Je bois
A la joie!
La joie est le seul but
Ou je vais droit . . . lorsque j'ai bu!
Ah! Ah! Ah! la joie
La . . la . . la . . je bois
A la joie!
Foin du jaloux, brune maîtresse,
Qui geind, qui pleure et fait serment
D'être toujours ce pâle amant
Qui met de l'eau dans son ivresse!
Ah! Je bois
A la joie!
La joie est le seul but
Ou je vais droit . . lorsque j'ai bu!
Ah! Ah! la joie!
La, la, la, je bois
A la joie!

It is strange to think that this boisterous drinking-song was
Ravel's swan song—his farewell to music. Although already
a sick man when he carried out this commission, he found, as
usual, the right language in which to convey the mood, and
the result is a very spirited, if slightly ironical drinking-song,
that moves to the rhythm of the *Jota*. Some Ravelian harmonies and rhythmic subtleties lend distinction to one of the
most extrovert pages he ever penned.

2. THE PIANO WORKS

Ravel's contribution to the literature of the piano was of the greatest importance, both on the technical and the aesthetic plane. While pianistically he was in the direct line of descent from Liszt and Chopin, his researches into the possibilities of the keyboard carried him into regions which had not hitherto been explored. He made full use of the discoveries of his predecessors, but added some of his own, for example, his very individual way of submerging elaborate and *recherché* harmonic progressions and internal pedals under a cascade of dazzling " runs " and figuration whose function is purely ornamental. The French pianist, Henri Gil-Marchex, thought that Ravel's finger technique was derived from the clavecinists, especially Scarlatti, and certain refinements of touch from the Chopin of the *Preludes* and the *Etudes*. Gieseking considered his keyboard works to be " the most pianistic ever written, making the most perfect and universal use of the resources of the modern piano ". Their execution calls for the greatest accuracy and precision, both as regards *nuances* and the use of the pedal.

Ravel was careful to make his intentions quite clear by marking his scores with plentiful indication as to tempo, dynamics, phrasing, etc., and had no patience with performers who failed to carry out his instructions to the letter. It was for this reason that the critic Vuillermoz declared that while there were several ways of interpreting the music of Debussy, there was only one way to play Ravel. The mechanism is so meticulously adjusted, the sonorities so carefully calculated, that the slightest deviation from the composer's original conception will upset the delicate balance of the work. The " Swiss watch-maker " left little margin for fantasy.

Ravel himself was, from all accounts, a competent pianist, but by no means a virtuoso—although he might have been one had he ever seriously worked at the instrument. He had agile fingers and a supple wrist and thumbs which he could turn well into the palm of the hand, a peculiarity which enabled him to strike three keys simultaneously with the thumb and to execute such difficult passages as this descending sequence of seconds that occurs in *Scarbo* (No. 3 in *Gaspard de la Nuit*):

Ex. 17

It seems probable that his pianistic style was conditioned to some extent by certain personal idiosyncrasies and physical limitations (or peculiarities), but there is no doubt that he opened up a new era in the history of the keyboard, not only consolidating, but carrying still further the transcendental technique of Liszt in such a way as to influence profoundly the pianistic style of a whole generation of twentieth-century composers. And it is clear that Debussy himself was the first to profit by Ravel's discoveries; one has only to compare everything he wrote for the piano *after* 1901 (the date of Ravel's *Jeux d'Eau*) with the earlier works, including *Pour le Piano* (written in the same year as *Jeux d'Eau* but quite unadventurous in comparison) to see that a great change has taken place in his style of writing for the piano which, in such works as, for example, *Estampes*, shows quite clearly the influence of the younger composer. Later on, however, Debussy was to develop a very distinctive style of his own quite different from Ravel's; and even if it was developed along lines which had been initially suggested by Ravel's earliest compositions for the instrument, I think we must admit that Ravel wrote nothing for the piano as profoundly original and rich in purely musical content as Debussy's masterly *Douze Etudes*.

We have already dealt with the incident of Debussy's alleged plagiaristic adaption of Ravel's famous *Habanera* in *Soirées dans Grenade*; of the originality of the *Habanera* itself, written in 1895 when the composer was only twenty, there can be no doubt. The style and harmonic treatment already bear the authentic Ravelian stamp, and a certain maturity and sureness of touch which are quite remarkable in view of his age at the time and the fact that he had previously written only two small works for the piano—a *Sérénade grotesque* (1893, unpublished) and the little *Menuet antique* (1895, Enoch). This was his first published work, written while he was still a student at the Conservatoire, and represents the old order giving way to the new; archaism mingled with modern dissonances—major ninths and sevenths—in a classic framework. It was first performed by Ricardo Viñes on April 13, 1901, at a *Société Nationale* concert, and orchestrated in 1929.

The *Menuet antique* was followed in the same year by a work for two pianos to which Ravel gave the rather whimsical title (which might have been inspired by Satie) of *Sites Auriculaires*. It consisted of two pieces: *Habanera* and *Entre cloches*. Unpublished in its original form, the *Habanera* was later incorporated in the orchestral *Rapsodie Espagnole*; *Entre Cloches* has not been preserved.

The *Pavane pour une Infante défunte* brought the name of Maurice Ravel before the general public for the first time; it had a drawing-room success, although the composer himself (see p. 23) judged it somewhat severely in later life. It has undeniable charm and atmosphere, but is not otherwise significant in Ravel's production. Composed in 1899 and dedicated to the Princess Edmond de Polignac, it was orchestrated in 1910 and first performed in that version in Paris under the direction of Alfredo Casella on December 25, 1911. Ricardo

Viñes had played it for the first time at a *Société Nationale* concert on April 5, 1902. (Published by Eschig, after Demets.)

With Ravel's next work for the piano we are on very different ground. *Jeux d'Eau*, as we have seen, made history. The composer described it as follows: " *Jeux d'Eau* is at the origin of whatever pianistic innovations my works may be thought to contain. This piece, inspired by the noise of water and the musical sounds emitted by fountains, waterfalls and streams, is based on two themes, on the model of a sonata first movement, but without conforming to the classical plan of key relations." (B.S.) Two themes, it is true, may be distinguished, but they are very freely treated and the piece can hardly be described as in sonata form. It calls for the greatest technical agility and the player is faced with every kind of difficulty. It is, for example, essential to keep the harmonic structure clear underneath the brilliant figuration where almost every note carries an accidental. The following example is typical of the piano writing throughout the piece:

Ex. 18

Reproduced by permission of Editions Max Eschig.

Note especially the extraordinary A natural at the bottom of the *glissando* run which is sustained throughout the next bar under quite alien harmony.

Jeux d'Eau is dedicated to " Mon cher Maître Gabriel Fauré " and bears a quotation from the Symbolist poet Henri

de Régnier: " Dieu fluvial riant de l'eau qui le chatouille "—
(" a river-god laughing at the water which tickles him ").
Composed in 1901, it was first performed at a *Société Nationale*
concert on April 5, 1902, by Ricardo Viñes. (Demets-Eschig.)

In the *Sonatine*, in contrast to the Lisztian exuberance of
Jeux d'Eau, Ravel assumes again the mantle of classicism. It
has something of the chiselled perfection and nonchalant grace
of the *String Quartet*, with the addition of a faintly archaic
flavour. There are three movements: *Modéré, doux et expressif*
in F sharp minor; *Mouvement de Menuet* in D flat major; and
Animé in F sharp minor, ending in the major. The movements
are well contrasted, and the *Sonatine* presents no great technical difficulties. Composed in 1905, it is dedicated to Ida
and Cipa Godebski. (Durand.) First performed by Paule de
Lestang at Lyons on March 10, 1906.

In *Miroirs*, composed in the same year as the *Sonatine*, Ravel
adopts a freer, more impressionistic style, and the writing for
the piano is sometimes of an extreme complexity calling for
even greater dexterity on the part of the performer than *Jeux
d'Eau*. The five pieces that make up the set are all inspired by
some sort of external image or impression " mirrored " in
sound. Thus the first is entitled *Noctuelles* (a kind of moth);
the second, *Oiseaux Tristes*, is an evocation, to quote the composer's own words, of " birds lost in the torpor of a dark
forest during the hottest hours of the summer—to my mind
the most typical of the set "; the third is entitled *Une Barque
sur l'Océan*; the fourth is the well-known *Alborada del Gracioso**
(The Jester's Serenade), and the fifth, *La Vallée des Cloches*, is
an impression of distant bells heard in a valley. It will be recalled that Ravel said later that even musicians who were
accustomed to his manner up till then were somewhat disconcerted by the marked change in his harmonic development
so noticeable in *Miroirs*.

(1) *Noctuelles*. Dedicated to Léon-Paul Fargue.† Definitely

---

* A sort of " Andalucian Petrushka " (Jankélévitch.)

† A phrase by the author suggested the title to Ravel: " Les noctuelles des hangars
partent d'un vol gauche cravater d'autres poutres " (" The owlet-moths fly clumsily
out of the old barn to drape themselves round other beams ").

" impressionistic " with its shifting harmonies, indeterminate rhythm and fleeting, unsubstantial figuration. Marked: *Très léger*.

(2) *Oiseaux Tristes*. This piece is said to have been inspired by birds singing at dawn in the forest of Fontainebleau. Marked *très lent* and *très doux* the musical texture is much more " open " than in *Noctuelles* and is built round a persistently repeated note, interspersed with bird-like trills against which can be heard, at the beginning and again at the end, a plaintive descending major third suggesting the voice of a distant cuckoo. Dedicated to Ricardo Viñes.

(3) *Une Barque sur l'Océan*. The piano writing here recalls *Jeux d'Eau* with its rushing arpeggios covering the entire keyboard. Marked: *D'un rythme très souple—très enveloppé de pédales*, it is the longest of the set and with the *Alborada* one of the most difficult to perform. Dedicated to Paul Sordes.

(4) *Alborada del Gracioso*. Brilliantly effective in Ravel's Spanish manner. The outlines are sharper and the accent more pronounced than in the other numbers of *Miroirs*; the impressionist mists of the north have here given way to a burst of strong Mediterranean sunlight. *Glissando* runs in fourths and thirds are among the hazards that await the performer in this tempestuous piece. The dedication is to M. D. Calvo-coressi.

(5) *La Vallée des Cloches*. Here the music is conditioned by the subject, being built on the harmonics produced by bells. A poetic and imaginative evocation of the sound of bells heard in the open air and inevitably inviting comparison with Debussy's *Cloches à travers les feuilles*. Dedicated to Maurice Delage.

Miroirs was performed for the first time by Ricardo Viñes at a *Société Nationale* concert on January 6, 1906. (Demets–Eschig.) Nos. 3 and 4 are orchestrated.

In *Ma Mère l'Oye*, Ravel's next composition for the piano, the accent, in contrast to the increasing complexity of the works that preceded it, is on simplicity. It is as if he wished to relax for a moment and find distraction in that other world of fantasy and legend to which he had always been attuned. He was at

easc with children and found no difficulty in entering their
world of make-believe and detachment from reality, which
corresponded to something fundamental in his own character.
For in spite of the sophistication, intellectual refinement and
love of complexity manifested in his art, he was simple and
sincere in all his human contacts and took pleasure in childish
things. It was therefore only natural that he should have conceived the idea of writing for the children of his best friends,
Ida and Cipa Godebski, a set of pieces for piano duet to illus-
trate some well-known fairy-tales. These were published
under the general title of *Ma Mère l'Oye* (Mother Goose) and
dedicated to Mimi and Jean Godebski. " It was my intention ", said Ravel in referring to this work, " to evoke in these
pieces the poetry of childhood, and this naturally led me to
simplify my manner and style of writing." (B.S.)

Ma Mère l'Oye: 5 Pieces enfantines

1. *Pavane de la Belle au bois dormant* (Charles Perrault).

Twenty bars only of limpid melody, in the Aeolian mode,
of an extreme simplicity and haunting beauty, so contrived that
each of the four hands has only single notes to play; there are
no chords in either hand.

2. *Petit Poucet.*

> Il croyait trouver aisément son chemin par le moyen de son
> pain qu'il avait semé partout où il avait passé; mais il fut bien
> surpris lorsqu'il n'en put retrouver une seule miette: les
> oiseaux étaient venus qui avaient tout mangé.
>
> (Ch. Perrault.)

The right hand (*prima*) sings a gentle melody against a
counterpoint in thirds traced by the two hands (*seconda*) consisting of a steadily moving quaver figure representing Tom
Thumb wandering in the forest. The cheeping of the little
birds who had eaten the crumbs Tom Thumb had strewn
about to help him find his way out is heard in the piano's
highest register.

3. *Laideronette, Impératrice des Pagodes.*

> Elle se déshabilla et se mit dans le bain. Aussitôt pagodes et
> pagodines se mirent à chanter et à jouer des instruments: tels
> avaient des théorbes faits d'une coquille de noix; tels avaient
> des violes faites d'une coquille d'amande; car il fallait bien pro-
> portionner les instruments à leur taille.
>
> (Mme d'Aulnoy: *Serpentin Vert.* 1650–1705.)

The little Empress taking her bath to the sound of viols and
lutes made of nutshells played by mandarins and mandarin-
ettes under a Chinese pagoda was a perfect subject for Ravel
to embroider with appropriate chinoiseries—which he does
to perfection in this exquisite page in which the pentatonic
scale is used to great effect.

4. *Les Entretiens de la Belle et la Bête.*

> " Quand je pense à votre bon cœur, vous ne me paraissez pas
> si laid."—" Oh! dame oui!; j'ai le cœur bon, mais je suis un
> monstre."—" Il y a bien des hommes qui sont plus monstres
> que vous."—" Si j'avais de l'esprit, je vous ferais un grand com-
> pliment pour vous remercier, mais je ne suis qu'une bête." ...
> " La Belle, voulez-vous être ma femme? "—" Non, la Bête! "
>
> .   .   .
>
> " Je meurs content puisque j'ai le plaisir de vous revoir encore
> une fois."—" Non, ma chère Bête, vous ne mourrez pas: vous
> vivrez pour devenir mon époux! "...
> La Bête avait disparu et elle ne vit plus à ses pieds qu'un prince
> plus beau que l'Amour qui la remerciait d'avoir fini son en-
> chantment.
>
> (Mme Leprince de Beaumont. 18th cent.)

This charming dialogue between Beauty and the Beast
ending in the deliverance of the Beast from the spell which
had transformed him from a handsome prince into a monster
is translated into music both humorous and tender. The influence of Satie is so evident that Roland-Manuel has credited
Ravel here with writing a " fourth *Gymnopédie* ".

5. *Le Jardin Féerique.*

A kind of sarabande, slow and solemn, beginning *pianissimo* and ending in a brilliant peroration with a fanfare and *glissando* runs in the highest register of the piano.

Ma Mère l'Oye is one of Ravel's happiest achievements, a masterpiece in miniature and very typical, in the purity and nostalgic quality of its melody and modal harmonies, of a certain aspect of his genius that is sometimes lost sight of, namely his ability to achieve perfection with the simplest as well as with the most complex means. As has been well said by Roland-Manuel: ". . . the Ravel of *Ma Mère l'Oye* reveals to us the secret of his profound nature, and shows us the soul of a child who has never left the kingdom of Fairyland, who makes no distinction between nature and artifice, and who seems to believe that everything can be imagined and carried out on the material plane provided everything is strictly controlled and regulated on the mental or spiritual plane."

The work was performed for the first time at the inaugural concert of the newly founded *Société de Musique Indépendante* by two young students, Mlles Jeanne Leleu and Geneviève Durony, on April 20, 1910. Orchestrated in 1911, *Ma Mère l'Oye* was produced as a ballet at the *Théâtre des Arts* in Paris on January 28, 1912, on a scenario written by the composer. The ballet has six tableaux and is preceded by a short Prelude. The first scene, which, like the *Prelude*, does not appear in the original piano version, is *Danse du rouet* (Spinning-wheel dance) introducing Princess Florine (the Sleeping Beauty). An old woman is spinning at her wheel; Florine stumbles and pricks her finger on the spindle and falls into a deep sleep. The courtiers and maids of honour try to arouse her, but in vain.

Scene 2 (Pavane). While the Princess is sleeping the old woman throws off her sordid garments and appears in dazzling raiment as the Good Fairy. She orders two little negro boys to watch over Florine while she sleeps.

Scene 3 (La Belle et la Bête). Same argument as in the Piano Suite.

Scene 4 (Petit Poucet). The woodcutter's seven children are lost in the forest at night. Tom Thumb consoles his brothers and sisters by showing them the crumbs he has strewn along their path to help them find their way out. While they are asleep the birds come and eat up all the crumbs. When they wake up the children discover this and go sadly on their way.

Scene 5 (Laideronette). *Pas de deux* and general dance in the Chinese setting as described in the Piano Suite.

Scene 6 (Le Jardin Féerique). Prince Charming, guided by a Cupid, arrives at dawn just as the Princess is waking from her deep sleep. All the characters in the ballet group themselves round the royal pair as the Good Fairy appears to give them her blessing. Apotheosis.

The Ballet is scored for: 2 fl., 2 ob., 2 cl., 2 bn., 2 horns, kettledrums, harp, strings, triangle, cymbals, side-drum, bass drum, xylophone, celesta and glockenspiel. (Durand.)

Dating from the same year as *Ma Mère l'Oye*, but in a very different vein, *Gaspard de la Nuit*, described as " trois poèmes pour piano à deux mains d'après Aloysius Bertrand ", is one of Ravel's most important compositions. We are still in the realm of fantasy, but the scene has shifted from Fairyland to another plane of the supernatural—more sophisticated and literary and, in the case of one of these pieces, definitely macabre.

Aloysius (Louis) Bertrand (1807–1841) was born at Ceva, in Piedmont, his father being a Frenchman from Lorraine and his mother Italian. He enjoyed a certain vogue as a Romantic writer during his lifetime, and was well thought of by Sainte-Beuve. In his preface to *Gaspard de la Nuit* (published posthumously at Angers) the author relates that he once asked a stranger to tell him what were the laws of a literary aesthetic, whereupon the stranger, " Gaspard de la Nuit ", alias Satan, gave him in reply the manuscript of these poems in prose.* The romantic and somewhat mysterious background of these poems and the personality of their author obviously had a strong attraction for Ravel, and he accepted the challenge to his genius for finding the exact musical equivalent for images and concepts expressed in words. The " Verb " was, in fact, for him

---

* In a letter to Ida Godebski dated July 17, 1908, Ravel, after announcing the successful completion of the work " after too many long months of gestation ", alludes specifically to the alleged diabolic authorship of the poems in the following terms: " *Gaspard* has been the very devil to write, which is only logical since He is the author of the poems."

a powerful catalytic, stimulating his powers of musical invention. In the exacerbated romanticism of these " poems " of
Bertrand he saw an opportunity for a display of virtuosity,
and he told Delage he intended to write something for the
piano that would be more difficult than *Islamey*. Certainly
Gaspard is a monument in the literature of the piano and, to
quote Alfred Cortot, " one of the most astonishing examples
of instrumental ingenuity to be found in the work of any
composer ".

The three prose poems are entitled respectively *Ondine*, *Le
Gibet* and *Scarbo*, and the texts are printed in the musical score.

1. ONDINE

. . . Je croyais entendre
Une vague harmonie enchanter mon sommeil.
Et près de moi s'épandre un murmure pareil
Aux chants entrecoupés d'une voix triste et tendre.

(Ch. Brugnot: *Les Deux Génies*.)

" Ecoute! Ecoute! C'est moi, c'est Ondine qui frôle de ces
gouttes d'eau les losanges sonores de ta fenêtre illuminée par les
mornes rayons de la lune; et voici, en robe de moine, la dame
châtelaine qui contemple à son balcon la belle nuit étoilée et le
beau lac endormi.

" Chaque flot est un ondin qui nage dans le courant, chaque
courant est un sentier qui serpente vers mon palais, et mon palais
est bâti fluide, au fond du lac, dans le triangle du feu, de la terre
et de l'air.

" Ecoute! Ecoute! Mon père bat l'eau coassante d'une branche
d'aulne verte, et mes sœurs caressent de leurs bras d'écume les
fraîches îles d'herbes, de nénuphars et de glaïeuls, ou se moquent
du saule caduc et barbu qui pêche à la ligne."

Sa chanson murmurée, elle me supplia de recevoir son anneau
à mon doigt, pour être l'epoux d'une Ondine, et de visiter avec
elle son palais pour être le roi des lacs.

Et comme je lui répondais que j'aimais une mortelle, boudeuse
et dépitée, elle pleura quelques larmes, poussa un éclat de rire, et
s'évanouit en giboulées qui ruisselèrent blanches le long de mes
vitraux bleus.

(I thought I heard music vaguely in my sleep, and near me the
murmur of a tender and sad voice singing.

Ch. Brugnot.

" Listen! It is I, Ondine, sprinkling with drops of water your window-pane lit by the pale moon's rays while over there the Lady of the Manor is gazing from her balcony at the beauty of the starry night and slumbering lake.

" Every little wave is a water-sprite swimming with the current, and every current is a path that leads to my palace, and my palace is built of water at the bottom of the lake in the triangle formed of fire, earth and air.

" Listen! My father is dipping a branch of green alder into the bubbling water while my sisters are caressing with their foam-transparent arms the cool islands of herbs and water-lilies and flags, or laughing at the weeping-willow fishing in the stream."

Having finished her murmured song, she begged me to put her ring upon my finger to show that I was wed to an Ondine, and to go with her to her palace to be the king of the lakes.

And when I told her that I loved a mortal woman, chagrined and discomfited she wept a little, then laughed and disappeared, dissolving into a shower of drops that glistened on my blue window-pane.)

Under a cascade of scintillating arpeggios and iridescent harmonies a quiet melody weaves it way, rising and falling like the " murmur of a sad voice singing ". This is one of Ravel's most elaborately wrought and at the same time imaginative pictures in sound. The texture is both rich and translucent, and the structure, though episodical in character, is firm and homogeneous. It is interesting to compare this with Debussy's *Ondine* (*Preludes*, Book 2. 1913) which is on a much smaller scale, and more fragmentary and impressionistic. But Debussy, of course, was not illustrating any particular text.

2. LE GIBET
Que vois-je remuer autour de ce Gibet? (Faust.)

Ah! ce que j'entends, serait-ce la bise nocturne qui glapit, ou le pendu qui pousse un soupir sur la fourche patibulaire?

Serait-ce quelque grillon qui chante tapi dans la mousse et le lierre stérile dont par pitié se chausse le bois?

Serait-ce quelque mouche en chasse sonnant du cor autour de ces oreilles sourdes à la fanfare des hallali?

Serait-ce quelque escarbot qui cueille en son vol inégal un cheveu sanglant à son crâne chauve?

Ou bien serait-ce quelque araignée qui brode une demi-aune de mousseline pour cravate à ce col étranglé?

C'est la cloche qui tinte aux murs d'une ville, sous l'horizon, et la carcasse d'un pendu que rougit le soleil couchant.

(What do I see stirring round this gibbet? Faust.)

Ah! What is that sound I hear? Is it the night wind howling, or the sighing of the corpse that hangs from yonder gibbet?

Is it a cricket singing in the moss and barren ivy in which the gallows stand?

Is it a fly sounding its hunting-horn in those deaf ears?

Is it perchance some blundering cockchafer trailing a hair plucked from that bald head?

Or would it be some spider weaving a length of muslin as a cravat for that strangled neck?

. . . It is the sound of a bell tolling from the walls of a town far away on the horizon, and a corpse hanging from a gibbet reddened by the rays of the setting sun.)

This macabre theme has provided Ravel with a pretext for what is nothing less than a musical *tour de force*. Constructed most ingeniously round an internal pedal—a persistent octave B flat that suggests the tolling of a bell—upon which successive waves of intricate harmony surge and break, like the sea swirling round a rock, *Le Gibet* stands out as one of Ravel's supreme achievements. The following extract gives some idea of the complexity of the writing and the difficulties it presents to the performer.

Ex. 19

During the last twelve bars the pedal is sustained in the bass as well as in the middle register of the piano.

3. Scarbo

Il regarda sous le lit, dans la cheminée, dans le bahut;—personne.
Il ne put comprendre par où il s'était introduit, par où il s'était
évadé.   (Hoffman: *Contes Nocturnes.*)

Oh! que de fois je l'ai entendu et vu, Scarbo, lorsqu'à minuit la
lune brille dans le ciel comme un écu d'argent sur une bannière
d'azur semée d'abeilles d'or!

Que de fois j'ai entendu bourdonner son rire dans l'ombre de
mon alcove, et grincer son ongle sur la soie des courtines de mon
lit!

Que de fois je l'ai vu descendre du plancher, pirouetter sur un
pied et rouler par la chambre comme le fuseau tombé de la
quenouille d'une sorcière!

Le croyais-je alors évanoui? Le nain grandissait entre la lune
et moi comme le clocher d'une cathédrale gothique, un grelot
d'or en branle à son bonnet pointu!

Mais bientôt son corps bleuissait, diaphane comme la cire d'une
bougie, son visage blémissait comme la cire d'un lumignon—et
soudain il s'éteignait.

(He looked under the bed, up the chimney and in the cupboard
—nobody there. He could not understand how he had got in
or from where he had escaped.

How many times have I seen and heard Scarbo when, at midnight, the moon is shining in the sky like a piece of silver on an
azure banner sprinkled with golden bees.

How many times have I heard him laughing in the shadow of my
alcove or scratching at the silk curtains round my bed! How
often have I seen him descend from the ceiling, pirouette on one
foot, and roll across the floor like a bobbin from a witch's distaff!

And if I expected him then to disappear, the little dwarf would
grow taller and taller and stand towering between me and the
moon like a cathedral spire, with a golden bell jingling at the tip
of his pointed cap! But soon his body would turn blue, and
translucent like the wax in a candle, and his face grow pale—then
suddenly he would vanish.)

If *Ondine* is remarkable for its melodic character and *Le Gibet*
for its harmony, then *Scarbo* completes the trinity by placing
the accent on rhythm. It is a brilliant *bravura* piece, like *Jeux
d'Eau* and the *Toccata* in *Le Tombeau de Couperin*, and immensely
difficult to perform. As to the mood Ravel intended to con-

vey, the pianist Henri Gil-Marchex records that when he was
studying the piece with the composer, Ravel wrote under the
three notes of the principal theme the three syllables " Quelle
horreur! "—thus:

The famous semiquaver " runs " in consecutive seconds, to be
played with the thumb, are only one of the technical difficulties with which Ravel has plentifully besprinkled these
pages. Scarbo, the malicious little goblin, seems to have been
standing at the composer's elbow when he wrote these dazzling
studies, urging him to have no pity on any performer rash
enough to tackle them.

Modern pianistic technique can hardly be carried further than
it has been in *Gaspard de la Nuit*, in which Ravel has certainly
fulfilled his declared intention of writing " pieces of transcendental virtuosity "; and nowhere else in his works, as Roland-
Manuel has pointed out, has " artifice assumed with greater
ease and power the appearance of being natural and inevitable ".

The three movements of the suite are dedicated respectively
to Harold Bauer, the pianist, Jean Marnold, critic of the
Mercure de France, and Rudolph Ganz. It was first performed
by Ricardo Viñes at a *Société Nationale* concert on January 9,
1909. (Durand.)

When in the following year, 1909, Ravel was invited to contribute to a special number of the *Revue S.I.M.* in commemora-
tion of the centenary of the death of Haydn, he decided to
write a minuet on the letters of his name, thus:

In the course of the piece the little theme is played backwards, and then upside down:

Apart from these little scholastic devices which must have given great pleasure to the composer, this brief piece of only fifty-four bars contains some typical Ravelian harmonies and in mood is not unlike the Minuet in the *Sonatine*. First performed *Société Nationale*, 1911. (Durand.)

We come now to one of the most important works in Ravel's pianistic production, the *Valses Nobles et Sentimentales*. The title, as the composer himself is at pains to explain, " indicates clearly enough my intention of composing a chain of waltzes, following the example of Schubert. The virtuoso element which was the basis of *Gaspard de la Nuit* is here replaced by a style of writing of greater clarity which has the effect of sharpening the harmony as well as the outline of the music." (B.S.) The circumstances in which the first performance took place have been described in Chapter III; the authorship of the waltzes, which were performed anonymously, was recognized by only a small majority of the audience who had been asked to guess it. At the head of the score Ravel had inscribed a quotation from the poet Henri de Régnier: ". . . le plaisir délicieux et toujours nouveau d'une occupation inutile." This provides a significant clue to the composer's mood and intentions at the time. These eight waltzes (or rather seven and an epilogue) contain all the essential ingredients of Ravel's style and harmonic language. Deceptively simple in appearance, they are, in fact, a treasure-house of subtleties and refinements of all kinds, melodic, harmonic and rhythmic. Debussy paid tribute to these qualities when he said of Ravel, referring to the *Valses*: " C'est l'oreille la plus fine qui ait jamais existé."

No. 1 is definitely " noble "—vigorous, almost brutal with its acid, clashing major ninths and seconds and hammered, incisive rhythm. It bears the indication: " *très franc* ".

No. 2, "*Assez lent—avec une expression intense* " (an unusual direction for Ravel), is clearly a " sentimentale ". More subdued, more melodic than the first, it has a nostalgic charm. Ravel has marked some passages *rubato*, which is very rare in his music. Ricardo Viñes said that he had created a " rubato en place: le rubato dosé " which he evidently intended here to suggest a kind of Viennese waltz " hesitation ".

No. 3, " *Modéré* ", and smoothly flowing, is characterized by the displaced accents within the 3/4 bar, producing the effect: *one*, two, *three*, one, *two*, three, etc., which, moreover, is carried on into No. 4, " *Assez animé* ".

No. 5, " *Presque lent—dans un sentiment intime* ", marks a change of mood, calmer and more voluptuous, again with displaced accents, the stress (melodic) falling at times on the first and fourth of six quavers in ternary time.

No. 6, *Vif*, sets another problem of combined binary and ternary rhythm divided between left and right hand, thus:

Ex. 24

No. 7, *Moins vif*, the longest of the set, begins with a curious little preamble recalling the theme of the preceding waltz, leading into a theme with a strong Viennese flavour and accentuation which is worked up to a big climax, followed by a quiet middle section which leads back again to the initial theme, the last bars being a reminiscence of the opening rhythmic figure of the first waltz.

No. 8, the *Epilogue*, marked *Lent*, is a kind of résumé of all the seven preceding waltzes, disembodied fragments of which come floating to the surface in the course of this highly evocative movement in which Ravel passes in review, as it were, what has gone before, not insisting on, but alluding discreetly and nostalgically to, the seven links which have formed his golden chain. In the concluding bars the music dies away imperceptibly, " en se perdant ", a feathery *appoggiatura* descending on the final tonic chord.

Composed in 1911, the *Valses Nobles et Sentimentales* are dedicated to Louis Aubert, who performed them for the first time at a concert of the S.M.I. on May 9, 1911. (Durand.) The music was also orchestrated to accompany a ballet on a scenario written by the composer and produced during Mlle Trouhanova's season of ballets at the Châtelet on April 22, 1912, under the title: *Adélaïde ou le Langage des Fleurs*. The action takes place in the Paris salon of a courtesan named Adélaïde round about 1820. There are seven scenes and an epilogue, as in the original.

Scene 1. While the couples are waltzing or engaged in tender conversation Adélaïde comes and goes. She is wearing a tuberose, the symbol of sensual pleasure.

Scene 2. Enter Lorédan in melancholy mood. He offers her a buttercup, and the exchange of flowers that follows symbolizes Adélaïde's coquetry and her suitor's love for her.

Scene 3. Adélaïde sees from the flower offered her that Lorédan's love for her is sincere, but the marguerite she gave to Lorédan tells him that his love is not returned. Lorédan tries a second time, and this time the reply is favourable.

Scene 4. The lovers dance together affectionately, but are interrupted by the entrance of The Duke.

Scene 5. The Duke presents Adélaïde with a sunflower (a

symbol of empty riches) and a diamond necklace, which she puts on.

Scene 6. Lorédan in despair presses his suit, but is repulsed coquettishly.

Scene 7. The Duke begs Adélaïde to give him the last waltz. She refuses, and goes in search of Lorédan, who strikes an attitude of tragic despair. Finally he yields to her insistence and they go off together.

Epilogue. The guests retire. The Duke, hoping to be asked to stay, receives from Adélaïde's hands a branch of acacia (symbol of Platonic love) and departs in high dudgeon. Lorédan approaches looking very sad. Adélaïde gives him a poppy (an invitation to forget), but he rejects it and goes off, bidding her farewell for ever. Adélaïde goes to the window and breathes the scent of the tuberose. Suddenly Lorédan appears on her balcony in a state of agitation, falls on his knees and presses a pistol to his head. But Adélaïde smilingly produces from her corsage a red rose and falls into his arms.

The orchestration is as follows: 2 fl., 2 ob., 2 cl., 2 bn., 4 horns, 2 trp., 3 trb., tuba, kettledrums, side-drum, cymbals, triangle, drum, tambourine, celesta, glockenspiel, 2 harps, strings.

In 1913 Ravel wrote only two slight works for the piano; these were *A la manière de . . .* and *Prélude*. The first contains two clever parodies of Borodin (a waltz) and Chabrier (paraphrase on an air from Gounod's *Faust*). They were first played in public by Casella at the S.M.I. on December 10, 1913. The second piece was written for a sight-reading test at the Paris Conservatoire, and is dedicated to Mlle Jeanne Leleu (one of the two little girls who gave the first performance of *Ma Mère l'Oye* and who later became a well-known pianist and Prix de Rome. Only a few bars long, this little piece nevertheless involves some interlocking of the hands, but otherwise presents no difficulties, apart from a few unexpected harmonies, being very simply written. (Durand.)

Ravel's last work for solo piano (apart from the two concertos) was *Le Tombeau de Couperin*, begun just before the first world war in the summer of 1914, and finished, after having been interrupted by the composer's war activities and illness, in 1917. It was intended as a homage, not only to Couperin " le Grand ", but to the whole seventeenth- and eighteenth-century French school of " clavecinists ". In mood and style it most resembles the *Sonatine*. It has six movements, each bearing a dedication in memory of a friend killed at the front. The rapidly moving *Prélude*, built on a recurring semiquaver group of six notes, is inscribed " to the memory of Lieutenant Jacques Charlot ". The *Fugue* that follows, constructed on a theme derived from the *Prélude*, is orthodox and rather dry, but most ingeniously wrought. It is the only example of a fugue in all Ravel's published works. In order to write it he studied fugue intensively, and wrote several exercises to ensure that this one should be a perfect example of the form. He even rewrote a fugue of Bach, which he proudly claimed to have improved! The dedication is to the memory of Second Lieutenant Jean Cruppi. The third movement, a *Forlane*, dedicated to the memory of Lieutenant Gabriel Deluc, is a version of the Italian dance-form, the *Forlana*, said to be a favourite with Venetian gondoliers. It is in 6/8 time throughout, in the ornamental style of the eighteenth-century harpsichord composers, the very acid modern harmonies forming a piquant contrast to the staid and rather formal character of the dance. The *Rigaudon* that follows, " to the memory of Pierre and Pascal Gaudin ", is lively and vigorous, with a pastoral middle section over a drone bass. The stately and graceful *Menuet*, " *à la mémoire de Jean Dreyfus* ", is followed by a brilliant *Toccata*, the most pianistic of all the pieces in the suite, in the same virtuoso category as *Jeux d'Eau* or *Scarbo*. It is dedicated to the memory of Captain Joseph de Marliave, the husband of Mme Marguerite Long who gave the first performance of *Le Tombeau* at the S.M.I. on April 11, 1919.

Four of the six movements exist in an orchestral version: *Prélude, Forlane, Menuet* and *Rigaudon*. This orchestral suite was first performed under Rhené-Baton, conducting the Pasdeloup orchestra on February 28, 1920; later in the same year, on

November 8, it provided the music for a ballet produced by
Rolf de Maré's Swedish Ballet at the *Théâtre des Champs-Elysées,*
conducted by D. E. Inghelbrecht. It was scored for 2 fl., 2 ob.,
2 cl., 2 bn., 2 horns, trp., harp and strings. The suite has also
been arranged for piano duet and for two pianos. (Durand.)

In 1918 Ravel wrote a short piece for two pianos, four
hands, entitled *Frontispice,* for inclusion in a book of poems by
Canudo. This was subsequently published in the now
extinct *Feuillets d' Art* but nowhere else, so that this extract
from it (the concluding bars) is of especial interest in so far as
the work from which it is taken is virtually unknown.

Ex. 25

After this, Ravel wrote no more for the piano until 1931, when
he composed, in the same year, the two concertos which
are perhaps his crowning achievement in this field. The

circumstances in which they came to be written, together with Ravel's own comments on their general style and character, have been described in Chapter VI (p. 84–5).

That in G major is dedicated to Mme Marguerite Long, who gave the first performance with the Lamoureux orchestra, with the composer conducting, on January 14, 1933. It has three movements: *Allegramente, Adagio assai* and *Presto*. In marked contrast to the two lively outer movements, the *Adagio* reflects a mood of tranquil meditation. A long melody unwinds itself slowly over a steadily pulsing accompaniment figure in the left hand, the piano playing alone for thirty-three bars before the orchestra enters. The theme is then developed until the piano embarks on florid figuration in the right hand over the original accompaniment figure, and continues to weave arabesques against a simple counterpoint in the orchestra, finally bringing the movement to an end with a prolonged trill. In spite of the apparent spontaneity of this movement, especially the long, flowing melody, it cost Ravel a great effort to compose; in fact, as he himself confessed, he made up the tune laboriously, two bars at a time, taking the slow movement of Mozart's Clarinet Quintet as a model. There is nothing else in his whole production quite like this movement; its classic serenity and simplicity stand out in sharp contrast, not only to what precedes and follows it in this work, but to everything that we consider typical of this essentially sophisticated composer.

The concerto was originally conceived as a *divertissement*, which accounts for the gay, almost frivolous character of the first and last movements which evolve in an atmosphere of 'Kermesse' and joyous, if somewhat self-conscious exuberance. The orchestral palette is bold and bright, and the scoring, as usual with Ravel, is masterly and full of original and striking effects. The highly spiced, acidulous harmonies are typical of Ravel at his most adventurous, and full of quips and quirks. A bi-tonal passage in the very first bar bears an unmistakable resemblance to a similar passage in Stravinsky's *Petrushka*—no doubt an unconscious reminiscence:

Ex. 26

Ravel

Ex. 27

Stravinsky

But this is only the piano's accompaniment to the theme given out by the piccolo—a kind of " bransle gay " with a definitely rustic flavour:

Ex. 28

Another contrasting theme is soon announced by the piano, making its first solo entry:

Ex. 29

which seems to come from far away, like an echo of some languorous dance measure from the southern seas. Note especially the dying fall of the last two bars, with its characteristic " false relation ", so typical of Ravel's melodies (cf. the *Sonatine, Pavane pour une Infante défunte, Ma Mère l'Oye*, etc.). These two themes provide most of the material for this movement, in which Ravel transforms his orchestra into a dazzling *feu d'artifice*.

The final *Presto* is a frenzied galopade in which piano and orchestra pursue one another in a blaze of brilliant virtuosity.

The percussion section of the orchestra is heavily reinforced and includes triangle, drum, cymbals, side-drum, gong, woodblock and a whip. For the rest, the instrumentation is as follows: 1 fl., 1 picc., 1 ob., cor anglais, 1 B flat cl., 1 small E flat cl., 2 bn., 2 horns, 1 trp., 1 trb., 2 kettledrums and harp. (Durand, who also publish an arrangement for 2 pianos.)

The D major Concerto, for the left hand alone, is music of a very different kind. Sombre and tragic, it is perhaps Ravel's finest achievement. Composed for and dedicated to the Austrian pianist Paul Wittgenstein, who had lost his right arm in the 1914 war, it had its first performance in Vienna on November 27, 1931, and in Paris on March 19, 1937, with Jacques Février as soloist and the Orchestre Philharmonique de Paris conducted by Charles Munch.

Accepting the challenge of the purely technical problem of writing for the left hand alone a concerto for piano and orchestra, Ravel deliberately set out to make a concerto on a grand scale in a style, as he put it, more akin to that usually associated with the traditional concerto, " since in a work of this kind it is essential not to make the musical texture sound thin, but on the contrary to give the impression of a solo part written for two hands." On this score alone the Concerto must be considered an extraordinary *tour de force*; and Ravel's profound knowledge of the resources of the keyboard and consummate skill in writing for it under the limitations imposed have nowhere been more convincingly displayed. No one listening to a record of this prodigious work, not knowing anything about it, could possibly guess that the pianist is using only one hand.*

The D major Concerto is in one movement—a *Lento* followed by an *Allegro*—played without a break. Ravel has outlined its general form in these terms: "After a first section, imbued with the spirit of the 'traditional' concerto, an episode in the nature of an improvisation makes its appearance introducing a kind of jazz music. Not until later will it be seen that the 'jazz' episode is in reality constructed on the themes of the first section." Ravel is here being deliberately as uncommunicative as possible; he is evidently unwilling to disclose what lies beneath the surface in this profoundly moving but disturbing work.

It opens mysteriously with a theme on the double-bassoon that emerges slowly from a bustling murmur on the lower strings:

Ex. 30

soon to be succeeded by a sort of anguished complaint announced by the horns:

Ex. 31

Tension increases as the orchestra develops these two themes, and at the moment of crisis the piano makes its entry in an unaccompanied cadenza, forceful and dramatic, a feature of which is a new variant of the anguished second theme which now takes on heroic proportions:

* Before writing it Ravel had studied, among other things, the *Six Etudes pour la main gauche* of Saint-Saëns.

Ex. 32

After the orchestra has reaffirmed the opening theme, the piano enters with a nostalgic melody of ineffable sadness; there is no suggestion here of preciosity or artificiality; it is as if, for once, in an unguarded moment, Ravel has allowed his feelings to betray him, and is speaking direct from the heart under the stress of some deeply felt emotion—regret—or premonition?

Ex. 33

But the piano is not allowed to sustain for long this calm and reflective mood; the opening theme reappears in the orchestra while the solo instrument embroiders with rapid figuration in octaves *crescendo* and *accelerando*. A climax is reached, and there is a sudden change of mood and style: the " jazz " episode is ushered in on the brass, and soon the piano is hammering away at a sort of devil's dance in a furious 6/8, parodying the first theme with a sarcastic vehemence echoed in the orchestra. The heroic version of the second theme recurs *fff* in the orchestra while the pianist's left hand sweeps the keyboard with soaring and plunging arpeggios, before settling down into a solo cadenza of great power and beauty in which all the themes are passed in review, with special insistence on the second theme. After a poignant climax, the 6/8 episode is recalled in a brief coda of five bars, and the Concerto ends, as it were, in a burst of sardonic laughter.

It seems extraordinary that Ravel should have written in the same year two piano concertos so completely different in character—the one gay and *insouciant* (apart from its contemplative slow movement), the other violent and tragic, with sombre undertones which all the frenzied exuberance of the " jazz " section cannot conceal. The *Concerto for the Left Hand* throws fresh light on Ravel's artistic personality and gives the lie to those who maintain that his music is entirely soulless. Although the dandyism and aloofness of the supreme craftsman are elsewhere in his *œuvre* often most in evidence, could it not be that they served to some extent as a mask to conceal a hypersensitive nature determined at all costs to avoid anything in the nature of self-revelation? The stratagem worked in nearly every instance, but in the *D major Concerto* one cannot help feeling that for once the barriers are down. And the result?—one of the great masterpieces of twentieth-century music.

The *Concerto for the Left Hand* requires the following orchestra: 2 fl., picc., 2 ob., cor anglais, 2 cl. in B flat, small E flat cl., bass cl., 2 bn., double bn., 4 horns, 3 trp., 3 trb., tuba, kettledrums, triangle, drum, cymbals, side-drum, woodblock, gong, harp, and usual strings. Also arranged for two pianos. (Durand.)

After the two concertos Ravel wrote no more for the piano, an instrument for which he had a particular predilection and to the literature of which he made a contribution of great originality and historical importance.

3. Chamber Works

The *String Quartet*, composed in 1902–1903 while Ravel was still a student at the Conservatoire, was his first essay in this field and to this day remains a model of its kind. The influence of Debussy, who had made history with his string quartet written ten years earlier, is unmistakable, especially in the second movement, but the work is nevertheless one of Ravel's most perfect achievements. It is remarkable not only for its freshness and melodic charm but even more for its astonishing technical maturity. It bears the dedication: " à mon cher maître Gabriel Fauré ", and was performed for the first time at the *Société Nationale* by the Quatuor Heymann on March 5, 1904.

There are four movements: *Allegro moderato*; *Assez vif*; *Très lent*; *Vif et agité*. The first is pastoral in character and in more or less strict sonata form, the first and second subjects:

Ex. 34

Ex. 35

undergoing various transformations in the course of the exposition and development sections.

The second movement, marked " *très rythmé* " (like the corresponding movement in the Debussy quartet) is a scherzo.

It opens with all the strings playing *pizzicato*; the middle section has a " *bien chanté* " melody not unlike theme 2 in the first movement; Ravel here shows great skill and ingenuity, and the string writing is most effective. The slow movement is rather rhapsodical in character, proceeding episodically with more than one allusion to themes heard in the first movement. The *finale*, in alternating 5/8, 5/4 and 3/4 time, is vigorous and emphatic, abounding in rapid *tremolo* passages, arpeggios and spread chords, bringing the work to a brilliant conclusion.

The quartet is most effective in performance and displays a sureness of touch altogether remarkable when one considers that the composer was still a student at the time. Though in no way revolutionary, the Quartet was considered by the pundits to be too unorthodox and was actually counted against him when Ravel was a candidate for the Prix de Rome. Even Fauré found fault with the last movement, which he thought was badly balanced; but Debussy (see Chapter I) thought highly of the work and advised Ravel not to alter a note. The Quartet has been arranged for piano solo, and two pianos (four hands), by Lucien Garban; and for piano duet (four hands) by Maurice Delage. (Durand.)

Ravel's next work for a chamber ensemble was the *Introduction et Allegro* for Harp, accompanied by a quartet of strings, flute and clarinet. This Septet, composed in 1906, was probably written as an exercise or test piece for the Paris Conservatoire, and was not even included in the composer's own catalogue of his complete works. It is really a miniature concerto for harp, and was first performed at a semi-private concert (Cercle Musical) with Micheline Kahn as soloist on February 22, 1907. It is an agreeable minor work, but does not call for any special comment. It has been arranged for piano solo, piano duet and two pianos. (Durand.)

The *Piano Trio* (violin, 'cello and piano) on the other hand is one of Ravel's most important and original compositions. Since 1908 it had been among his projects, but it was not until 1914 that he started seriously to work at it. As usual when he felt the need for solitude, he left Paris at the end of 1913 and retired to St. Jean-de-Luz where he could work in peace without fear of being disturbed, especially in the off-season. And so we find him writing to Mme Casella on March 21, 1914: " I am working at the *Trio* in spite of the cold and stormy weather, rain and hail." By the end of the month the first movement was finished, but a little later he writes to Mme Godebska that he can think of nothing but the piano concerto, *Zaspiak-Bat*, he was planning to write on themes derived from Basque folk-lore. The project was soon abandoned, however (see Chapter IV), and by the summer he was working again at the *Trio,* although, in a letter to Mme Casella dated July 21, 1914, he complains that " in spite of the fine weather, for the last three weeks the *Trio* has made no progress and I am disgusted with it. Today, however, I have decided that it's not too nauseating. . . and the carburettor is now repaired."

A fortnight later the outbreak of war stimulated Ravel to redouble his efforts to finish the *Trio* so that he would be free to volunteer for military service, and on August 4 he wrote in great agitation to Delage: " If you only knew how I am suffering. From morning to night I am obsessed with one idea that tortures me . . . if I leave my poor old mother, it will surely kill her. . . But so as not to think of all this, I am working—yes, working with the sureness and lucidity of a madman. At the same time I get terrible fits of depression and suddenly find myself sobbing over the sharps and flats! "

But on August 29 he wrote to Jacques Durand to tell him the *Trio* was ready and asking where he should send it. Considering the conditions under which the work was composed, one can only marvel at its perfection and apparently unruffled equilibrium—with the possible exception of the last movement which shows some signs of nervous tension, although it is exultant and not at all tragic. But this is only another example of Ravel's determination to keep his music uncontaminated by any infiltration of personal feelings—a faculty he shares to some extent with his illustrious predecessor, Mozart.

The *Trio* is in four movements: *Modéré*; *Pantoum* (assez vif); *Passacaille* (Très large); and *Final* (animé).

The opening theme, described by Ravel as "Basque in colour", is announced on the piano and then repeated by the strings in unison:

Ex. 36

The rhythm, harmony and type of melody are all characteristic of the composer, and the initial rhythm dominates the movement, which is in fairly free sonata form.

The second movement is described as a "Pantoum", a poetic form sometimes used by Baudelaire and said to be of Malay origin, in which the second and fourth lines of one stanza become the first and third in the next, though this procedure is not, and hardly could be, strictly applied here. A feature of this movement is the combination of binary and ternary rhythms in the middle section. While the strings continue in 3/4, playing the main theme in quavers, the piano announces a new subject, in spaced chords of a chorale-like nature, in 4/2, thus:

Ex. 37

The positions are then reversed, the 4/2 theme going to the strings while the piano plays the 3/4 quaver figure. The construction is ingenious and the writing extremely effective in this brilliant movement. Contrast is provided by the soberly classical *Passacaille* that follows the *Pantoum*, the basic theme being announced in the piano left hand and repeated on the 'cello and violin in that order. After some transformations and elaborations of the theme, the short movement ends with the theme of the Passacaglia being announced in reverse order, first by the violin, then by the 'cello and lastly by the piano. The formal construction and consistent tonality create an impression of dignity and repose which is soon dispersed by the dazzling display of fireworks provided in the *Final*, written throughout in 5/4 and 7/4. Trills, artificial harmonics, arpeggios and double-stops abound in the strings, while the piano pursues a more or less independent but equally animated course of its own. It would not be too fanciful to see in this variant of the main theme:

Ex. 38

an allusion to the theme of the first movement (see Ex. 36), but there is no deliberate cyclic formation, such details merely serving to stress the unity of the composition as a whole. The emphasis in this movement, and indeed throughout the work, is on colour and contrasts in timbre and rhythmic variety, and the problem which Ravel set himself in composing a Trio for piano and strings, whose tone colours he always felt to be incompatible, has here been triumphantly resolved. For this reason alone, apart from the intrinsic musical interest of the work, the Trio in A must be considered a model of its kind and an outstanding example of how ingenuity and inspiration combined can breathe fresh life into the most refractory forms of instrumental combination.

The only reproach that could be levelled against the Trio is its excessive difficulty, which makes it almost impossible for amateurs to perform. Many of Ravel's works are open to the same reproach, and the tendency always to over-elaborate and pile ingenuity on ingenuity is a fault which prevents his music from making a direct appeal to the average unsophisticated listener. It was this, too, that led " Les Six " in the 1920's to criticize Ravel's " *écriture artiste* " as being artificial and lacking in spontaneity, while Erik Satie used to say that " Ravel puts in all the punctuation but forgets to write any music underneath ". Nevertheless, the *Piano Trio* must be counted as one of the composer's most successful achievements and a very notable contribution to twentieth-century chamber music, although Ravel himself used to say, modestly: " C'est du Saint-Saëns." It was first performed on January 28, 1915, by Georges Enesco, Alfredo Casella and the 'cellist Feuillard, and is dedicated to André Gédalge, with whom Ravel, like so many other distinguished musicians of his generation and after, studied composition at the Paris Conservatoire. An arrangement exists for piano duet (four hands). (Durand.)

Almost as if in answer to the criticism I have just quoted and to show that he, too, could if need be write in the " *dépouillé* " or barebone, " wrong-note " style affected by the neoclassicists in the twenties, Ravel's next chamber work was the *Sonata for Violin and 'Cello*, composed in 1922. The asperities and angularities of this controversial work created something of a scandal at the time, and caused many of Ravel's admirers to revise their opinion of the composer of *Daphnis* and the *Rapsodie Espagnole*. Gone are the scintillating sonorities and rich texture of the *Piano Trio*; the solo violin and 'cello are now exposed, naked and unadorned, in a pitiless two-part counterpoint, vying with one another in the execution of perilous acrobatics and almost perpetually in motion; antagonists frequently, rather than partners.   No concessions are made to either instrument; at times the style is almost percussive.   Mme Jourdan-Morhange, who studied the Duo Sonata with the composer and gave the first performance with Maurice Maréchal in 1922, tells us* that Ravel attached great importance to obtaining a correct balance between the different sonorities of the two instruments, and found that the accompaniment figuration in the 'cello generally needs to be made more prominent than is usually the case, as it supplies the harmonic substructure on which the whole edifice depends.   He considered the Sonata marked a turning-point in the evolution of his career, with its abandonment of harmony in favour of melodic line.   The *Sonata* (originally christened *Duo*) is in four movements: (1) *Allegro*; (2) *Très Vif*; (3) *Lent*; (4) *Vif*.   If is dedicated: " To the memory of Claude Debussy."

(1). The theme is announced by the 'cello in the treble over a simple arpeggio figure on the violin, harmonically ambiguous owing to an alternating C sharp and C natural.   The position is then reversed and the two instruments pursue a closely knit argument with scarcely a rest till the end of the movement.

(2) A rapid scherzo-like movement, with alternating *pizzicati* and *arco* passages, many of them bi-tonal.

(3) A calm eight-bar melody, not unlike the theme of the *Passacaille* in the *Trio*, announced by the 'cello alone is taken up by the violin and soon leads to a heated argument with both instruments playing *fortissimo* in their highest registers with some fiercely discordant clashes.   At the end peace is restored.

(4) The long final movement bristles with every kind of difficulty and is perhaps the harshest of the four; one has the impression of an epic struggle being conducted without mercy on either side.   Ravel has nowhere come nearer to complete atonality; there is even an almost complete twelve-note row:

* *Ravel et Nous*, pp. 180-188.   Ed. du *Milieu du Monde*, Geneva, 1945.

However, the movement, and with it the *Sonata*, ends on a chord of C major.

As Ravel said, it marked a turning point in his evolution, for in none of the later works shall we find the same opulent harmonic texture and iridescent colours as those displayed in, for example, *Daphnis* or *L'Heure Espagnole* or even *Gaspard de la Nuit*. The *Chansons Madécasses*, as we have seen, strike a new note of quasi-barbarism and a greater economy of means, and in the *Violin and Piano Sonata* this *dépouillement* is carried to still greater lengths. Not only is the mood less aggressive, but the style of writing is simpler and the texture more transparent. Especially noticeable is the extreme independence of the parts which results at times in some curious sonorities.

The composition of this Sonata gave Ravel a great deal of trouble and took him four years, from 1923 to 1927, to complete, though this may be partly accounted for by the fact that he was engaged at the same time on the composition of *L'Enfant et les Sortilèges*, a work, incidentally, which shows him in a very different light and is poles apart from the *Sonata* in feeling and style. It is said that he had planned the general form of the first movement even down to the number of bars, key changes, modulations, etc., long before he had any idea of what the musical content was going to be. This, of course, is typical of Ravel's approach to composition, which meant, for him, a canvas to be filled, and some particular technical problem to be solved in every work he undertook. In this instance he wished to see how far it would be possible to write a concerted work allowing the maximum independence to both instruments: " It was this independence I was aiming at ", he declared, " when I wrote a Sonata for violin and piano, two incompatible instruments whose incompatibility is emphasized here, without any attempt being made to reconcile their contrasted characters." (B.S.) The result is a work which has no emotional or decorative content at all and must be counted as one of Ravel's most purely cerebral compositions, despite the excursion into Jazzland in the second movement.

Dedicated to Hélène Jourdan-Morhange, the *Violin Sonata* has three movements: (1) *Allegretto*; (2) *Blues* (moderato); (3) *Perpetuum mobile* (allegro).

(1) A dry little theme is first announced by the piano and repeated in a slightly different form and in a different key by the violin:

Ex. 40

This is soon answered by a short, *staccato*, strongly accented little phrase rapped out by the piano and presently echoed by the violin. The piano writing is bare, consisting in places merely of sequences of open fifths or major sevenths, with more than a hint of Satie's elliptical harmonies, especially in the final cadence which recalls *Socrate*.

(2) The title here ("Blues") speaks for itself—another example of Ravel's preoccupation with jazz rhythms (cf. the foxtrot in *L'Enfant et les Sortilèges* and the middle section in the *Concerto for the Left Hand*). Violin and piano give an excellent, if somewhat sophisticated, imitation of saxophone and guitar, and the characteristic, morbidly nostalgic atmosphere of the blues is enhanced by the acid harmonies and perverse contortions in which both instruments indulge. Ravel always insisted that the *staccato* chords with which the piano accompanies the violin's first entry should not be played quietly and unobtrusively, but on the contrary should give the impression of metallic strings being plucked by the fingers, imposing an implacable rhythm with no suggestion of *rubato*. There is no doubt that this movement, if played as the composer directed, can be extremely effective.

(3) In this brilliant *Perpetuum mobile*, which is introduced by a repetition of the little *staccato* phrase occurring in the first movement, the violin takes the lead and without a bar's rest from beginning to end embarks on a breath-taking display of pyrotechnics to which the piano lends a somewhat grudging support, harking back from time to time to the theme of the *Blues*, or supplying a few spiky harmonies as an undercarriage to the rushing flight of its partner in this musical marathon.

The *Sonata* was given its first performance by Georges Enesco and the composer at the Salle Erard on May 30, 1927. (Durand.)

Dating from the same period, 1924, and providing further evidence of Ravel's interest in virtuosity for its own sake, is the *Tzigane* dedicated to the Hungarian violinist Jelly d'Aranyi who with H. Gil-Marchex at the piano gave the first performance in London on April 26, 1924, having had only two days in which to study it. The composer described it briefly as " a virtuoso piece in the style of a Hungarian Rhapsody "; on the title-page it is described as " Rapsodie de Concert ". It is everything that its name implies, a virtuoso piece calculated to tax the skill and bravura of even the most accomplished technician, but is at the same time an extremely clever *pastiche* of the authentic tzigane style. In writing it Ravel took as his model the 24 *Caprices* of Paganini which he asked Mme Morhange to play to him while he was composing it.

Originally written for violin with piano (or " lutheal ") accompaniment, it was orchestrated by Ravel the same year for Jelly d'Aranyi to play with the Colonne orchestra (November 30, 1924). The instrumentation is as follows: 2 fl., 2 ob., 2 cl., 2 bn., 2 horns, 2 trp., triangle, glockenspiel, cymbal, harp and strings. (Durand.)

Before closing the chapter of Chamber music, mention should be made of a little *Berceuse* on the name of Gabriel Fauré for violin and piano, composed for the special number of *La Revue Musicale* devoted to Fauré and published in 1922. Arrangements exist for piano solo, piano duet, 'cello and piano, flute and piano. (Durand.)

4. ORCHESTRAL WORKS

We come now to a field in which Ravel was an undisputed master—the orchestra. In view of this fact, it seems somewhat paradoxical that so few of his works were written originally for orchestra. If we exclude the Ballet *Daphnis et Chloë* and the two operas, there are only three purely symphonic works (he never wrote a symphony) originally scored as such —the *Rapsodie Espagnole*, *La Valse* and *Boléro*. On the other hand, many of his piano works exist in an orchestral version, while he also orchestrated works by other composers. Among these may be cited *Menuet Pompeux* by Chabrier, *Danse* and *Sarabande* by Debussy, and *Tableaux d'une Exposition* by Mussorgsky. Unpublished orchestrations include *Prélude du Fils des Etoiles* by Erik Satie and (in collaboration with Stravinsky) *La Khovantschina* by Mussorgsky.

Ravel came at a time when the art of instrumentation had been brought to the highest pitch of refinement by Debussy, and of opulence by Rimsky-Korsakov and Richard Strauss. Yet he contrived to gild the already gilded lily with a fresh coat of dazzling veneer and extract from the almost limitless resources of the twentieth-century orchestra new and unheard sonorities and hitherto untried effects. He was perhaps the last exponent of what might be called the phosphorescent school of orchestration, though his scoring, in comparison to Debussy's glitters rather than glows. Its edges are sharper, its timbres more incisive. He had a fondness, too, for using instruments in unfamiliar registers, following here the example of Stravinsky; but no composer ever had a finer ear for instrumental balance or for rare and subtle combinations of timbre. All his orchestral effects, in fact, are calculated with meticulous precision and depend for their realization on the most faithful observance by the conductor of the indications marked in the score. All that Ravel demanded from his interpreters was that they should play or sing the notes as written and not indulge in any " personal " interpretation of their own. His orchestral scores are as highly organized as a piece of intricate machinery and as delicately balanced; nothing is left to chance or to the caprice of the individual player or conductor. In this context the remark attributed to Stravinsky about the " Swiss watchmaker " is seen to be apposite in so far as it is a tribute to Ravel's consummate craftsmanship, to which there would seem to be no parallel in the history of music, the two exceptions that spring to mind being Mozart and Igor Stravinsky himself. It was Stravinsky who later gave the *coup de grâce* to the type of orchestration perfected by Debussy and Ravel; after the *Sacre* there was no more room for nostalgic Spanish rhapsodies or languorous evocations of Mallarméan preciosities. From now on orchestral sound is modelled in the block; the sculptor's chisel has replaced the etcher's needle or the painter's brush, while the delicately graded palette of the Impressionists is discarded in favour of a cruder and more sharply contrasted gamut of orchestral colours. What was predicted by Cocteau in 1918*—" We may hope soon for an orchestra where there will be no caressing strings; only a rich choir of woodwind, brass and percussion "—has, in fact, come to pass as the result of a changing aesthetic and a revulsion on the part of both musicians and the public against " music in which one lies and soaks ", to quote Cocteau again. Be this as it may, one can only be thankful that Debussy and Ravel were able to enrich our musical heritage with works of lasting beauty which are at the same time masterpieces of scoring and an object lesson in the art of instrumentation.

If we except his early unpublished Overture *Shéhérazade* (1898), Ravel's first symphonic work for full orchestra was the *Rapsodie Espagnole*, composed in 1907. He wrote it in a month, and at one stroke revealed himself a master of the orchestra, that " nervous and feline orchestra ", of which Roland-Manuel speaks, " whose transparency, clarity and vigour are exemplary and the quality of whose sound, dry but at the same time as smooth as silk, is so characteristic of Ravel. No other composer's instrumentation shows *tutti* so sharply defined or

* In *Cock and Harlequin*.

more delicate *piani*. A geometer of mystery, Ravel knows how to weigh the most imponderable substance of sound on the most sensitive and most accurate scales in the world ".*
The *Rapsodie* is in four parts: (1) *Prélude à la Nuit*; (2) *Malagueña*; (3) *Habanera*; (4) *Feria*. It is dedicated: " à mon cher maître Charles de Bériot."

(1) *Très Modéré*. The movement is built on a simple *motif* of four descending quavers: F, E, D, C·sharp, heard first on the strings and then on the woodwind and horns. This is presently combined with another theme that establishes the Spanish atmosphere, the orchestral colour being applied with delicate brush strokes, as it were. A cadenza for two solo clarinets is echoed a few bars later by two solo bassoons while the divided violins trill and perform arpeggios in harmonics in the highest register. The creeping *motif* returns on the strings and the movement dies away on a mysterious chord whispered by the 'cellos and basses divided and softly accented by two notes sounded *ppp* on the celesta. A feature of this movement is that its range of dynamic intensity lies entirely between *ppp* and *mezzo forte*.

(2) *Assez Vif*. (For a malagueña " assez modéré " would have been more usual, and Ravel replaces the customary 3/8 by a 3/4.) The theme proper is sounded by the trumpet, introduced by a little triplet figure on the sarrusophone. The rhythm is strongly marked and a climax is reached in a *tutti* employing a full percussion section, including castanets. Towards the end the four-note theme of the first movement is heard again *pianissimo* and the malagueña, as if exhausted, dies away, the basses marking the rhythm quietly to the end.

(3) *Assez lent et d'un rythme las*. This is the famous *Habanera* which Debussy was accused of having plagiarized in *Soirées dans Grenade* (see Chapter VII). Although written in 1895 (a date which, in view of the controversy referred to, Ravel was careful to indicate at the beginning of this movement in the *Rapsodie*), the *Habanera*, especially in its orchestral dress, remains one of Ravel's happiest inspirations. The subtle

* *Ravel*. Collection " Leurs Figures ". Ed. Gallimard, Paris.

rhythm, with the first beat held in suspense and the ingeniously contrived pedal point of C sharp appearing in every department of the orchestra and relentlessly maintained throughout (compare the B flat pedal in *Le Gibet*) make this movement irresistibly appealing, its effect being immeasurably enhanced by the marvellous instrumentation.

(4) *Assez animé*. The most extended movement of the suite, the *Feria* or *Fête*, is perhaps the most superficially brilliant. The spirit of the " fiesta " is conveyed by a sort of frenzied animation, with which the orchestra is convulsed, the movement consisting of a series of climaxes and anti-climaxes contrived with consummate skill and making great demands on the players' virtuosity. A luminous, scintillating tableau of Iberian exuberance, and one of the most forthright and uninhibited pages in the whole of Ravel's *œuvre*, the *Feria* brings the *Rapsodie* to an end in a blaze of colour and sound as brilliant as anything to be found in the whole repertory of the twentieth-century orchestra. And yet, from a purely musical point of view, Debussy's excursion into the same field in his *Iberia* is more rewarding in so far as it seems to penetrate more deeply beneath the surface, and to be animated by a warmer and more truly imaginative and poetic insight into the nature of the experience and sensations to be conveyed in purely musical terms. In other words, *Iberia* has a magic quality about it, an enveloping aura of sensuous beauty that transports us into a world of " *luxe, calme et volupté* " that is not perhaps evoked with quite the same intensity of emotion and imagination in the *Rapsodie Espagnole*. Nevertheless this work is a perfect example of Ravel's consummate craftsmanship, and reveals him as one of the great modern masters of the orchestra.

The *Rapsodie* was first performed under the direction of Edouard Colonne on March 19, 1908. The instrumentation is as follows: 2 fl., 2 picc., 2 ob., cor anglais, 2 cl., bas cl., 3 bn., sarrusophone, 3 trp., 3 trb., tuba, 4 kettledrums, side-drum, cymbals, triangle, tambourine, castanets, drum, gong, xylophone, celesta, 2 harps and strings. Arrangements exist for piano solo, piano duet and two pianos. (Durand.)

It was in 1906 that Ravel first conceived the idea of writing a symphonic poem which would be a kind of apotheosis of the Viennese waltz and to which he gave the provisional title of *Wien*. It was not, however, until after the 1914 war that Ravel was able to carry out this project, thanks to Serge de Diaghilev, who suggested to the composer, while he was convalescing after the war at Mégève in 1919, that he should turn the music he was planning to write on this theme into a ballet. Ravel accepted with enthusiasm the commission, and set to work on his score, which was completed early in the following year. For some reason, which has never been satisfactorily explained, Diaghilev refused to produce the work on the pretext that it did not lend itself to a choreographic interpretation. Ravel was deeply offended and from that moment broke off all relations with Diaghilev, with whom he had been, since *Daphnis et Chloë*, on amicable terms. Five years later, when the two men met at Monte Carlo on the occasion of the *première* of *L'Enfant et les Sortilèges*, Ravel not only refused to shake hands with Diaghilev but, according to Serge Lifar, challenged him to a duel. The encounter never took place, but the breach between them was never healed.

Ravel himself gives the following account of the circumstances in which *La Valse* (the original title *Wien* was no longer permissible after the 1914 war) came to be written and of what he had in mind when writing it: " After *Le Tombeau de Couperin* the state of my health prevented me from working for some time. When I started to compose again it was only to write *La Valse*, a choreographic poem the idea of which had come to me before I wrote the *Rapsodie Espagnole*. I had intended this work to be a kind of apotheosis of the Viennese waltz, with which was associated in my imagination an impression of a fantastic and fatal kind of Dervish's dance. I imagined this waltz being danced in an imperial place about the year 1855. This work, which I had intended to be essentially choreographic, has so far only been staged at the Antwerp theatre and at Mme Rubinstein's season of ballets." (B.S.) The score is prefaced by the following note, evidently intended as a stage direction: "Through whirling clouds can be glimpsed now and again waltzing couples. The mists gradually disperse, and at letter A (in the score) a huge ballroom is revealed filled with a great crowd of whirling dancers. The stage grows gradually lighter. At the *fortissimo* at letter B the lights in the chandeliers are turned full on. The scene is an imperial palace about 1855."

La Valse occupies in Ravel's *œuvre* a somewhat similar position to that of *La Mer* in Debussy's. Both works are in a sense untypical of their composers; here all restraint seems to have been thrown aside, and in place of the delicate, impressionistic brushwork of, say, *L'Après-midi d'un Faune* or *Ma Mère l'Oye*, we are treated to an exhibition of full-blooded romanticism that reminds us of the symphonic poems of Liszt or Richard Strauss. In the case of *La Valse*, however, it is obvious that Johann rather than Richard has been the source of the composer's inspiration. Some critics, including Roland-Manuel, profess to see in *La Valse* an expression of personal anguish or premonition, a nightmarish vision—in a word, a *danse macabre*. Others take a more objective view and see the work as a study in the art of creating a whole symphonic poem out of a brief germ-phrase subjected to all kinds of subtle rhythmic transformations and carried on the crest of successive *crescendi* to a frenzied, ecstatic climax. Certain it is, in any case, that from the mysterious opening bars in which a fragmentary wisp of waltz rhythm emerges bit by bit from the confused growlings and mutterings of the muted double-basses to the last in which the whole orchestra is unleashed in an orgy of triumphant (or is it despairing?) frenzy, the effect of this dynamic music is overwhelming. The tension and suspense created in the hearer, as with *Boléro*, is largely physical, and it is perhaps not altogether a coincidence that it is by these two works that Ravel is most widely known to the general public.

The instrumentation is as follows: 2 fl., picc., 2 ob., cor anglais, 2 cl., bass cl., 2 bn., double-bn., 4 horns, 3 trp., 2 trb., tuba, 3 kettledrums, triangle, tambourine, drum, side-drum, cymbals, castanets, gong, glockenspiel, *crotales*, 2 harps, strings.

Arrangements exist for piano solo, piano duet and two pianos. (Durand.) Dedicated to Misia Sert, *La Valse* was first performed in the concert-room at a Lamoureux concert conducted by Camille Chevillard on December 12, 1920, and, as a ballet, during the Ida Rubinstein season at the Paris Opéra on November 20, 1928, conducted by Walter Straram.

5. STAGE WORKS: BALLETS AND OPERAS

1. *Ballets*

WHILE several of Ravel's compositions, as we have seen, provided music for ballets to which they were adapted subsequently—e.g. *Ma Mère l'Oye, Adélaïde ou le Langage des Fleurs, Le Tombeau de Couperin* and *La Valse*, two of his best-known scores were composed expressly for dancing and were first heard in that form. These are: *Daphnis et Chloë* and *Boléro*.

Ravel was engaged on the composition of *Daphnis* for two years—from 1909 to 1911. The work was commissioned by Serge de Diaghilev and interpreted by Karsavina, Nijinsky and Bolm, with choreography by Fokine and décors by Bakst. Monteux conducted the first performance on June 18, 1912, during the Russian Ballet's Paris season. Ravel has given the following account of his intentions in composing this ballet: " *Daphnis et Chloë*, a choreographic symphony in three parts, was commissioned by the Director of the Russian Ballet Company. My intention in writing it was to compose a vast musical fresco in which I was less concerned with archaism than with reproducing faithfully the Greece of my dreams, which is very similar to that imagined and painted by French artists at the end of the eighteenth century. The work is constructed symphonically, according to a strict plan of key sequences, out of a small number of themes, the development of which ensures the work's homogeneity." (B.S.)

The creation and production of the ballet was hampered by all sorts of difficulties and misunderstandings, and at one point

Diaghilev threatened to cancel his commission and call the whole thing off. Rehearsals were well under way when Diaghilev called one day on Jacques Durand, Ravel's publisher, to inform him of his decision on the grounds that he was not satisfied with the work and would prefer not to proceed with it; and it took all Durand's powers of persuasion to make Diaghilev change his mind. Up to the last minute the atmosphere during rehearsals was stormy, with Fokine and Nijinsky at daggers drawn, quarrelling over the choreography, and Diaghilev trying to keep the peace between them. The upshot of it all was a final rupture between Diaghilev and Fokine, who left the troupe as soon as the season was over. Another cause of trouble was the difficulty the *corps de ballet* had in performing Ravel's music; Serge Lifar* records that the only way in which they could manage the 5/4 rhythm in the Finale was by saying out loud the syllables of Diaghilev's name: " Ser-guei-Dia-ghi-lev, Ser-guei-Dia-ghi-lev."

In spite of the beauty of the music and the collaboration of so many distinguished artists, *Daphnis* was not a great success, largely no doubt because it was felt that there was a lack of harmony between the music, the scenery and the choreography which could have been avoided if the composer, the producer and the interpreters had been able to agree on questions of style and presentation. For one thing Ravel's vision of ancient Greece as seen through the eyes of eighteenth-century French painters did not fit in with Diaghilev's more classical conception of Hellenic art and legend, with the result that scenically the ballet was felt to be a rather unsatisfactory compromise.

In spite of all these difficulties and misunderstandings, there was at this time no open breach between Diaghilev and Ravel; but I am unable to find any confirmation of the statement made by Mr. Serge Grigorieff in his book *Diaghilev's Ballet, 1909–1929* that Ravel was invited by Diaghilev during the winter of 1911–1912 to visit St. Petersburg and meet some Russian musicians, to whom he played extracts from the still unfinished

* *La Revue Musicale*, December 1938.

score of *Daphnis*. So far as is known—and here all Ravel's biographers are in agreement—he never went to Russia at any time, and it seems difficult to believe that what would have been for him, especially at such a time, an important incident in his life should have gone unchronicled until now. Nevertheless, it would appear that Diaghilev did on another occasion invite Ravel again to write the music for a new ballet which he was planning to produce during the war in 1917, and that Ravel, according to Lifar* accepted in the following terms:

> My dear Diaghilev,
> Confirming our conversation of yesterday, I agree to compose the music for a ballet on the subject you described to me, the scenario to be written by the Italian poet Cangiullo. The piano score must be finished by the end of 1917, and the orchestral score by April 1, 1918. Exclusive performing rights in all countries will be vested in you for a period of five years dating from the first performance. For this work I shall receive the sum of Frs. 10,000, payable as to one half on delivery of the piano score, and the remainder on delivery of the orchestral score. As regards the orchestral parts, you will come to an agreement with my publisher, M. Jacques Durand. You will retain concert performing rights, provided the ballet has already been performed in the town where the concert will take place. Yours very sincerely, Maurice Ravel.

What became of this project and whether any of the music was ever written remains a mystery; and this letter, which was discovered by Mr. Lifar among Diaghilev's papers after his death, is the only evidence that such a contract had ever been drawn up.

The scenario of *Daphnis et Chloë* is by Michel Fokine, after the Greek poet Longus, and the work is dedicated to Serge de Diaghilev. It is in three parts, and in addition to the orchestra there is a chorus (*ad lib.*).

Scene 1. A clearing on the outskirts of a sacred wood dominated by a huge rock in the form of the god Pan. A procession of young men and girls enters, bearing offerings to the nymphs whose effigies are carved at the entrance of a grotto. They

* *Loc. cit.*

dance a solemn dance. Daphnis and Chloe when they appear are surrounded respectively by the girls and young men, one of whom, the goatherd Dorcon, presses his attentions on Chloe, to the annoyance of Daphnis, who challenges him to a contest of dancing. Dorcon's " *danse grotesque* " is followed by Daphnis' " *Danse légère et gracieuse* ", and, as the winner, he is awarded a kiss from Chloe. The crowd goes off, taking Chloe with them, and Daphnis is left alone. Lycenion, a seductive young woman, appears and dances for Daphnis, who repulses her. Left alone again, Daphnis is aroused by warlike cries: pirates have invaded the island and the women are fleeing in terror. Chloe is carried off, and Daphnis, going in pursuit, finds her sandal which she has abandoned in the struggle. He falls unconscious at the entrance of the grotto, and the nymphs come down from their pedestal and dance a slow, mysterious dance. They call on the god Pan, who appears out of the clouds as darkness falls.

Scene 2. The pirates' camp. A warlike dance is in progress when Chloe is brought in and ordered by the pirate chief to dance. Afterwards she is carried off in his arms. Suddenly the atmosphere grows threatening, strange apparitions appear and under the darkening sky the huge shadow of Pan is seen silhouetted against the mountain top. Seized with panic, the pirates flee.

Scene 3. The clearing in the wood. Daphnis is still lying in front of the nymphs' grotto. Dawn is breaking; birds begin to sing and the sound of water gushing from the spring is heard. After a long symphonic interlude, Daphnis is roused by shepherds who have found Chloe safe and sound, thanks to the intervention of Pan. The old shepherd Lammon explains that it was because of his love for the nymph Syrinx that the god has saved Chloe. Daphnis and Chloe then perform a dance representing the loves of Pan and Syrinx. They fall into one another's arms amidst general rejoicing and all join in a frenzied *Bacchanale*.

The score of *Daphnis* is one of the richest in the whole repertoire of ballet and shows clearly the influence of the

Russian Ballet aesthetic with which the whole of civilized Europe was permeated in those years before the first world war. For the first time the arts of music, painting and the dance were united on a footing of equality and, thanks to Diaghilev's genius for detecting talent and his extraordinary ability to sense in what direction artistic trends of the day were moving, the Russian Ballet became the focal point of all the arts and attracted like an irresistible magnet the leading *avant-garde* musicians and painters of the day. It was therefore inevitable that Ravel should have been drawn into the magic circle, along with Stravinsky and Debussy, and equally inevitable that the Russian Ballet atmosphere should have influenced his style, however slightly, and caused him to make certain concessions to the taste of the new public he was now addressing. At times one feels the Polovtsian dances are not very far away, while in the final *bacchanale* there are unmistakable echoes of Rimsky-Korsakov's *Scheherazade*.

At the same time Ravel had no intention of allowing his music to be subservient to the dancers, but rather the other way about; nor did he have a very high opinion of Fokine's scenario. It was to underline the autonomous nature of his score, indeed, that he entitled it " *symphonie choréographique* "; Roland-Manuel even refers to it as his " Symphony in A ". It took him three years to write, in spite of the apparent spontaneity of much of the music, especially the famous " *lever du jour* ", the long symphonic interlude that introduces the third part, without doubt one of the finest pages in the whole of Ravel—the most full-blooded, the most eloquent and the most stirring evocation of Nature with its myriad voices and of the might and glory of the rising sun flooding the whole earth with warmth and light. This is wonderful, exhilarating music, and Ravel wrote nothing else like it in any other of his works. Other memorable pages in *Daphnis* are the solemn dance of the nymphs in Part I and their invocation to the god Pan; the pirates' dance in Part II, ending with the apparition of Pan; the Pan and Syrinx miming dance by Daphnis and

Chloe and the final *bacchanale* in Part III. Running through the whole ballet like a *leitmotif* is the haunting phrase, so typically Ravelian, representing the love of Daphnis and Chloe:

Ex. 41

For this ballet, which in length is Ravel's most important work, he demands a very large orchestra, the instrumentation being as follows: picc., 2 fl., fl. in G, 2 ob., cor anglais, E flat cl., 2 B flat cl., 1 bass cl., 3 bn., double-bn., 4 horns, 4 trp., 3 trb., tuba, kettledrums, side-drum, castanets, *crotales* (kind of castanet), cymbals, wind machine, bass drum, drum, tambourine, gong, triangle, celesta, glockenspiel, xylophone, 2 harps, strings (double-basses tuned down to C obbligato). Mixed chorus (off stage). There are arrangements for piano, two and four hands, and for two pianos, and two orchestral suites for performance in the concert room. (Durand.)

Boléro, Ravel's only other purely choreographic work—i.e. written originally for dancing—was composed in 1928, and first performed on November 22 the same year during the Ida Rubinstein ballet season at the Paris Opéra, conducted by Walter Straram. The circumstances which led to its composition and the composer's own attitude to the work have been described in some detail in Chapter VI (see p. 80–81) and the music is too well known to need a detailed analysis. It depends entirely for its effect on timbre and dynamics; the material is of the simplest, but the skill shown in its instrumentation and the way in which the long crescendo is contrived without the slightest variation in tempo or key, until the wonderful modulation to E major shortly before the end, make *Boléro* what it is—an orchestral *tour de force* in a class entirely by itself. The whole work is constructed, it could be said, on two sixteen-bar phrases, each divided into two sections of eight bars, thus:

Ex. 42

There is no other thematic material, but the rhythm is relent-lessly tapped out from the first bar to the last on the drum. Some unusual orchestral colour is provided by rarely used instruments such as the oboe d'amore, the E flat (sopranino) clarinet and three saxophones. The full instrumentation is as follows: 2 fl., picc., 2 ob. (1 d'amore), cor anglais, E flat cl., 2 cl. in B flat, 2 bn., double-bn., 4 horns, 3 trp., small trp. in D, 3 trb., tuba, sopranino saxophone, soprano saxophone, tenor saxophone, 3 kettledrums, 2 drums, cymbals, gong, celesta, harp and strings.

Arrangements exist for piano solo, piano duet and two pianos. (Durand.)

2. Operas

L'Heure Espagnole was Ravel's first stage work. Composed in 1907, it had its first performance at the Opéra-Comique in Paris on May 19, 1911. It was through the intermediary of Claude Terrasse (1867–1923), the light opera composer, that Ravel made the acquaintance of the Parisian poet Franc-Nohain, author of *Poèmes amorphes*, which had been set to music by Terrasse. Ravel had seen Franc-Nohain's light comedy, *L'Heure Espagnole*, at the Odéon, where it was having a successful run, and conceived the idea of setting it to music.

Its artificiality, verbal conceits, equivocal situations and, above all, its setting—a clockmaker's shop in Toledo—appealed to his imagination, while in the superficially unmusical nature of the piece he saw, as he had seen in Jules Renard's *Histoires Naturelles*, a challenge of a kind he was always ready to accept. Here, it seemed to him, was a perfect subject for an *opéra-bouffe*—the only kind of opera he was likely to want to write. Moreover his father's health was giving him some anxiety at the time, and it was largely on this account that he felt impelled to write a work which, if successful in the theatre, would give pleasure to his father during the last years of his life and prove to him that his son could be a successful composer. He therefore lost no time in setting to work—contrary to his usual practice—and completed the opera in five months. But long before he could get it produced—it took Albert Carré, Director of the Opéra-Comique, four years to make up his mind—his father died, so that his haste had been in vain.

The story has often been told that when Ravel went to play over his score to Franc-Nohain, the latter's only comment at the end was to remark dryly, after glancing at his watch: " Fifty-six minutes." And fifty-six minutes it is, of the most delightful entertainment, which needs, however, to be most carefully produced and calls for a cast and orchestra of exceptional proficiency. But it was not only the technical difficulties of the work that caused Albert Carré to hesitate over its production at the Opéra-Comique; he was afraid lest its somewhat *risqué* subject might offend his essentially *bourgeois* public. When finally the opera was mounted, it had a generally favourable reception, although, as we shall see, it aroused considerable controversy among the critics.

The scene is a humble clockmaker's shop in eighteenth-century Toledo. It is full of mechanical toys, marionettes and automata of all kinds, as well as clocks. It belongs to Torquemada and his wife Concepcion. A muleteer, Ramiro, brings in his watch to be repaired on the day when Torquemada is about to go out to wind up and regulate the town clocks. Ramiro, much to the annoyance of Concepcion, who is

looking forward to her one free day, decides to await his return. To get rid of him, Concepcion asks the muleteer to
carry up to her room one of the big grandfather clocks.
While he is gone her lover Gonzalvo enters, and she has the
idea of concealing him in another clock, which she then asks
Ramiro to carry up and to bring the other down again. While
Concepcion is upstairs, another of her admirers, Don Inigo
Gomez, a portly and pompous personage, comes in and, for a
joke, conceals himself in the empty clock Ramiro has just
brought down. Concepcion returns in a great state of agitation, and Ramiro offers once more to bring down the clock
with Gonzalvo in it and carry up the one in which Don Inigo
is hiding. Ramiro, of course, is unaware all the time that there
is anyone in the clocks, but the ease with which he transports
such weighty objects fills Conception with admiration.
Finally, when both clocks have been brought down, she asks
the muleteer if he would like to go up to her room again, and
to his naïve query, " Which clock this time? ", she answers
simply: " Without a clock." When Torquemada comes back,
he finds Gonzalvo and Don Inigo in his shop, the latter trying
vainly to extricate himself from his self-imposed prison. The
old clockmaker seizes the opportunity of making his visitors
buy the clocks in which they seem to be so interested—which,
in the circumstances, they can scarcely refuse to do. Meanwhile Concepcion and Ramiro re-appear, and help Torquemada and Gonzalvo to pull Don Inigo out of the clock in
which he is still imprisoned. The five of them then address
the public in a satirical Quintet, citing the moral of Boccaccio:
" There comes a moment in the pursuit of love when the muleteer has his turn! "—and the curtain falls. It is perhaps not
only a coincidence that this ending should recall inevitably
the finale of another, even more famous, *dramma giocoso*.

L'Heure Espagnole follows no formal design; the music
throughout is conditioned by the text, each of the twenty-one
scenes growing naturally out of the preceding one, while
the music comments on and underlines the action. The characters for the most part express themselves in a kind of *quasi*

parlando; but the dandified and foppish Gonzalvo is given some set arias in which to exhibit his command of *bel canto*, notably an eloquent *habanera*. There are no *leitmotivs*, but each character is presented in an appropriate musical dress, with many touches of humour. The orchestration throughout is masterly, abounding in novel effects and strange new sonorities. Especially remarkable is the orchestral prelude, in which Ravel displays an almost uncanny ingenuity in evoking the ticking of clocks and the whirring and creaking of the mechanical toys with which the shop is filled. The clocks all strike a different hour; a mechanical cock crows; an automaton sounds his little trumpet; marionettes strut and turn their little hurdy-gurdies, and an artificial bird twitters and trills, all this forming a marvellous symphony of brittle, inhuman sounds. The trumpet is imitated by the horn, the marionettes' musical box by the celesta, the cock's crow by the sarrusophone deprived of its mouthpiece, and when Ramiro speaks of his mules the xylophone imitates the click-clack of their hooves.

In the pages that follow the clockmaker's charming but inconstant wife, the muleteer who is so willing to carry out her commands but who " has no conversation ", the unenterprising lover who prefers to express his passion by singing serenades, the elderly beau whose ardour is handicapped by his portly physique, and the shrewd clockmaker with an eye to the main chance go through their motions of stock characters in the tradition of the *commedia del' arte* and provide the composer with perfect material for an *opera buffa* in which he is free to indulge in every musical artifice, unhampered by the need to treat his characters as anything other than puppets without a soul. Ravel rises to the occasion, and the result is fifty-six minutes of dazzling vocal and orchestral pyrotechnics, a *tour de force* which for sheer virtuosity is without a parallel in the history of the operatic stage.

The orchestration is as follows: picc., 2 fl., 2 ob., 2 cl., bass cl., 2 bn., double bn., 4 horns, 2 trp., 3 trb., *tuba contrebasse,* kettledrums, battery, celesta, 2 harps, strings. (Durand.)

It is a curious comment on the state of musical taste and

appreciation in France at that time that *L'Heure Espagnole*
makes a much greater appeal to modern audiences than it
apparently did to the public, and even the critics, in the year
1911. As usual, Pierre Lalo in *Le Temps* (May 28, 1911) was
uncompromising in his hostility to Ravel's latest score. " His
characters could not be more lacking in life and soul . . . the
declamation reminds one of that in *Pelléas*, repeated on a gramophone turning at an excessively slow speed. Everything is
stilted and glacial—small, petty, narrow, wizened . . . like
china dolls or figures on a musical clock. That M. Ravel owes
much to Debussy is manifest. But the spirit of his music and
of his art is entirely different. M. Debussy is all sensibility;
M. Ravel all insensibility."

Emile Vuillermoz, in *S.I.M.* (June 15, 1911) speaks of " an
adventure that leads nowhere ", and suggests that Ravel would
do better to exercise his talents of illusion and leave it to others
to arouse laughter by means of facile instrumental tricks ".
Criticizing the *quasi parlando* recitative, he accuses Ravel of
" stripping the language of music not only of its international
and universal qualities, but of its simple humanity, transforming it into a purely local and personal idiom whose
inflexions are without charm or meaning, except to the
initiated ".

Henri Ghéon, on the other hand, writing in *La Nouvelle
Revue Française* of July 1, 1911, takes up a different attitude,
stressing the fact that Ravel's " innate and most characteristic
gift, which he cultivates, is his ability to transmute into music
the least musical subjects. The charm and gaiety of this music,
in my opinion, is essentially vocal; in spite of all the ingenuity
lavished on harmonic texture and combinations of timbre,
I maintain that the orchestra here is too much in evidence and
too loud, and that this would have been a good opportunity
to react against the massive orchestration which, ever since
Wagner, has been crushing us; what I would like to see would
by a lyrical comedy by M. Ravel, with a lively little band consisting of strings, a bassoon, two flutes, a triangle and, if you
like, a drum. No one is better equipped than he to lighten

our music materially, just as he has lightened it spiritually and intellectually ".

The " lyrical comedy " referred to might well be taken as a prophetic allusion to *L'Enfant et les Sortilèges* which was, in fact, to be Ravel's only other contribution to the lyric stage. Indeed, the terms in which the composer speaks of his new work seem almost an echo of the advice proffered by Ghéon in the passage we have quoted: " The preoccupation with melody which predominates throughout is accounted for by the subject which it amused me to treat in the spirit of an American operetta. Mme Colette's libretto justified this licence in dealing with a fairy story. Here, it is singing that must come first. The orchestra, although some instrumental virtuosity is not excluded, nevertheless remains in the background." (B.S.)

Some account of Ravel's collaboration with Colette has already been given in Chapter IV (p. 56-9). The surprising thing is that this somewhat unnatural partnership should have been so successful in its final results. But Colette's typical mixture of naïvety and sophistication appealed to Ravel, who saw opportunities of doing ingenious and amusing things with animals and insects and inanimate objects and fairies with which the naughty child is involved in this story of bewitchment and magical transformations. In spite of the work's undoubted charm and the consummate skill with which the composer has met the challenge inherent in such a text, I do not share the view expressed in some quarters that this is one of Ravel's major achievements. It is brilliantly clever; it even has an undercurrent of sentiment such as is rarely found in Ravel's works; but it is fundamentally, I feel, a pretext for some dazzling musical legerdemain, brilliantly executed and faultlessly presented, yet, in the last resort, more " *Malerei* " than " *Empfindung* ".

L'Enfant et les Sortilèges, described as a " *fantaisie lyrique en deux parties* ", was first performed at Monte Carlo on March 21, 1925, conducted by Victor de Sabata; and it had its Paris *première* a year later at the Opéra-Comique, on February 1,

1926, under Albert Wolff. In the first Tableau the action takes place in the child's room; in the second, in the garden. In the first scene the child is in open revolt: he refuses to do his lessons, is rude to his mother, pulls the cat's tail, ill-treats the tame squirrel in its cage, upsets the kettle, breaks the teapot, lacerates the wallpaper, swings on the pendulum of the clock and finally falls exhausted into a big armchair. Gradually the room grows dark, and one by one the creatures and the furniture and all the inanimate objects come to life and scold the child for his atrocious conduct. He is surrounded by apparitions, including a terrible old man personifying arithmetic, attended by a crowd of figures, and a fairy-tale princess from the child's favourite story-book. He pleads with her not to abandon him, and says he will defend her against her enemies who want to destroy her; but as he has torn up the book, she tells him he will be powerless to help her, and the ground opens under her feet as she is dragged away by her enemies Night and Sleep. After the mad dance of the figures, which rise from the pages of the torn-up school books, the black cat appears, but refuses to play with the child. He is soon joined by a white she-cat, and together they sing their famous love duet. As they do so, the wall of the room dissolves, and the child finds himself in the garden, the scene of the second Tableau. Bats and owls, dragon-flies and frogs, trees and plants reproach the child with his cruelty and crowd round him threatening and striking him. In the scuffle the squirrel is wounded, and the now thoroughly terrified child binds up its wounded paw and then falls exhausted, calling on his mother for help. But the creatures have heard the strange word he pronounces: " *maman* ", and are filled with wonder and consternation. With pity and gratitude too; for has he not bandaged the wounded squirrel? They think he is going to die, and carry him to the house, leaving him standing and holding out his arms to his mother who appears in the lighted doorway. Once more he calls softly: " *Maman!* " and the curtain falls.

In addition to the child and his mother, there are solo parts for the Bergère, the China Teacup, the Fire, the Princess, the

She-Cat, the Dragon-fly, the Nightingale, the Bat, the Owl, the Squirrel, a Shepherdess, a Shepherd, the Armchair, the Grandfather Clock, the Wedgwood Teapot, the Little Old Man, the Black Cat, a Tree and a Tree-frog. (Many of these roles can be doubled in performance.) There is also a chorus of children's voices representing some of the animals and furniture.

Although a large orchestra is used, the scoring is for the most part transparent, with the emphasis on melody. A great deal of the writing is, owing to the nature of the subject-matter, frankly descriptive—the ticking of the clock, the croaking of the frogs, the mewing of the cats, the staccato recitation of the figures out of the arithmetic book, etc., may be cited as examples—and once again Ravel, in the duet between the Wedgwood Teapot and the China cup, makes use of jazz rhythms, choosing this time the foxtrot (see his correspondence with Colette on this subject on p. 58). The Cup and Teapot are made to sing the most extraordinary gibberish, a mixture of what is supposed to sound like Chinese and American— e.g.: " Black and costaud, black and chic; jolly fellow, I punch your nose, I knock out you, stupid chose " . . . and: " Keng-ça-fou, Mah-jong, Ca-oh-ra, Cas-ka-ra, hara-kiri, Sessue Hayaka, chi-no-a." At the same time there are passages of simple, lyrical beauty such as the child's address to the Princess, " *Toi, le cœur de la rose* . . . ", which might have come from Fauré's pen, the Waltz of the Dragon-flies and the final chorus of the animals, leading to the child's last murmured " *Maman* " on the characteristic Ravelian descending fourth, B–F sharp. (Incidentally, the unwonted vein of sentiment, bordering on sentimentality, running through this score could no doubt be attributed, in the light of what we know about Ravel's exclusive and dominating affection for his mother, to a " mother-fixation ", combined perhaps with subconscious recollections of his own childhood.)

Despite the essential simplicity and sobriety of the actual musical material, there is as much wizardry in Ravel's brilliant projection of Colette's little fantasy in terms of sound as there is in the subject-matter of the story itself. While in *L'Heure Espagnole* we are in a world of marionettes, in *L'Enfant et les Sortilèges* we are in Fairyland. In the words of Fred Goldbeck: " If everything here is exquisite and refined to the last degree, it is thanks to a gift, an act of grace, because the artist who invented this music was an Ariel by nature and could speak no other language."*

The orchestration is as follows: 2 fl., picc., 2 ob., cor anglais, E flat cl., 2 cl., bass cl., 2 bn., double bn., 4 horns, 3 trp., 3 trb., tuba, kettledrums and small kettledrum in D, triangle, drum, cymbals, bass drum, gong, whip, rattle, cheese-grater, woodblock, wind machine, *crotales*, slide-flute (*Flûte à coulisse*), xylophone, celesta, harp, *luthéal* (or piano with the strings muffled with paper to imitate a harpsichord), usual strings. (Durand.)

The opera had, on the whole, a favourable press, but Messager reproached the composer for sacrificing too much to " imitative music ", while Dézarneaux in *La Liberté* summed up his impressions as: " A lot of notes and a lot of science expended for a meagre result." The work has nevertheless established itself in the repertory of the lyric theatre and, together with *L'Heure Espagnole*, must be considered as one of the most original and characteristic manifestations of the peculiar genius of Maurice Ravel.

We have now come to the end of our detailed examination of his works—all rare in quality, even if numerically his output was relatively small—some sixty works, mostly of modest dimensions—during roughly forty-five years of active life. Ravel himself was sensitive on this point and used to say that his career had been a failure because, in comparison to Mozart for example, he had produced so little. Few composers, on the other hand, have achieved so high a percentage of flawless works by which to be remembered, a rare distinction which in itself is enough to ensure him a place of eminence in the annals of the music of our time.

* " Les Fées et les Marionettes "; *La Revue Musicale*, December 1938.

A PORTRAIT OF THE MAN

Le cœur ironique et tendre qui bat sous
Le gilet de velours de Maurice Ravel.
TRISTAN KLINGSOR

THE physical features of artists often bear a surprising resemblance to what we imagine to be the essential features of their art. Thus, the red hair and blue eyes of a van Gogh seem to live again in the fierce brush-strokes of his flaming cornfields; the aristocratic, melancholy countenance and bearing of Chopin are mirrored in almost every nostalgic bar of his Mazurkas or Nocturnes; and we should find it no less difficult to associate the elfin music of Papageno with the stocky, red-faced, choleric figure of an L. van Beethoven than to imagine, behind the turbulence of the *Eroica* or Fifth Symphonies, the elegant silhouette of a Wolfgang Amadeus Mozart. And, to come nearer our own times, who but the heavy-lidded, faun-like Claude Debussy could have written the *Prélude a l' Après-midi d'un Faune*?

With Maurice Ravel the parallelism between the physical man and his art seems even more complete. His small, taut frame, neat and precise movements, large head with its high cheek-bones, long nose and straight, tight-lipped mouth, suggest iron self-control and intellectual integrity—both qualities that are conspicuous in his music; while the dry and rather distant manner we are told he affected seems to indicate a non-emotional approach to people and things, combined with a certain fastidious reserve. The craftsman and the formalist are revealed again in the composer's dandyism— both vestimentary and intellectual: Ravel could never have been in an " unbuttoned " mood. To be correctly dressed was for him as important in its way as writing impeccable music; and he would choose a cravat as carefully as a chord. The incident of the mislaid patent leather evening shoes which delayed a concert has been related; in the reminiscences of his friends many similar instances of this sartorial punctiliousness recur, such as the occasion on which he refused to wear a friend's breast-pocket handkerchief to replace his own, which had been forgotten, because it was not marked with his own monogram. He kept a vigilant eye on trends in masculine fashions and, as an example of the importance he attached, or pretended to attach, to such things, even at times when most artists would have been otherwise preoccupied, the true story is told of his meeting a friend in the foyer of the Opéra during the first performance of *L'Heure Espagnole* and exclaiming: " Have you noticed, *mon cher*, that you and I are the only people wearing *black* dress clothes instead of the new midnight blue? "

To some extent, of course, this preoccupation with trivialities and external conventions may have been a protective barrier thrown up to discourage any attempt on the part of strangers to establish contact with the real Ravel whose inmost aspirations and ideals were his own secret. The *homme du monde* pose was useful as a protection against indiscreet attempts to penetrate behind the mask which the composer habitually wore in his dealings with the outer world. Only in the company of trusted friends was the mask discarded. Yet even those nearest to him always admitted that it was almost impossible to know his inmost thoughts or feelings. And always in his eyes there was a look that suggested some inner sadness—not near the surface, but deep down, as if to accentuate his essential loneliness. The same sadness, in fact, that underlies so much of his music, even when it is most brilliant, colouring his favourite bitter-sweet harmonies and wistful, drooping cadences. But all agree that he was the surest and most faithful of friends, loyal and generous, and full of consideration for those around him. He cultivated friendship, but there is no evidence of his ever having formed a " romantic " attachment of any kind; the only woman he ever loved seems to have been his mother. Whatever psychological complex he may have suffered from has never been satisfactorily explained.

He was full of contradictions. The solitary recluse, the " hermit of Montfort " as he was called, could also be the gayest of companions in congenial company; and Ravel was often to be seen in fashionable night-clubs and cafés in the capital. He liked entertaining his friends in the country too; but when he was composing he demanded absolute solitude. A great deal of his work was done in his head during long walks in the forest of Rambouillet or in the Bois de Boulogne; but no one ever saw him actually at work, nor were there any visible traces on his desk of manuscript paper, pens or pencils. It was, as Roland-Manuel observed, as if by depressing the keys of his piano he set in motion, by invisible means, the machinery which produced the printed page, eliminating all intermediate stages. For he used the piano freely when composing, and especially when orchestrating. Widor's *Technique de l'Orchestre moderne* was always at his hand, as well as miniature scores of the piano concertos of Saint-Saëns and the symphonic poems of Richard Strauss. His favourite composers were Mozart, Weber, Chopin, Mendelssohn, Liszt, Saint-Saëns, Borodin and Chabrier, and among his immediate contemporaries, Debussy, Stravinsky, Satie.

Although fundamentally modest in the sense that he hated to be treated as a " celebrity " and acclaimed as such in public, he had no illusions as to his own worth; he was even mortally offended when a critic ventured to assert that his piano concertos, fine though they were, were not quite on the same level as those of Mozart. He knew himself to be a highly professional artisan, the product of a long and carefully nurtured tradition; and it was this knowledge that prompted him on one occasion to say of a contemporary composer, Stravinsky: " He can take liberties I could not allow myself because he is less of a musician than I am." Ravel, indeed, was the type of artist who seems to have been created expressly to create; the

highly specialized faculty he had in him to make music left little
room for any other kind of interest or activity. That he was fully
aware of this is shown by the remark he once made to his friends
the Delages: " It's lucky that I've been able to write music,
because I don't think I could ever have done anything else."

His attitude towards his own music was completely objective; once a composition was finished, he lost interest in it
and was thinking only of the next. Each one of his works was
for him a new venture, a new problem to be tackled. But
even if the approach to each is different, and the accent is now
on virtuosity, now on simplicity—think of the contrast between, for example, *Gaspard de la Nuit* and *Ronsard à son âme*,
or between the *Chansons Madécasses* and *L'Enfant et les Sortilèges*
—a fundamental unity runs through and permeates his whole
œuvre. Ravel's fingerprints are unmistakable and would betray
him anywhere.

But the detachment of the man from his music was complete.
It was something he preferred not to discuss and upon which
he was determined not to allow his own personal feelings and
ordinary human emotions to encroach. What Baudelaire said
of Delacroix, Roland-Manuel has pointed out, is extraordinarily applicable to Ravel, especially the allusion to the " manteau
de glace recouvrant une pudique sensibilité " and the assertion
that " une des grandes préoccupations de sa vie, c'était de
dissimuler les colères de son cœur et de n'avoir pas l'air d'un
homme de génie ".

In this it could be said he was successful. In fact the extreme
sophistication of the musician was matched by the essential
simplicity of the man. No one could have been less of a
poseur. Except where music was concerned, he had the
ingenuous outlook on life of a child. Small things gave him
pleasure and excited in him wonder and surprise. He liked
children and animals and young women for their decorative
qualities, and adored mechanical toys. What he liked about
these was the illusion of life they create. " You can feel its
heart beat ", he said once of a little plush-covered bird that, on
being wound up, hopped about and pecked. The *illusion* of

life—that was perhaps more important to him than life itself, with all its mundane obligations and restrictions. It was in the free world of fantasy that the composer of *Mother Goose* and *L'Enfant et les Sortilèges* felt most at home, or in the company of the *Peacock*, the *Kingfisher* and the *Cricket*. He was not, however, by any means a miniaturist and nothing more; the *Piano Trio*, *Daphnis*, *La Valse* and the *Concerto for the Left Hand*, to name only a few examples, are there to prove the contrary. But in all he did his vision was never obscured by sentiment; he saw everything clearly and saw it whole.

Ravel has few parallels in the annals of music or, indeed, of any other art, because few artists have succeeded in detaching themselves so completely from their art. We may feel that in consequence his music is sometimes lacking in human warmth, and that there is even something glacial in the very perfection of his craftsmanship. This music may have the clarity of crystal, but the clairvoyant will seek in it in vain a clue to the ultimate mysteries of love and life and death. But although in the hierarchy of the great creators the place of Maurice Ravel is not among the Titans, the beauty and perfection of his art, and the single-minded devotion with which he served it, are sufficient guarantee that, so long as music lives, his name and works will never be forgotten.

Ex. 43

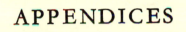

APPENDICES

APPENDICES

THE BIOGRAPHICAL SKETCH

ROLAND-MANUEL has given the following account of how this sketch came into being at the request of the artistic director of the Aeolian Co. in connexion with a series of recordings on perforated rolls to be used on the new automatic pianos, or " pianolas " as they were called. The idea was that each piece should be prefaced by a descriptive or informative note printed on a card incorporated in the roll for the information of the player—a system which had been inaugurated by Stravinsky, who was at that time interested in these mechanical reproductions. Ravel at first wanted these notes to appear in the form of an " interview " with Roland-Manuel, but in the end it was decided that the latter should take down from dictation the notes improvised by Ravel and put them into shape for his approval afterwards. This was done, but it appears the notes were never printed on the rolls and, indeed, were not published until ten years later in the special number of *La Revue Musicale* issued after the composer's death. I am now able to give the text of some general reflections on music which Ravel, at the request of Roland-Manuel, added to the " biographical sketch ", but which remained unpublished until they appeared in the *Revue de Musicologie* (Vol. XXXVIII, July 1956). In presenting them, Roland-Manuel explains that this time Ravel insisted on the " interview " form, and that therefore the text as published does not claim to be a reproduction of his actual words, although containing the essence of his thoughts.

" SOME REFLECTIONS ON MUSIC "

" I have never felt the need to formulate, either for the benefit of others or for myself, the principles of my aesthetic. If I were called upon to do so, I would ask to be allowed to identify myself with the simple pronouncements made by Mozart on this subject. He confined himself to saying that there is nothing that music cannot undertake to do, or dare, or portray provided it continues to charm and remains always music.

" I am sometimes credited with opinions which appear very paradoxical concerning the falsity of art and the dangers of sincerity. The fact is I refuse simply and absolutely to confound the *conscience* of an artist, which is one thing, with his *sincerity*, which is another. The latter is of no value unless the former helps to make it apparent. This conscience compels us to turn ourselves into good craftsmen. My objective, therefore, is technical perfection. I can strive unceasingly to this end, since I am certain of never being able to attain it. The important thing is to get nearer to it all the time. Art, no doubt, has other *effects*, but the artist, in my opinion, should have no other aim."

As this is one of Ravel's rare pronouncements on the subject of his art, it is of more than ordinary interest; furthermore it has not, so far as I am aware, until now been made available in English.

"LIGUE NATIONALE POUR LA DEFENSE DE LA MUSIQUE FRANCAISE"

" Zone des Armées." June 7, 1916.

" *To* The Committee of the National League for the Defence of French Music.

" Gentlemen,

" An enforced repose enables me at last to reply to your communication enclosing the notice and statutes of the *Ligue Nationale pour la défense de la musique française* which reached me after being considerably delayed *en route*. I beg you to excuse me for not having replied sooner, but various transfers and my active service duties have left me little leisure until now.

" Excuse me, too, for not being able to subscribe to your statutes; having studied your notice carefully I feel unable to do so.

" I naturally have nothing but praise for your *idée fixe* concerning a victory for our country, by which I, too, have been haunted ever since the outbreak of hostilities. Consequently I fully approve the ' need for action ' which has inspired the *Ligue Nationale*. I felt this ' need for action ' so keenly that it made me give up civilian life, although I was in no way obliged to do so.

" Where I am unable to follow you is when you affirm as a matter of principle that: ' the role of the art of music is economic and social '. I had never considered music, or any other art, from that point of view.

" I have nothing to say about the ' films ' you mention, or the ' gramophone records ', or the ' popular song-writers '; all that has only a remote connexion with the art of music. I grant you also your ' Viennese operettas ' which, however, are more musical and better written than works of a similar nature in this country. These, like all the rest, would appear to belong to the sphere of ' economics '.

" But I do not believe that ' in order to safeguard our national artistic inheritance ' it is necessary to ' forbid the public performance in France of works by contemporary German and Austrian composers still under copyright '.

" ' Though there can be ', as you say, ' no question, so far as we and the young generations are concerned, of repudiating the classics which are one of humanity's immortal monuments ', still less should there be any question of ' keeping out of our country for a long time ' interesting works which, in their turn, may one day become monuments, and from which, in the meantime, we may learn much that is useful.

" It would even be dangerous for French composers to ignore systematically the production of their foreign colleagues and form themselves in this way into a sort of national coterie; for then our music, at present so rich, would soon become degenerate and bogged down with academic formulae.

" The fact that M. Schoenberg, for example, is of Austrian nationality is of no importance. This does not prevent him from being a very fine musician whose very interesting researches have had a beneficial influence on some Allied composers, including our own. Moreover I am even delighted that MM. Bartók, Kodály and their disciples are Hungarian and show it so unmistakably in their works.

" In Germany, apart from M. Richard Strauss, there appear only to be composers of the second rank whose equivalent could easily be found without going outside our frontiers. But it is possible that soon some young artists may be discovered there whom we should be interested to know here.

" Moreover, I do not think it necessary that French music, regardless of its quality, should predominate in France, or that we should seek to diffuse it abroad.

" You will see, Gentlemen, that my views on many of the points raised are so different from your own as to make it impossible for me to become a member of your organization. I hope nevertheless to continue to ' act like a Frenchman ' and to ' count myself among those who will always remember '.

" I have the honour to be, Gentlemen,

" yours etc.,

" (signed) Maurice Ravel."

The question was evidently very much in Ravel's mind, for a few weeks later he returned to the charge and wrote as follows to Jean Marnold, music critic of the *Mercure de France* (whom he had already had occasion to congratulate for his article " Le Cas Wagner " [*Mercure de France*, May, 1915] opposing the movement to ban Wagner in France during the war). Marnold had asked Ravel for permission to publish the letter he had written to the Ligue (see above).

" My letter? I hesitate . . . but I believe you are right. Obviously these gentlemen are not going to publish it; it is even probable that it will not be read before the assembly. As you say, everyone will know who their supporters are, but the name and the reasons of those who protest will never be known. After all, it is true I am as well qualified as anyone to speak in the name of French music. I may not have been in the trenches; I have at least done as much to defend my country as those who have stayed in the rue d'Assas (the headquarters of the League). The dangers were not quite the same —that's the only difference.

" But we must not forget that I am a soldier and am not allowed to write anything for publication—especially as this may well become a controversial question. It is annoying, because when we come back we may be obliged to hold our tongues in the presence of a *fait accompli*. Well then! publish it without my signature; a few hints will be enough to make your readers understand the situation. . . The effect will be the same.

" What is regrettable is that these gentlemen will be able to carry on their propaganda undisturbed; the *Mercure* only appeals to an *élite*, while they will have no difficulty in winning over the public of the big dailies. . . It would really be too bad if, after having fought against the militarism of Germany today, we are to be dictated to by our own people and told what to admire and what not to. What a lot of trenches we shall have to clean out when we come back! For my part I have made up my mind to ride into the assembly at the rue d'Assas on a horse—on twelve horses! . . .

" With best remembrances, Maurice Ravel."

In the end this letter was never published, and the League failed to make much headway, the majority of disinterested composers having declined to have anything to do with it. It is amusing to recall that when in June 1919 Wagner appeared on the programme of a concert in the Jardin des Tuileries Ravel made a point of attending and applauded loudly.

(The above documents were first published in *La Revue Musicale* of December 1938.)

LIST OF WORKS IN CHRONOLOGICAL ORDER

(U, unpublished; P, piano; V, voice; Vn., violin; Vc., violoncello; O, orchestra; Op., opera; B, ballet; Ch., chorus; Orch., orchestrated)

1893. *Sérénade Grotesque*, P. (U.)
1894. *Ballade de la Reine Morte d'Aimer*, V. & P. (U.)
1894. *Le Rouet*, V. & P. (U.).
1895. *Menuet Antique*, P. (Orch.)
1895. *Un grand sommeil noir*, V. & P. (U.)
1895–96. *Sites Auriculaires*, 2 P. (U, except for *Habanera* included in *Rapsodie Espagnole*.)
1896. *Sainte*, V. & P.
1898. *Deux Épigrammes*, V. & P.
1898. *Shéhérazade*, O. (Overture.) (U.)
1899. *Pavane pour une Infante défunte*, P. (Orch.)
1899. *Si Morne*, V. & P. (U.)
1901. *Myrrha*, Rome Cantata. (U.)
1901. *Jeux d'Eau*, P.
1902. *Alcyone*, Rome Cantata. (U.)
1902–03. String Quartet.
1903. *Alyssa*, Rome Cantata. (U.)
1903. *Shéhérazade*, V. & P. or O.
1904–06. *Mélodies populaires grecques*, V. & P. (Harmonized by Ravel.)
1905. *Le Noël des jouets*, V. & P. (Orch.)
1905. *Sonatine*, P.
1905. *Miroirs*, P.
1905–06. *Introduction et Allegro*. (Harp, Str. Qt., Fl. & Cl.)
1906. *Les Grands Vents venus d'Outre-mer*, V. & P.
1906. *Les Histoires Naturelles*, V. & P. (Orch.)
1907. *Sur l'herbe*, V. & P.
1907. *Vocalise—Etude en forme d'Habanera*, V. & P.
1907. *Rapsodie Espagnole*, O.
1907. *L'Heure Espagnole*, Op.

1908. *Ma Mère l'Oye*, P. 4 hands. (Orch. & B.)

1908. *Gaspard de la Nuit*, P.

1909. *Nocturnes* (Debussy), transcribed for 2 P.

1909. *Menuet sur le nom de Haydn*, P.

1909. *Tripatos* (Gr. dance), V. & P.

1910–17. *Chants Populaires*, V. & P. (3 U.)

1910. *Prélude à l'Après-midi d'un Faune* (Debussy), transcribed for 2 P.

1911. *Valses Nobles et Sentimentales*, P. (Orch. for B. *Adélaïde*.)

1909–12. *Daphnis et Chloë*, B. (And 2 orchestral suites.)

1913. *Trois poèmes de Mallarmé*, V., P., str. qt., 2 fl., 2 cl.

1913. *Prélude*, P.

1913. *A la manière de. . .*, P.

1913. *Le Prélude du Fils des Étoiles* (Erik Satie), Orch. (U.)

1914. *Deux mélodies hébraiques*, V & P.

1914. *Trio* (Vn., Vc., P.)

1914. *Carnaval* (Schumann), Orch. (U.)

1915. *Trois Chansons*. (Ch. *a cappella*.)

1917. *Le Tombeau de Couperin*, P. (Orch. & B.)

1918. *Menuet Pompeux* (Chabrier), Orch.

1919. *Frontispice*, 2 P. (Pub. in *Feuillets d'Art*, out of print.)

1919–20. *La Valse*, O. (And B.)

1920–22. *Sonate*, Vn., Vc.

1920. *Sarabande* (Debussy), Orch.

1922. *Berceuse sur le nom de Fauré*, Vn. & P.

1922. *Tableaux d'une Exposition* (Mussorgsky), Orch.

1923. *Danse* (Tarantelle styrienne) (Debussy), Orch.

1924. *Ronsard à son âme*, V. & P.

1924. *Tzigane*, Vn. & P. (Orch.)

1920–25. *L'Enfant et les Sortilèges*, Op.

1925–26. *Chansons Madécasses*, V., P., Fl. & Vc.

1927. *Rêves*, V. & P.

1923–27. *Sonate*, Vn. & P.

1927. *Fanfare* (for B. *L'Éventail de Jeanne*).

1928. *Boléro*, O. & B.

1931. *Concerto* in D for L. H., P. & O.

1931. *Concerto* in G, P. & O.

1932. *Don Quichotte à Dulcinée*, V. & P. (Orch.)

PROJECTED WORKS, NEVER COMPLETED

In addition to *La Cloche engloutie* Ravel at one time or another had contemplated writing:

1. An opera based on Maeterlinck's *Intérieur*;
2. An opera-ballet to be called *Morgiane* (an Ali Baba story) of which he said: " Ce sera magnifique; il y aura du sang, de la volupté et de la mort . . . je ferai du Massenet. . .";
3. A work inspired by Alain-Fournier's celebrated novel, *Le Grand Meaulnes*, which he had read in hospital during the 1914 war and which, according to some, would have been in the form of a piece for 'cello and orchestra; according to others, a piano work, a kind of pendant to *Gaspard de la Nuit*;
4. A setting of the *Fioretti* of St. Francis of Assisi, in an adaptation by the Italian poet Canudo, part of which, St. Francis preaching to the birds, he had even begun to put on paper (Falla believed that the second part of the Finale of *Ma Mère l'Oye* contains some of this music);
5. *Dédale VI*, described by Ravel as an " outsider " in a letter to Mme Casella dated December 27, 1929. The allusion is obscure, and nothing is known about the work in question;
6. A piano Concerto on Basque themes *Zaspiak-Bat*;
7. *Les Chansons du Valois* (for which he had asked Jean Marnold to supply him with some documentation);
8. An *Olympia*, taken from Hoffmann's *Marchand de Sable*, some of the music for which was used in the first act of *L'Heure Espagnole*;
9. A grand opera, or " opera-oratorio " on the *Jeanne d'Arc* of Joseph Delteil. This had occupied his thoughts from 1928 onwards and he intended to write the libretto himself. He even got as far as planning the various scenes, which would have been as follows: Joan with her sheep; at the Court; meeting with the King; the siege of Orleans; capture of Orleans; the trial before the French ecclesiastics and the British officials (" sarcastic music "); the stake and death of Joan, and finally her entry into heaven.

His idea was to have the chorus massed on either side of the stage to comment on the action, and he had envisaged having two singers to represent Joan as a child and Joan as a soldier. He was familiar with Bernard Shaw's *Joan of Arc* and was so little afraid of anachronisms that he intended to introduce *Tipperary*, the *Marseillaise* and *Madelon* during the siege of Orleans. These plans he confided to Mme Morhange and Jacques de Zogheb, but of the music he intended to write it would seem that not a note was ever committed to paper.

BIBLIOGRAPHY

I. BOOKS

ACKERE, Jules van, *Maurice Ravel* (Ed. Elsevier, Brussels, 1957).

AKERET, Kurt, *Studien zum Klavierwerk von Maurice Ravel* (Zürich, 1941).

BRUYR, Jose, *Maurice Ravel, ou Le Lyrisme et les sortilèges* (Lib. Plon, Paris, 1950).

CALVOCORESSI, M. D., *Musicians' Gallery* (Faber & Faber, London, 1933).

CHALUPT, René, *Ravel au miroir de ses lettres* (Laffont, Paris, 1956).

DEMUTH, Norman, *Ravel* (Dent, London, 1947).

FARGUE, Léon-Paul, *Maurice Ravel* (Coll. " Au voilier ", Domat, 1949).

GOSS, Madeleine, *Bolero* (The life of Maurice Ravel) (Holt, New York, 1940).

JANKÉLÉVITCH, Vladimir, *Maurice Ravel* (Ed. du Seuil, Paris, 1956).

JOURDAN-MORHANGE, Hélène, *Ravel et nous* (Ed. " Le Milieu du Monde ", Geneva, 1945).

——, (in collaboration with Vlado Perlemuter) *Ravel d'après Ravel* (Ed. du Cervin, Lausanne, 1957).

LANDOWSKY, W. L. *Maurice Ravel, sa vie, son oeuvre* (Editions Ouvrières, Paris, 1950).

MACHABEY, Armand, *Maurice Ravel* (Ed. Richard-Masse, Paris, 1947).

ONNEN, Frank, *Maurice Ravel* (Amsterdam; Eng. trans. Continental Book Co., A. B. Stockholm).

ROLAND-MANUEL, *Maurice Ravel et son oeuvre* (Durand, Paris, 2nd. ed. 1926).

——, *Maurice Ravel et son œuvre dramatique* (Lib. de France, Paris, 1928).

——, *Ravel* (*Nouvelle revue critique*, Paris, 1938; revised edition, Gallimard, 1948. Eng. trans. of 1st ed., Dobson, London, 1947).

SEROFF, Victor, *Maurice Ravel* (Holt, New York, 1953).

SHERA, Frank, *Debussy and Ravel* (Oxford, 1925).
TAPPOLET, Willy, *Maurice Ravel, Leben und Werk* (O. Walter, Olten, 1950).

MAURICE RAVEL *par quelques-uns de ses familiers* (Colette, Maurice Delage, Léon-Paul Fargue, H. Jourdan-Morhange, Tristan Klingsor, Roland-Manuel, Dominique Sordet, Emile Vuillermoz, Jacques de Zogheb) (Ed. du Tambourinaire, Paris, 1939).
MAURICE RAVEL (Tony Aubin, Léon-Paul Fargue, Arthur Hoérée, Hélène Jourdan-Morhange, Georges Pioch) (Les Publications techniques et artistiques, Paris, 1945).

II. *PERIODICALS*

1. *Obituaries*

AURIC, Georges, *Maurice Ravel.* (*Nouvelles Littéraires*, December 29, 1937.)
BRUSSEL, Robert, *La mort de Maurice Ravel.* (*Le Figaro*, December 29, 1937.)
CASELLA, Alfredo, *Maurice Ravel.* (*Musica d'Oggi*, March 1938.)
DUMESNIL, René, *Maurice Ravel.* (*Mercure de France*, February 1938.)
MANTELLI, A., *Maurice Ravel.* (*La Rassegna Musicale*, Turin, 1938.)
MILHAUD, Darius, *Maurice Ravel.* (*Ce Soir*, December 29, 1937.)
ROLAND-MANUEL, *Le génie de Maurice Ravel.* (*Les Temps Présents*, January 7, 1938.)
SAMAZEUILH, G., *Maurice Ravel.* (*Le Temps*, December 29, 1937.)
VUILLERMOZ, E., *Maurice Ravel est mort.* (*Excelsior*, December 29, 1937.)
——, *Une grande figure de la musique française.* (*L'Illustration*, January 8, 1938.)

2. *General*

La Revue Musicale. Three special numbers: April 1925, December 1938; January–February 1939.
CALVOCORESSI, M. D., *Les Histoires naturelles de Maurice Ravel et l'imitation debussyste.* (*Grande Revue*, May 1907.)
——, *Maurice Ravel.* (*Bulletin de la S.I.M.*, April 1909.)
DONOSTIA, P., *Hommage à Maurice Ravel.* (*Gure Herria*, 1937.)
FARGUE, Léon-Paul, *Maurice Ravel* (*Plaisir de France*, August 1936.)
HUGO, Valentine, *Trois souvenirs sur Ravel.* (*Revue Musicale*, January 1952.)
LALO, P., *Maurice Ravel.* (*Le Temps*, June 13, 1899.)
——, *Maurice Ravel et le Debussysme.* (*Le Temps*, March 19, 1907.)

LALOY, Louis, *Maurice Ravel.* (*Mercure Musical,* February–March
     1907.)
MARNOLD, Jean, *Le scandale du Prix de Rome.* (*Mercure de France,*
     June 1905.)
——, *L'Affaire Ravel.* (*Revue musicale de Lyon,* May 1, 1907.)
——, *L'Affaire Ravel.* (*Mercure de France,* January 16, 1908.)
MORRIS, R. O., *Maurice Ravel.* (*Music and Letters,* July 1921.)
ROLAND-MANUEL, *Maurice Ravel.* (*L'Echo Musical,* February 1913.)
——, *Maurice Ravel et la jeune école française.* (*Nouvelles Litteraires,*
     June 1937.)
——, *Réflexions sur Ravel.* (*La Grande Revue,* April 1938.)
VALLAS, Léon, *Le nouveau style pianistique.* (*Revue musicale de Lyon,*
     January 6, 1907.)
——, *Encore l'affaire Ravel.* (*Revue musicale de Lyon,* April 14, 1907.)
VUILLERMOZ, E., *Portrait de Maurice Ravel.* (*Cahiers d'aujourd'hui,*
     No. 10, 1922.)
——, *Défendons Ravel.* (*Candide,* January 13, 1938.)

III. *Articles by Ravel*

Réponse à une enquête sur Wagner. (*La Grande Revue,* May 10, 1909.)
Notices of Lamoureux and Colonne concerts. (*Revue musicale de la S.I.M.*
     February, March, April, November 1912.)
A propos des 'Images' de Claude Debussy. (*Les Cahiers d'aujourd'hui,*
     No. 3, February 1913.)
Reprise de Boris Godounov. (*Comoedia illustré,* 1913.)
Les mélodies de Gabriel Fauré. (*Revue Musicale,* special Fauré number,
     1922.)
Biographical sketch. (Dictated to Roland-Manuel in 1928, first pub-
     lished in *Revue Musicale,* October 1938.)
On Schoenberg. Contribution to "La Musique Autrichienne",
     special number of *La Revue Musicale,* Autumn 1929.

SELECTED DISCOGRAPHY

1. ORCHESTRAL

Daphnis et Chloë	Ansermet, Orch. Suisse, (R)ACL 53
(complete ballet)	Munch, Boston S.O., R.C.A. A. 630 294
	Monteux, L.S.O. SXL 2164 and LXT 5536
Rapsodie Espagnole	Munch, Boston S.O. SB 2019 -RB 16130
	Ansermet, Orch. Suisse, LXT 5424
La Valse	Munch, Boston S.O., ALP 1245
	Ansermet, Paris Conservatoire, LXT 5004
	(with *Boléro*)
Boléro	Munch, Boston S.O., SB 2019, RB 16130
	Ormandy, Phil. S.O., SBR 6201
Ma Mère l'Oye	Ansermet, (R)ACL 37

2. OPERAS

L'Heure Espagnole	Ansermet, LXT 2828
	Cluytens, 33CX 1076
L'Enfant et les Sortilèges	Ansermet, LXT 5019

3. CONCERTOS

Piano Concerto in G	V. Perlemuter, Vox PL 9220
	Monique Haas, DGM 18004, *or* 68324-6
	Marguerite Long, COL LX 194-6
	(Conducted by Ravel)
Piano Concerto in D	V. Perlemuter, Vox PL 9220
(Left Hand)	J. Février, COL LFX 631-3
	A. Cortot, HMV DB 3885-6

4. PIANO SOLO

Complete works   Walter Gieseking, COL 33CXS 1350
Walter Gieseking, COL 33CX 1351-2

5. CHAMBER MUSIC

Piano Trio   PMC 1035 (Trio des Beaux Arts)
String Quartet   DGM 18312 (Loewenguth)

6. VOCAL

*Trois Poèmes des
Mallarmé*   (Danco, Ansermet) LXT 5031
Shéhérazade   (Danco, Ansermet) LXT 5031
Chansons Madécasses   (Irma Kolassi) Decca LW 5246
(Madeleine Grey & Ravel conducting)
Polydor 561076-7
Histoires Naturelles   (Bernac and Poulenc) COL 33CX 1119

INDEX

INDEX